GW01605771

The Art and Technique of Pen Drawing

Frontispiece.

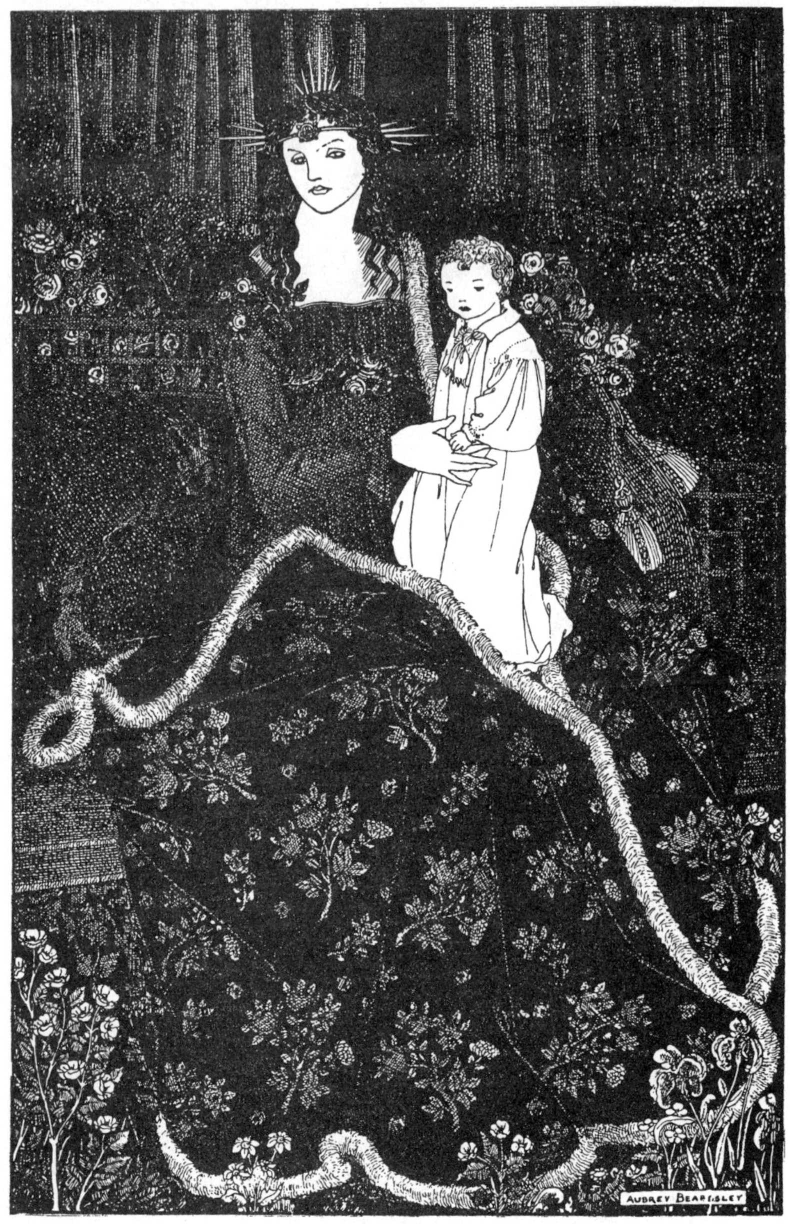

"A Christmas Card." A drawing from *The Savoy* by AUBREY BEARDSLEY.

The Art and Technique of Pen Drawing

G. Montague Ellwood

DOVER PUBLICATIONS, INC.
Mineola, New York

Bibliographical Note

This Dover edition, first published in 2003, is an unabridged republication of the work originally published by Charles Scribner's Sons, New York, in 1927 under the title *The Art of Pen Drawing: A Manual for Students, Illustrators, and Commercial Artists.*

Library of Congress Cataloging-in-Publication Data

Ellwood, G. M. (George Montague), 1875–1955.
[Art of pen drawing]
The art and technique of pen drawing / G. Montague Ellwood.
p. cm.
Originally published: The art of pen drawing. New York : Charles Scribner's Sons, 1927.
Includes index.
ISBN 0-486-42605-X (pbk.)
1. Pen drawing. 2. Pen drawing—technique. 3. Illustration of books. 4. Illustrators. I. Title.

NC905 .E5 2003
741.2'6—dc21

2002072873

Manufactured in the United States of America
Dover Publications, Inc., 31 East 2nd Street, Mineola, N.Y. 11501

FOREWORD

THE object of this little book is twofold. In the first place an attempt has been made to give as practical an account as is possible in cold print of the technique of drawing in pen and ink, setting down a variety of hints that, from the Author's experience of students' needs, are likely to prove of practical value in forestalling most of the usual pitfalls experienced by the beginner, and giving advice as to how the medium may best be applied to industrial work in illustration and advertising. Secondly, the aim is to provide in the illustrations a fairly comprehensive survey of the best contemporary pen work, with examples of the greatest masters of all periods, briefly commented upon in the text. This series should demonstrate far better than the written word the derivation of style and technique, and the main tendencies of present-day practice.

The beginner embarking upon a career as a pen artist will probably find that the most profitable opening for him is in commercial work. For this reason, considerable stress has been laid on what is wanted and expected of him by agents and advertisers. The standard of drawing for advertisement is rising steadily, whilst the demand for first-class drawings is always on the increase. Book illustration has reached a stage where commissions are only given to the chosen few, and it is usually necessary to graduate in periodical illustration or commercial work first.

In magazine illustration the editorial prejudice still inclines in favour of wash drawings as the next best things to photographs in realism; but the demand for page decorations and decorative treatment of head and tail pieces in the periodical press is on the increase, and signs are evident that the pen is likely to come fully into its own again in this vast field. Humorous drawing, however, has continued the exclusive ground of the pen draughtsman, and here *Punch* has for years set and led a high standard of drawing and style.

There is, then, immense scope for the pen artist, and a solid demand for good work which, if it inclines first in one direction and then in another, continually increases in volume. Given in the first place a sound knowledge of drawing, observation, imagination, and sufficient staying power to persevere, the artist is in a position to develop from these raw qualities an individuality of style and technical accomplishment that will ensure interesting and profitable work.

These necessary qualities, unless inborn, cannot be developed by any amount of labour; but should they be present in the first place, it is study and practice only that will develop them to their highest pitch. It is as an aid to this end that the present volume is planned, to facilitate the development of these qualities, and, so far as is possible, to smooth out the thorny path leading towards complete mastery and success.

G. M. E.

LONDON, *September* 1927.

NOTE OF ACKNOWLEDGMENT

THE Author must acknowledge his thanks to the following artists who have kindly permitted him to reproduce examples of their work, namely:—Mr Frank Brangwyn, R.A.; Mr E. J. Sullivan, A.R.W.S.; Mr Harold Nelson; Mr F. L. Griggs, A.R.A.; Mr L. Raven Hill; Mr John Austen; Mr Albert Rutherston; Mr Arthur Rackham; Mr W. Curtis Green, A.R.A.; Mr Randolph Schwabe; Mr E. H. Blampied, R.E.; Mr Sydney R. Jones, and Mr W. S. A. Gordon.

He is also indebted to Messrs John Lane (The Bodley Head) Ltd. for permission to reproduce the Frontispiece and the subjects on Figs. 2, 68A, 106, and 110; Messrs G. Bell & Sons Ltd. for Figs. 47, 53, and 54; the Authorities of the Architectural Association for Fig. 70, and those of the Victoria and Albert Museum for Figs. 13, 72, 97, 117, and 118; Messrs J. M. Dent & Sons Ltd. for Fig. 81; Messrs William Heinemann Ltd. for Fig. 94; Messrs G. Routledge & Sons Ltd. for Fig. 108; Messrs G. Duckworth & Co. Ltd. for Fig. 112; Messrs W. S. Crawford Ltd. for Figs. 35, 111, 139, and 143; The Sun Engraving Co. for Fig. 114; The London Press Exchange for Fig. 99; the Houghton Mifflin Co. for Fig. 98; and the Press of the American Institute of Architects for Fig. 85.

Thanks are also due to the proprietors of *The Christian Science Monitor*, *Vanity Fair*, *The Passing Show*, and *The Little Review* for permission to reproduce subjects that formerly appeared in these journals, and to Mrs E. A. Abbey for permission to reproduce the illustration by the late E. A. Abbey on Fig. 12.

A number of firms have kindly permitted the reproduction of original advertisement drawings made for them, and in some cases have courteously placed the blocks at the Publishers' disposal. Amongst the illustrations are original advertisements for Messrs John Dewar & Sons, Clark of Paisley, John Walker & Sons, Gill & Reigate, Bondman Tobacco Co., E. Brown & Son Ltd., Julius Kayser & Co., J. Lyons & Co. Ltd., Wallis of Holborn, Kerner Greenwood & Co., Waring & Gillow Ltd., The Erasmic Co., The Pepsodent Co., Lea & Perrins Ltd., Zambrene Weatherproofs, Mitchell's "Prize Crop" Tobacco, Bass & Co. Ltd., The General Electric Co. Ltd., Morny & Co., Carr's Biscuits, John Barker & Co. Ltd., Lincoln Bennett Ltd., Gera Fabrics, R. W. Forsyth Ltd., Compact Powder, etc., etc., to whom the Author must acknowledge his grateful thanks for their inclusion.

CONTENTS

The Art and Technique of Pen Drawing

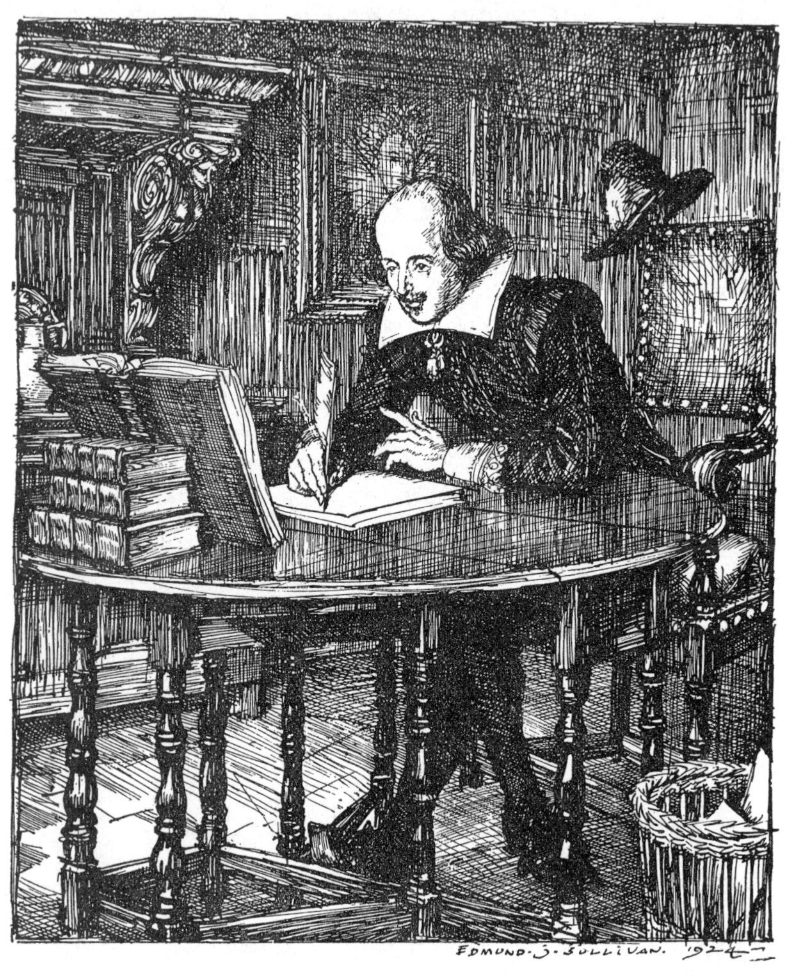

FIG. 1.—An Historical Illustration by EDMUND J. SULLIVAN.

THE ART OF PEN DRAWING

CHAPTER I

INTRODUCTORY

"ILLUSTRATION is an important, vital, living branch of the Fine Arts, and will live for ever."

The late Joseph Pennell concluded a book on "Modern Illustration" with the above words in 1895, some twelve years after the commercial adaptation of photo-zinco reproduction had made possible the use of comparatively cheap and rapidly produced blocks from line drawings.

"For ever" sounds a long time, even allowing for the pardonable enthusiasm of the author-artist in completing a monumental work on a congenial subject and intoxicated with the facilities which the new form of reproduction promised for the future; but it is fairly safe to prophesy that illustration in some form will persist while people are interested in one another and the world they live in.

Pennell saw a golden future for illustration which should have matured, if the promise of the older magazines had been fulfilled, into a pageant of fine drawings covering every aspect of affairs. Papers have multiplied exceedingly since the publication of his book; but although the demand for illustration is colossal now, compared to conditions in 1895, it is mainly for a totally different style of work. The overwhelming facilities of photography are largely responsible for this, in practically deleting illustration of current events from editors' commissions to artists. Some people, especially some artists, do not agree that the camera gives better results; but from an editorial point of view the matter does not admit argument insomuch as the ideal would be to put the reader in front of the actual happenings, and the camera is certainly the next best thing in giving the most faithful record of these.

America alone, with the courage of its huge circulations, has to some extent maintained a public appreciation of really well-produced magazines and weeklies dealing with things other than light fiction or relentless humour. In England, papers have increased in numbers and decreased in artistic interest. Reproductive methods have changed little in thirty years, but the requirements of editors have changed indeed with the expansion of the field of effort. *Punch* alone of the older papers maintains the tradition of the best procurable in pen drawing, and now carries on in friendly rivalry with many newcomers whose columns show work by some, but never by all, of the *Punch* men.

In the pages of *Punch* are to be found the finest flowers of pen artistry since the great times of Keene and Du Maurier in the early 'seventies, and its volumes offer examples of a succession of old and new fashions and styles in handling the pen which well repay serious study.

It cannot be too strongly insisted that study of the older work is the finest training in all essentials concerned with taste as apart from actual drawings ; but also, it cannot be too strongly emphasised that the method of study is equally important.

With some men, success, even fame, has come as the result of intensive study of the methods of a favourite master whose drawings were copied, dissected, and analysed until they were grafted anew and commenced to grow into very similar fruit. But this is hardly the process that is recommended, and study can with advantage cover a wider field, where personality may be reinforced rather than obliterated.

For personality is the very essence of enduring work, and the surest way to develop it is in an intelligent search into the principles of presenting things seen, in such a way that they are not only recognisable by others, but convey a sense of distinct pleasure in that recognition.

It has been said that the only things necessary for good pen drawing are personality and a pen. This is literally true, for it carries a deceptive load of reservations in the word personality. Accepted literally, it amply justifies the work of the modern non-representational schools in appealing mainly to the mind through the senses; for their intensely interesting penwork (in the case of the Nash's, for instance) shows the very essence of personality strewn over nature, adding a new fragrance to the many she has to offer.

The fragrance is generally a little difficult for the average person to detect; its charm does not reach his mind owing to severe artistic adenoids, all of which is merely mixed metaphor for the very hard fact that this kind of work has a very restricted appeal, and may be safely left to those who feel the definite urge to neglect tradition, verity, and the soft ways of the well-understood and universally wanted for the thorny path of the innovator at second hand. Innovators in art are the salt of the earth, but they are only blessed in offering their own brand, absolutely red-hot.

Freely interpreted, the personality and pen idea is a very workable definition of the right approach to study. The right personality can be very rapidly built up by a bowing acquaintance with the technique of the great masters of to-day and yesterday, together with a strong determination to surpass them all. The pen can be bought, together with a tempting block of paper. Then all that remains is to put the pen and paper together in such a way that the result is good to look upon. To do this it is usually necessary to cover much paper with the disappointing results of concentrated efforts, to make drawings of everything in sight, memory, or imagination, and not abandon hope because the coveted technique is shy in developing. Optimism and hard work are the breakfast foods of genius; it is only necessary to eat enough.

This is the whole art of pen drawing, but the road is rougher than the flippancy of this picture suggests, and it has been the aim throughout the following pages to smooth out the bumps as far as possible, so that the student may travel somewhat easier for having read it.

The infinite possibilities in pen drawing have never yet been dealt with from the standpoint of the interest they hold to the actual or intending producer of professional work. The few books on the subject published in England have been undertaken in the critical vein of the connoisseur, and their appeal is to the collector and amateur rather than the actual worker or student.

The opinions and preferences of a critic are of very little practical value to those who sigh for initiation into the mysteries of materials and handling, and seek guidance in the expression of their own observation or invention in definite lines or mass blacks for reproduction by the ordinary line process block, that wonderfully simple invention which called in the aid of photography to transfer the artist's drawing on to the metal plate, and by mechanical biting made it possible for the great public to see the work of draughtsmen exactly as it left their hands, without the inevitable change for better or for worse to which it had been previously liable at the hands of the wood-engraver.

The process block, according to Mr J. M. Bulloch's informative article on "British Pen Drawing" in the *Studio* Special Number for 1900, dates from about twelve years previous to that date, and he gives an idea of the progress in that period which seems absurdly small compared with the position of the process engraving business to-day. The following paragraph, quoted from Mr Bulloch's article, shows an almost uncanny prescience of the newer weekly journals: "I believe there are great possibilities for simple decorative effect that will make a direct appeal. Indeed, the only means of differentiation between one journal and another will be solved by decorative art, for the more photographic our illustration becomes, the less individual will be each journal, unless it undertakes some sort of decorative accompaniment capable of very rapid manipulation. Already the cheapest Sunday papers in America are availing themselves of the decorative artist in a more or less crude way. On this side the editors are chary and conservative, but they are bound to follow."

It has taken the editors until this last year or two to do it, but they have certainly come with a rush, and the policy indicated by Mr Bulloch is in full swing now, greatly to the advantage of artists of every kind, and especially to those who specialise in pen drawing, the ideal method of illustration for papers which aim at a high level of semi-decorative modernity.

Only in the last few years has technique in pen drawing been manifest to any appreciable extent; technique being understood as the conscious desire to interest our audience in the manner as well as the matter of our pictorial statement, not with the idea of creating a singular method or bizarre touch that will shout and compel instant attention to our work, but undertaken sincerely to add interest to the job of producing and also to the resulting drawings, quite apart from their subjects.

One of the best methods of acquiring ease in the manipulation of the pen, and thereby taking the first step in the cultivation of technique, is to draw direct from nature—the nude, landscape, flowers, or everyday costume studies—in pen and ink. Incidentally this is a sure method of discovering one's limitations, the best incentive to get rid of them.

Many examples exist of the early use of the quill pen as an instrument for purposes of study direct from nature, and such studies reproduce well in line, although they generally give a result strangely modern in effect when printed, caused by the elimination of gradations apparent in the lines of the old masters owing to the thin ink used. Conversely, it is very easy to impart an antique appearance to a quite fresh drawing by the use of antique paper and a quill pen used with diluted ink; a fact which has been recognised by the spurious art merchants and used to the detriment of many trusting collectors of old drawings.

It is not suggested that work direct from nature or memory should be the ideal of the budding pen draughtsman as a permanent method. There are many subjects that he will find much better if studied and composed in pencil first, either roughly, as a guide on the actual board or paper intended for the finished drawing, or in one or more separate studies and compositions to be finally translated into the ink state on this final board. But it cannot be too strongly insisted that this direct method is the best possible training for individuality of expression. Something indefinable seems ever to lead the adventurer in this method towards work that counts, and, moreover, it eliminates the ever present danger of following or attempting to follow the same technical method as an admired artist whose work is in demand.

The greatest asset of an illustrator or humorous artist is a sincere personal technique, allied with complete knowledge of the drawing and properties necessary for the range of work he undertakes. Specialism is almost inevitable to-day; things move too rapidly for the combined animal, figure, and marine artist to keep pace in the journalistic world.

There is danger in the fascination of facility, and many

great exponents of pen drawing have fallen victims to it. Herbert Railton's name occurs as an outstanding example of an architectural artist who degenerated by sheer executive ability into a weaver of patterns and reckless employer of stunts of omission which rob his drawings of stability and verisimilitude. He absolutely romped with the pen and undoubtedly enjoyed himself hugely in a way that is permissible only to a limited extent in art. His facility naturally attracted hosts of followers, who accentuated his mannerisms, without a trace of his mitigating brilliance.

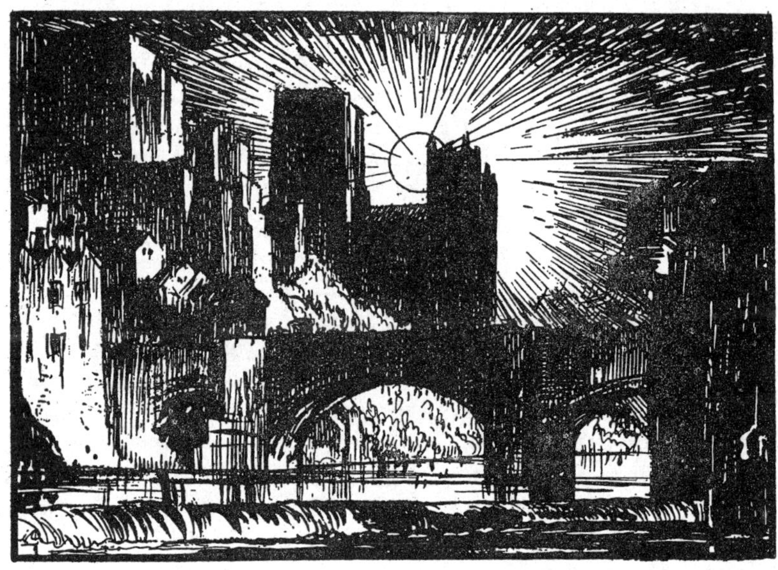

FIG. 2.—A Pen Drawing by FRANK BRANGWYN, R.A.

CHAPTER II

THE EVOLUTION OF PEN DRAWING

LINE was certainly the first method used by man for expressing his thoughts and recording his impressions of natural objects.

That the reindeer hunter of long ago was an artist is shown by the wonderful "La Madelaine" drawing on ivory of a mammoth (Fig. 3), so full of action, so indicative of bulk and power, and interesting as showing the practised self-

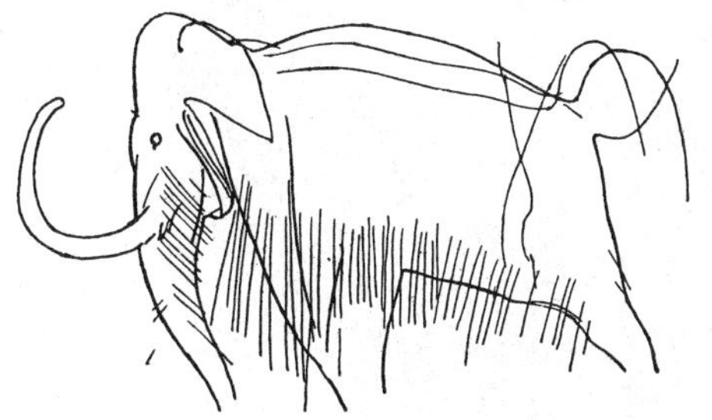

FIG. 3.—The La Madelaine Mammoth.

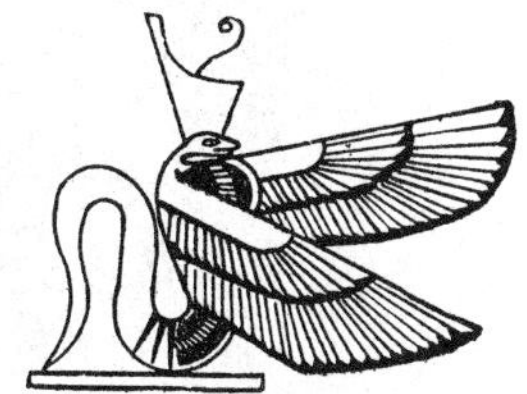

FIG. 4.—Egyptian Decorative Design.

criticism in the artist's corrections of his own first rendering, proving that the work is that of a really proficient student of line, equal in every respect to present-day animal draughtsmen.

Early civilisations, such as that of Egypt, evolved a more formal manner of treatment, adapting the subject to a decorative scheme to which it was subordinated, and rendering the human form, birds, animals, and the like according to a set code of rules (see Fig. 4). The Egyptians also acquired great power with the brush, using it much as the Japanese do at the present day.

Next in the line of great civilisations is that of Greece, which in its early stages came much under the influence of Egypt. Here again, in the many fine examples that have come down to us in the figured designs on vases, we see that Greek draughtsmanship, though freer and more fanciful than Egyptian, was ruled by certain conventions which again subordinated it to a general decorative effect (see Fig. 5). There is, however, an extraordinary charm and vigour in these drawings which in their delicacy of line and elimination of all but the essentials have found many disciples in modern French line work.

The first real stimulus to line drawing as we understand it

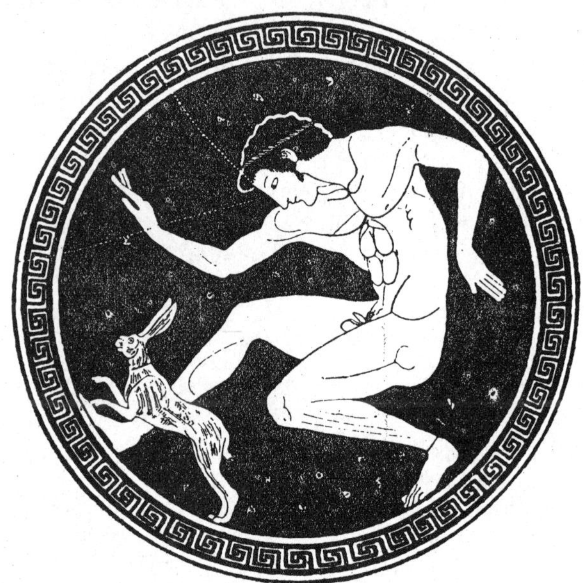

FIG. 5.—Greek Vase Decoration.

to-day came with the writing of "Missals." They were executed with a pen, and the instinct to decorate or in some way develop the use of the pen, led to drawing with it. Thus developed the notion of illustration, for the missal writers soon discovered that things drawn would save much time and labour in lengthy descriptions.

These old craftsmen, as members of strict religious houses, may be relied upon as having given their facts with all the accuracy their technical accomplishment allowed, and as records of customs, costume, and architecture, their crudely executed but often spirited drawings are of extraordinary interest at the present day.

With the introduction of printing, illustration of books by means of woodcuts was not long in developing. Fig. 6 shows a typical example of the rather crude methods employed by its early exponents. Though these woodcuts are often of the very poorest technique and childish in treatment, they brought about a veritable revolution, and in fact practically created the art of illustration along the lines on which we know it at the present day.

It only needed the work of a great innovator to raise this engraved illustration from its crude beginnings to a new and high standard, and such a one was found in Albrecht Dürer who, born in 1471, instigated a tradition in decorative line work which has hardly been surpassed at the present day. Besides his magnificent achievements as a painter, Dürer was absorbed in every process connected with his art. His extraordinary industry is shown in the stupendous tasks with which he constantly grappled in his paintings, engravings, and drawings, and one of the greatest lessons for the modern student to be learnt from his work is his thoroughness and stern determination to overcome all difficulties connected with technique. Fig. 7, taken from an actual pen drawing by the master, will give some idea of the vigour of his methods and of his masterly and accurate use of line to achieve the required effect. This entailed the elimination of anything approaching the haphazard in method ; each line was deliberate in aim and a definite item in a scheme of decoration as well as an essential factor in the illustration.

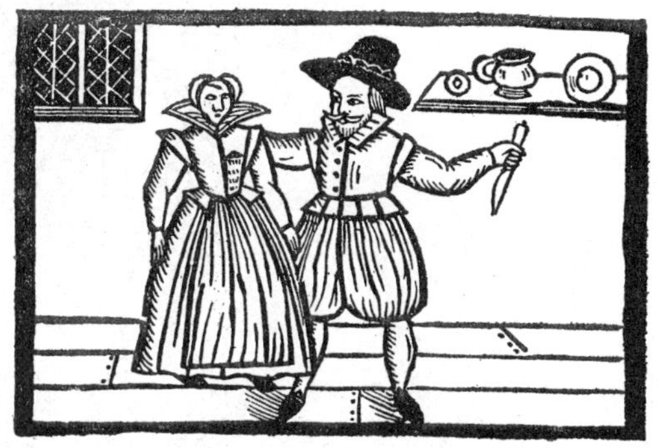

FIG. 6.—A Spirited Delineation of a Terrible Crime. (Early Seventeenth-Century Woodcut.)

The student is especially recommended to study some of Dürer's most famous works in wood-engraving, among which are the two series illustrating "The Passion of Our Lord," "The Apocalypse," and the large series illustrating "The

Triumph of the Emperor Maximilian." Keenly interested in the theory of all branches of his work, he elaborated a "drawing machine," which the illustration on Fig. 8, from an early woodcut, shows in action. This was mainly used to standardise the proportions of the human figure, much as his famous alphabet served to standardise the construction of letters.

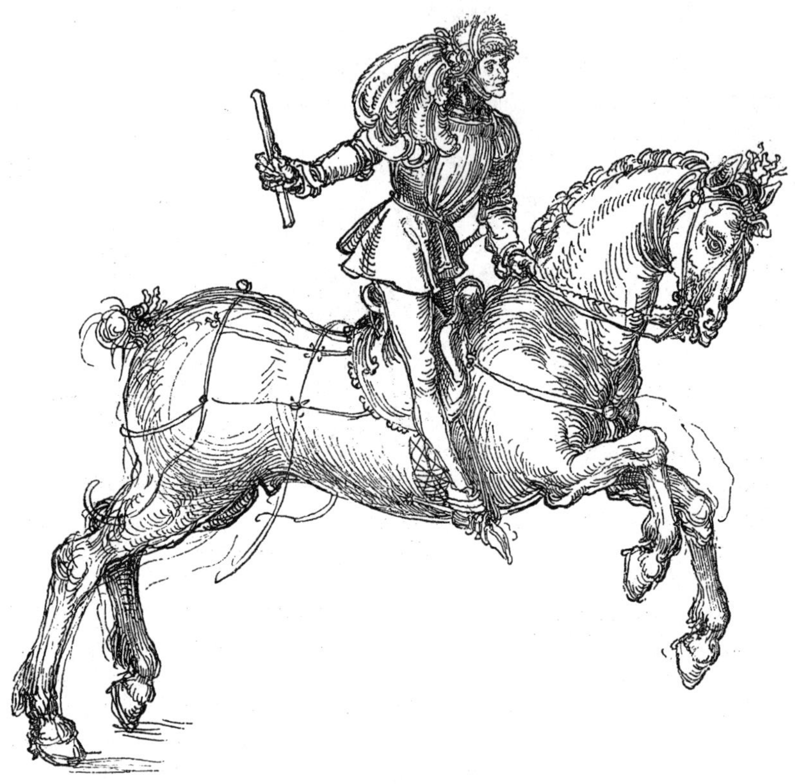

FIG. 7.—ALBRECHT DÜRER. "The Courier."

Meanwhile contemporary artists in Italy were making drawings for the wood-engraver, and in 1499 the "Hypnerotomachia Poliphili," or "Warring of Love in a Dream," one of the most famous of illustrated books, was published by Aldus Manutius of Venice, in which Virgil's "Eclogues" and "Georgics" were given a new pictorial life in graceful, sunny drawings, far removed from the austerity of the still Gothic North both in conception and execution (see Fig. 9). Many moderns, among them Anning Bell, have been to these as inspiration for similar drawings; as also to the contemporary Florentines for decorative conceits in borders, head and tail pieces, book-plates and initials, etc.

Hans Holbein carried on the Dürer tradition in association with the Basle printers. Born in 1498, his greatest work in illustration—the "Dance of Death"—was executed in 1538, and shows a tendency to simplification in blending the Italian

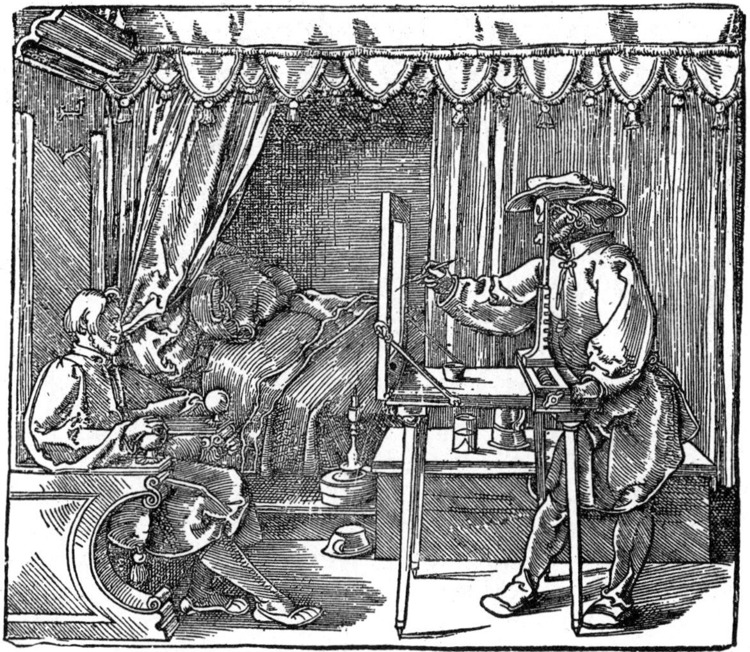

FIG. 8.—DÜRER'S "Drawing Machine" in Action.

treatment of line with Dürer's supernatural imagination. Holbein's directness and versatility, with his masterly appreciation of the value of expressive line applied to woodcuts, places him as the greatest book illustrator of his age.

The next outstanding name in the development of pen line is Rembrandt; but Holland produced two great men in the seventeenth century in Jan Lievens and Dirk de Bray. The former was born in Leyden a year before Rembrandt, and they must have worked much together. The black chalk drawing for the "Portrait of an Ecclesiastic Seated" is in the Boyman's

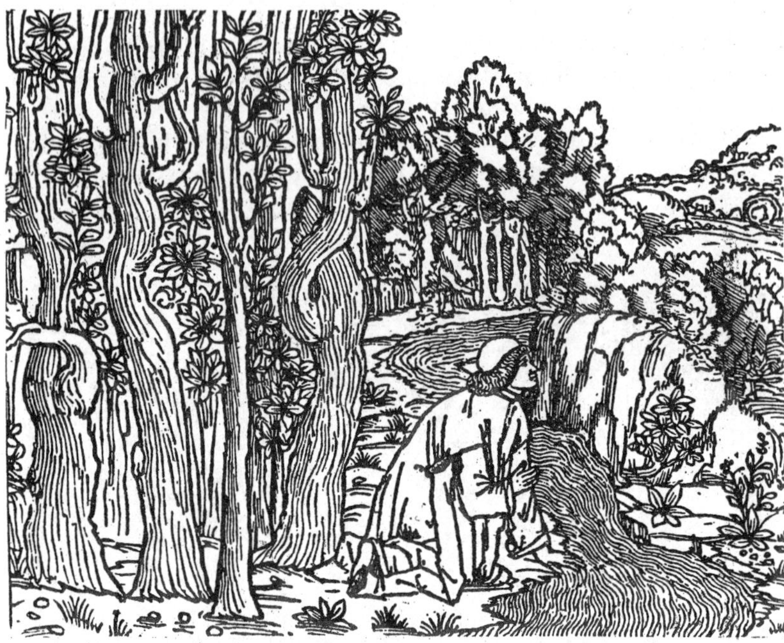

FIG. 9.—An Illustration from the "Hypnerotomachia Poliphili," published in Venice in 1499.

Museum, Rotterdam. Its principal lines show the marks of a stylus, proving that it was the actual drawing used in the transfer to wood for cutting. The engraving gave it a decided pen quality, and it ranks as one of his best portraits, an excellent example of the persistence of good quality in line. Dirk de Bray of Haarlem left only two portraits among the 146 miscellaneous subjects catalogued; but one of these, a portrait of his father, Salomon de Bray, is a technical masterpiece well worth the attention of modern portraitists in line.

Rembrandt, a red-hot revolutionist in art, stood for absolute freedom, and attained absolute perfection of style. Mainly concerned with problems of light, his figures are revealed by the light that envelops them, and shade is used as a means of searching out its source. He managed to render this in his etchings with an absolute success which has baffled his imitators. A number of his pen drawings, made generally as a preliminary to etchings, are preserved, and the two reproduced on Figs. 10 and 11 are splendid examples of his masterly use of this medium.

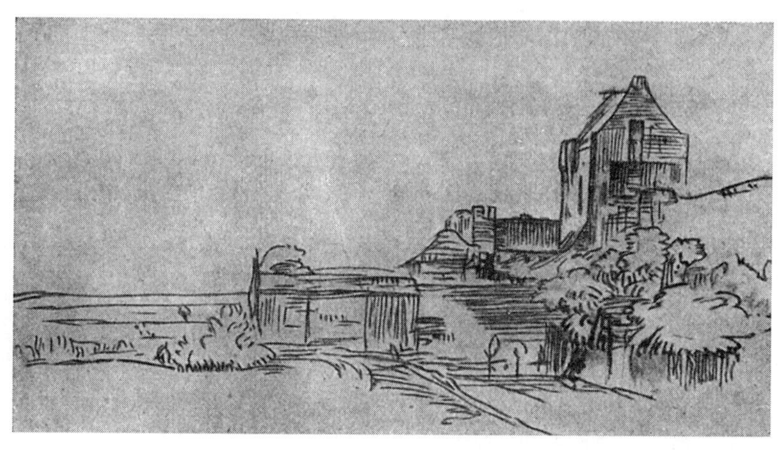

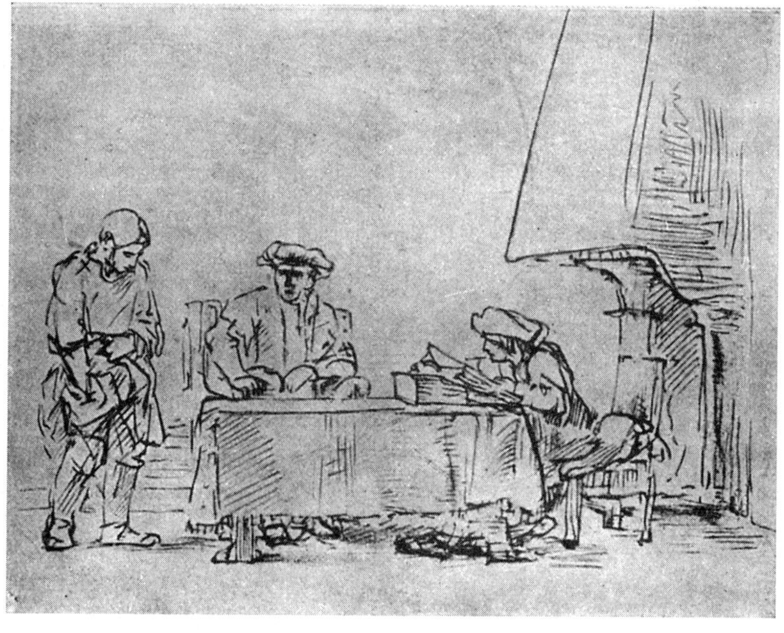

FIGS. 10 and 11.—Line Drawings by REMBRANDT.

[*To face p.* 14.

He remains unsurpassed for the expressiveness and economy of his line and for his wonderful rendering of chiaroscuro and shade.

These masters were in the main responsible for the evolution of line *technique* as we know it at the present day; but it was the men of the early nineteenth century, Goya, Menzel, Meissonier and, later, Vierge, who laid the foundations for modern line *illustration* which was only finally to be perfected by the introduction of the zinco-photographic process early in the present century. Amongst these innovators may be numbered the famous band of English illustrators of the 'sixties, Pinwell, Boyd Houghton, Small, Du Maurier, and the greatest of all, Charles Keene, still without a rival in the purely naturalistic use of the pen line, which he often employed in the manner of Rembrandt as a means of searching for effects of light. Keene's work in *Punch*, fine as it is, inadequately represents his tender and sensitive technique with the pen which, as Mr Emanuel says, "caressed the paper with fairy-like and almost invisible touches, leaving thereon faultless records of the dainty features of beautiful women and their immaculate early Victorian costumes; of male persons of every type and walk in life; of landscape and seascape, architecture and animals—all equally deftly and deliciously turned, and withal so surely, that as a rule pen and ink have been used right away without the aid of pencil preliminaries" (see Fig. 12).

The work of Keene and his contemporaries, Du Maurier, Sambourne, Millais, Tenniel, etc., inaugurated the formative period of a distinct English school of pen draughtsmen almost as brilliant as the French constellation which included Fortuny and Rico as stars of the first magnitude, with Doré, Detaille, De Neuville, and Jacquemart, the wonderful interpreter of furniture and decoration, scarcely less notable.

After Keene, the history of *Punch* runs almost parallel with that of line work in England, for all the new men of note have worked for it, Phil May being the next spectacular figure. In breaking with all tradition by exploiting the utmost possibilities of rigid economy of means in his finished drawings, he will live as the great eliminator—inimitable—for not one of his many would-be disciples penetrated the secret of his power, and his art remains an interlude in tradition (see Fig. 25). This does not mean that he had no influence on his

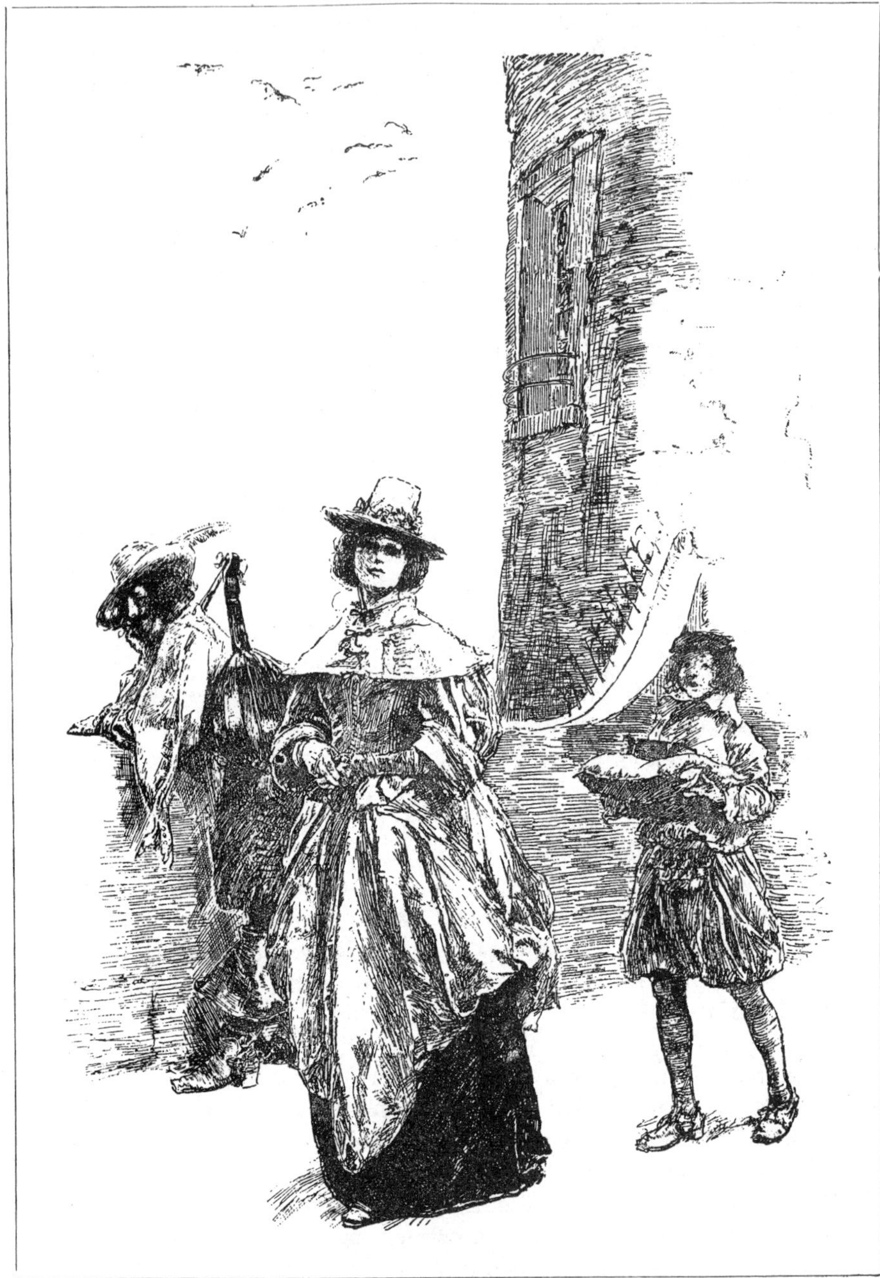

FIG. 12.—A "Costume" Illustration by E. A. ABBEY.

contemporaries and followers, but merely stresses the fact that his technique was temperamental to a degree which made it entirely elusive ; there was so much more in it than met the keenest eye. His influence was in the useful direction of broadening the outlook of both artists and editors to the possibilities of less labour and elaboration, impressing upon both that greatness is not necessarily found in quantity of line, but rather in quality.

A new and startling influence in pen illustration made a meteoric appearance in the late 'nineties in the shape of Aubrey Beardsley, who by the novelty of his technique and the curious and somewhat *macabre* personality that hall-marked his work created a controversy that was almost a scandal amongst his contemporaries. Savagely attacked in many quarters and enjoying only the appreciation of a group of artists and writers of the time, it was not until after his death that the full significance of his work was properly and widely understood. The extraordinary freaks of his imagination were conveyed by a stupendously clever use of delicate line combined with well-placed areas of solid black, a very personal method slightly reminiscent of the art of Japan. This manner formed a perfect expression of the strange and subtle imagination underlying all his work (see frontispiece and Fig. 106).

The history of the last forty years shows the rise of specialism in definite subjects, figure, animals, architecture, or decoration, and there is a wonderful record of achievement in each from many countries, France and Germany dividing the honours in strong figure men, the former with such names as Forain, Louis Morin, Vierge—of Spanish birth but French artistry—and Steinlen ; the latter with Menzel, Greiner, Max Bernuth, Bruno Paul, Heinrich Kley, and the "Simplicissimus" and "Jugend" crowd. England scores mostly with decorative and landscape work, though our record, both in pure illustration and humorous drawing, is certainly far from negligible. E. J. Sullivan, for instance, is a master both of illustration and decoration, with a curiously flexible technique, accomplished and fascinating in much the same way as the dangerous feats of an acrobat who keeps us wondering if he will avoid a cropper, and comes up smiling every time (see Figs. 1 and 17). Hartrick and Rackham show safer treatments of similar line, one in interpreting country types, the other in fantastic settings of trees for very real and charming children (see Fig. 94). Grieffenhagen, H. R. Miller, and Chas. Pears were representative, but have deserted pen work for larger expression.

America's finest effort in art has been in illustration, mainly in line. E. A. Abbey was her first great illustrator, triumphing over a pen technique of almost incredible fineness and redundancy of line, which he managed with evident enjoyment of its possibilities in suggesting colour (see Fig. 12). Reinhart, Blum, Pennell, and Howard Pyle were all contemporaries of Abbey in the early wood-engraving period, but his best work was done when it could be reproduced by process, and the famous series of the comedies of Shakespeare, together with Herrick and Goldsmith illustrations, were mechanically reproduced. Howard Pyle, a decorator of much strength, somewhat influenced by Vierge and in turn influencing our own Garth Jones, is another name of note. Piexotto and Pennell, almost parallel exponents of the charm of architecture, gardens, and landscape, attained wonderful dexterity with the pen in a technique often suggestive of lace in daintiness, especially when treating Gothic architectural detail (see Fig. 72).

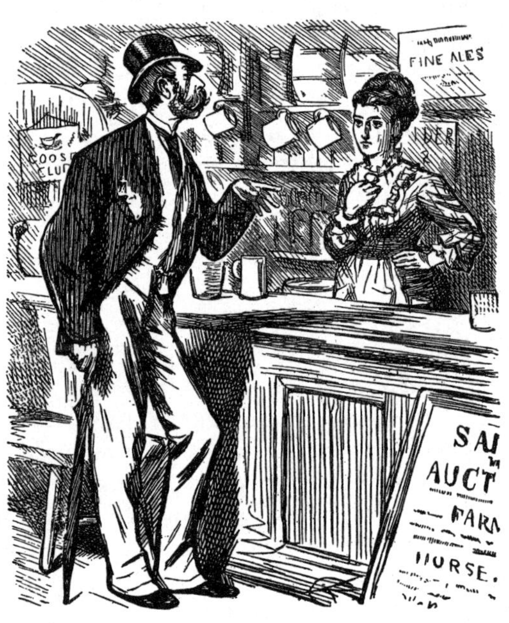

Fig. 13.—By CHARLES KEENE.

The evolution of line drawing has been a series of big jumps from giant to giant. No steady ordered growth can be indicated, supremacy going from one country to another to rest for yet another flitting. But there were great personalities all through, and there are giants among us to-day whose work will be competed for in the auction rooms of the future.

The evolution of opportunity, which formerly halted between the making of such great discoveries as the invention of printing blocks and the overcoming of difficulties in printing, has reached a stage where limits are hardly discernible. Opportunity knocks loudly at the door of the well-equipped pen artist to-day, and his range of usefulness is only limited by the power of his mind to direct the cunning of his hand in adding its quota to evolution of his fascinating and useful art.

Ruled with crow-quill pen.

Drawn slowly with same pen.

Drawn quickly with same pen (straight).

Drawn quickly in natural direction of stroke.

Accentuated strokes.

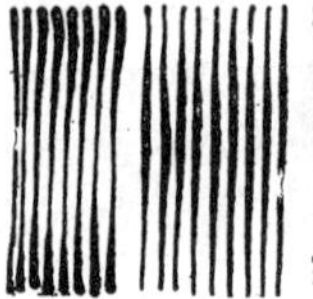

Contrast in accentuation.

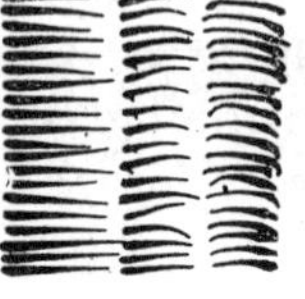

Diminished and increased from right hand.

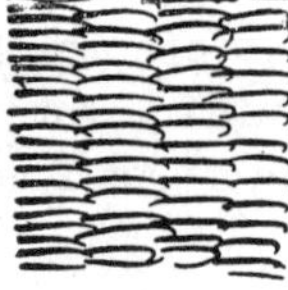

"Matting" effect.

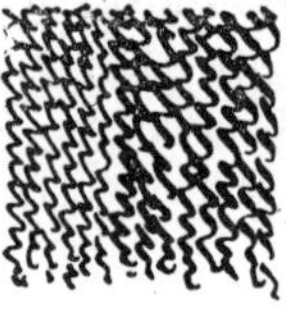

"Saw-tooth" texture.

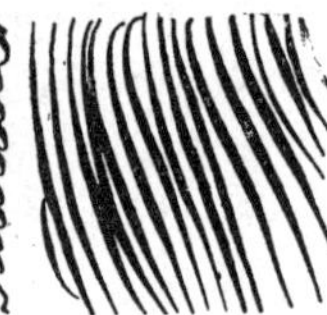

Rich swelled strokes.

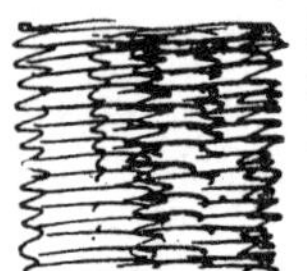

Reflections in water.

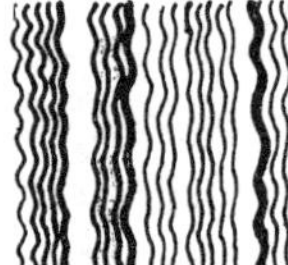

Wavy effect.

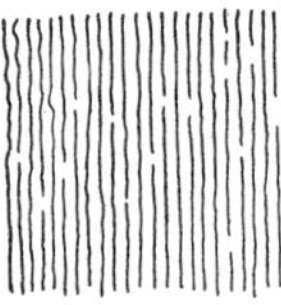

Interesting broken verticals.

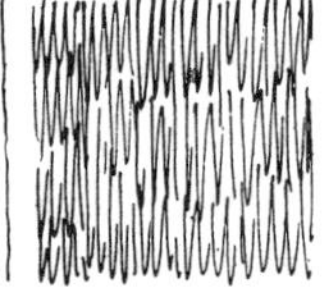

Rich quality in irregular wave effect.

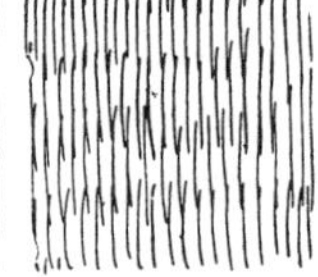

Overlapped verticals.

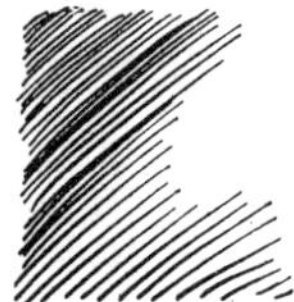

Shadow into light.

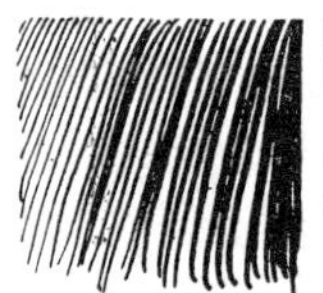

Light to dark (crow-quill pen).

Light to dark (Gillott's 303).

Thick strokes over thin.

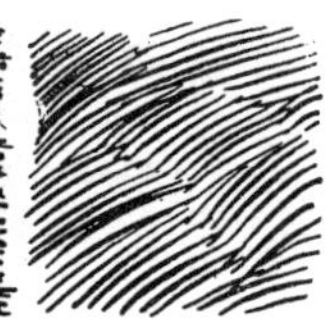

Batches of strokes in alternate directions.

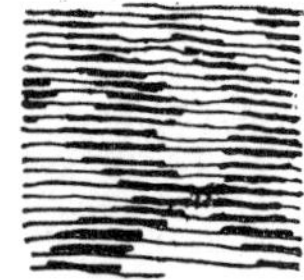

Reinforced lines have great possibilities.

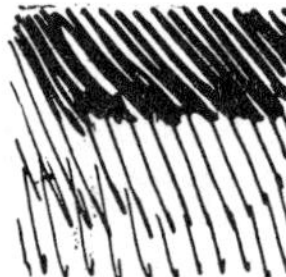

Shadow and shade.

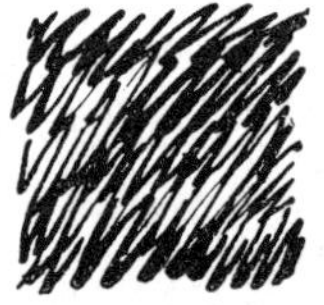

Quick horizontal wave with magnum pen.

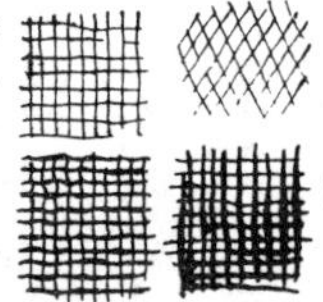

Cross-hatching always looks mechanical.

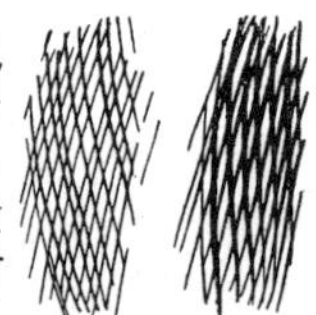

Unless at these angles.

FIG. 14.—PEN LINES.

CHAPTER III

LINE TECHNIQUE: ANALYSIS OF METHODS

STRICTLY speaking, the materials used in pen drawing are the pen or pens one draws with and the paper or card one draws upon ; but pencils and charcoal, india-rubber and duster, must certainly be reckoned with as influences on the average pen technique, although they fall out by the

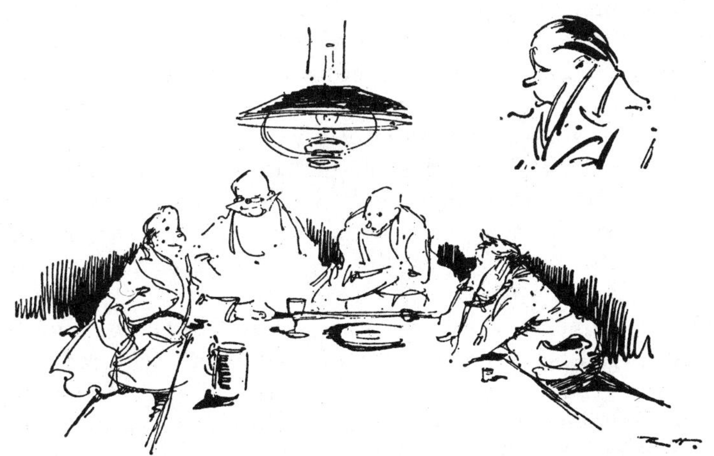

FIG. 15.—" Direct " Drawing with an Ordinary Pen by R. HESSE.

way and, like stage carpenters, are useful to the production as long as they do not show.

To students, especially young students newly attempting the art and (to them) mystery of pen drawing, the pen is something to be treated with much greater respect than the ever-accommodating lead pencil. They know that a mistake, or a round dozen mistakes, will easily fade away when recorded in pencil only, and they realise only too well that the pen line, right or wrong, once committed, is, like a post-war official, there until it is dug out ; consequently they tremble at the thought of recording it simply and naturally.

This early stage fright is easily mastered by the method of working direct from objects or people, and there is nothing better than an ordinary fountain pen for the purpose, preferably used on a smooth paper with a slight yield in its surface resistance ; a sketch book gives this delightful resilience, which to the practised executant is as grateful as a spring floor to the expert dancer.

For young students a *good* stylo (somewhat rare) is an excellent cheap substitute for a fountain pen ; with it they can express themselves in lines of uniform thickness and make dots. A good teaching method at this early stage is to encourage pupils to locate points and boundaries of areas by dots, linking these up and filling in shadows afterwards by single and series lines. An amazingly good result is often the outcome of quite tentative efforts in this method, which has at least the merit of being definite, insomuch as it indicates what to look for and offers a quite readily followed and interesting formula for transferring the impressions received to paper.

In using the stylo as this method dictates, the pupil loses terror of the pen's indelible line in the fun of searching for and fixing the essential points and seeing the drawing grow as these points are linked up by lines, the beginning, direction, and end of which they determine.

The usefulness of the stylo is purely academic, and the idea once grasped and facility of movement acquired, it is advisable to adopt the more sympathetic fountain pen and attempt drawings of everything, everywhere, and at all times—a practice which will inevitably develop a personal technique, influenced by the kind of pen used, just as handwriting is influenced.

Most artists whose wise habit is to sketch constantly from nature, use a pencil, mainly because every one has used pencils for making pictorial notes as a matter of course, without questioning its wisdom ; or because a specious statement soothes them—if one can draw with a pencil, one can draw with a pen—a half truth which the ambitious student will be wise to suspect.

Some of the older masters of pen drawing, whose triumphs

were achieved before the age of universal fountain pens, carried small unspillable bottles of ink in their waistcoat pocket, or slung from their coat lapel, and used ordinary pen holders with nibs for making their roving notes. That they found it worth while when it entailed such a complicated and messy proceeding, is surely a strong argument in favour of the use of its convenient modern substitute, so universal and clean in use.

A well-known contemporary artist habitually carries three fountain pens—one filled with black, one with red, and the other with green ink; his sketch books are most interesting and brilliant, showing some wonderful colour schemes made with the combination of the three inks.

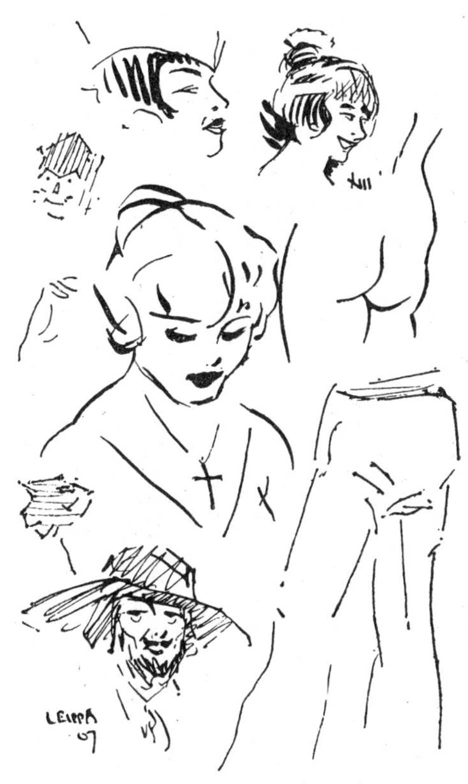

SKETCHES WITH A FOUNTAIN PEN

Fig. 16.

The habit of carrying more than one colour is not advocated, and is mentioned merely as the idea of one capable man who finds added interest in dealing with variety occasionally, for only about 5 per cent. of his notes reveal the use of more than one pen. The remainder consists of rapidly executed notes of moving objects, and anyone who has attempted this class of sketching will agree that one pen is quite enough to manipulate in catching action poses; the model makes all the rapid movement the duet can conveniently deal with.

In making these pen notes, do not attempt too much at

first, and do not aim at making the sketches look pretty or clever, for this is the surest way to render your work abortive to its real purpose. Fix it in your mind that the main object is to absorb facts, and the next to find a method by which you can convey your rendering of them to others in the most interesting way. Both objects will be best attained by direct observation and instant record of things actually seen—an eye, a nose, an ear, the lines made by the play of muscles in an elderly face, hats, boots, hands, and the folds in clothes are all vitally important details which you must find a way of representing. Rapid sketches from photographs are extremely useful, provided the photographs are regarded strictly as substitutes for the living model, and not as copies to be slavishly followed or even traced : for even the best photographs are static, and unintelligent drawings from them translate this quality of lifelessness. Work from motion photography is splendid practice, but is rendered difficult by the lighting conditions in the average cinema theatre, which impart to the ominous words " working in the dark " a too literal meaning.

This insistence on the study from nature in a particular way as a means of developing individuality and clarity of statement will be found of infinite use in practice, and there is little more to be said about it which the student will not discover in trying it out. A word on the selection of a suitable fountain pen may be useful. The nib will be gold, of course, iridium pointed, and a good one will last for years in constant use, giving an ever-increasing variety of line. With a medium point the finest lines are possible with light handling, and pressure brings wider lines as the pen gets broken in. A good notion is to adopt a pen which has already been broken in to your touch as a writing instrument.

It is rather difficult to see just how scientific analysis of the constituents of a line can assist students in finding an adequate pen technique, and it is questionable whether it is wise to search for an individual line. Maginnis commences his essay on technique with : " The first requirement of a good pen technique is a good individual line, a line of feeling and quality." It is certainly safe to try for a line of " feeling and quality " and leave individuality out of the initial calculations as something which must develop unconsciously or not at all. Feeling and quality in line must be temperamental, the subconscious mind

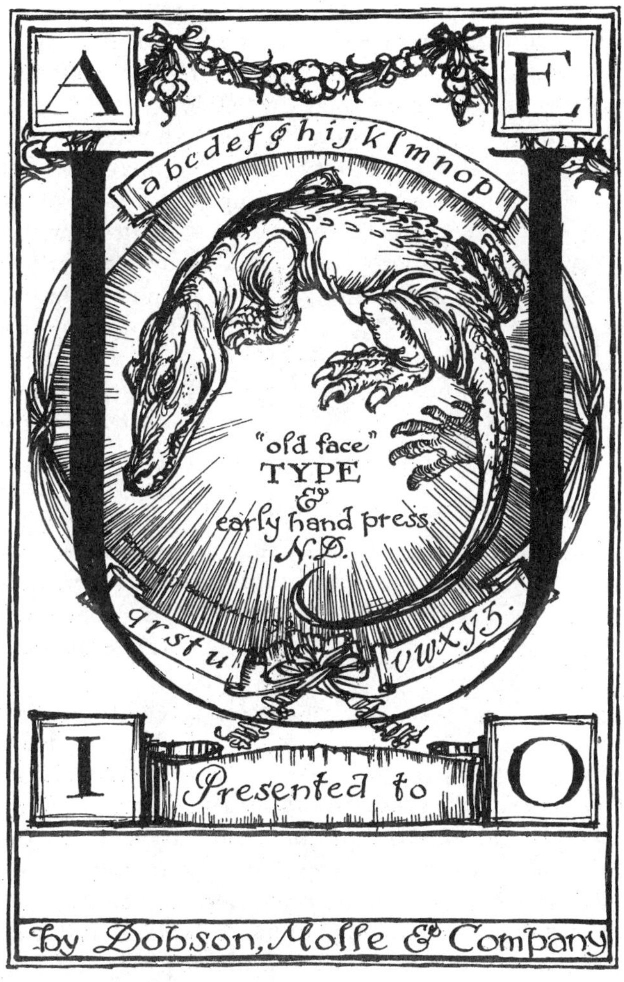

FIG. 17.—Richness of Line in a Book-plate by E. J. SULLIVAN.

acting upon the conscious desire to express something by an ungrudging expenditure of nervous energy. Individuality in actual stroke is not essential; many successful men ignore it completely; others deliberately work in the manner of a master they admire and yet produce work of marked originality; others, again, absorb the working methods of their favourite master and use them as a basis for their own style.

E. J. Sullivan, in his book "Line," shows an interesting analysis of the production of curves by combinations of straight lines, proving that the apparently impossible task of drawing a circle with a ruler is perfectly simple in execution. All that is necessary in drawing any curve by this method is that the sections of straight line building the curve be short enough to deceive the eye in combination as a series of "pressed in" tangents forming it. The notion apparently amuses Mr Sullivan intensely; but it is difficult to see any practical application of it. Everything it will do can be better done in a normal way, so even Mr Sullivan's tempting paragraph—"In the stealthy employment of a scarcely perceptible angle often lies the beauty of a curve, and its character of vigour or languor, its speed or slowness"—which evidently seeks to justify the many pages and diagrams given to its very thorough analysis, is a vague suggestion for the accomplished artist rather than a practical help to the student.

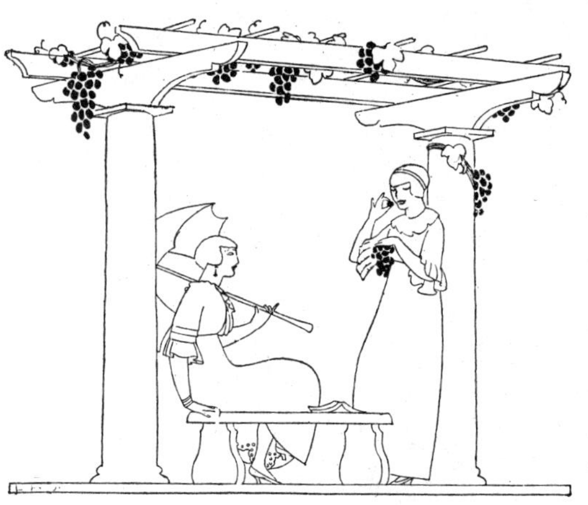

FIG. 18.—American Decorative Illustration by L. HELD, JUN., showing the Possibilities of Pure Outline.

An interesting line is the direct result of intense feeling and joy in concentration on actual execution. E. J. Sullivan's work is the best justification of this dictum; his line is pure revelry with the pen, consequently it shows a complete pen quality which is unique in modern illustration (see Fig. 17). The student who troubles to make a comparative analysis of the actual line of the great masters will find very definite qualities of beauty and strength peculiar to each, from the crisp perfection of Vierge to the riot of expressive and colourful line in Wilkinson and the repressions of Rutherston, Boutet de Monvel, Held, Benito, and John Nash.

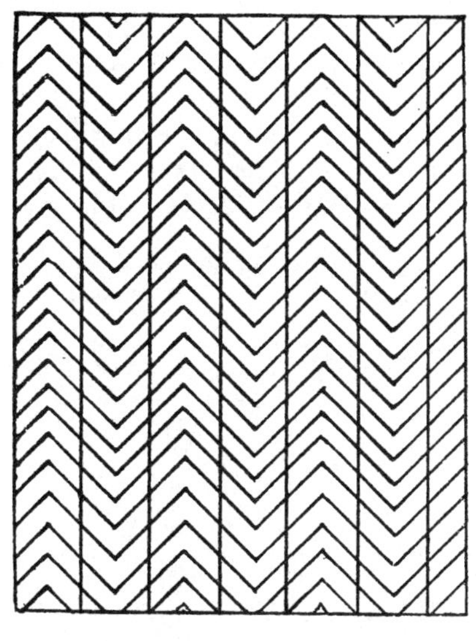

FIG. 19.—Diagram showing the effect of Intersecting Lines on Parallel Uprights.

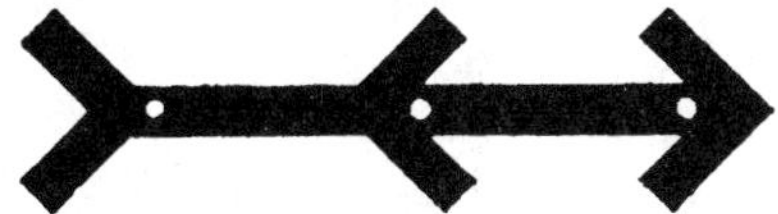

FIG. 20.—Diagram showing the effect of Intersecting Lines in making Equal Portions of another Line appear Short or Long.

The attempt to express something definite in line is interesting in itself, revealing individuality in the earliest effort of the student. The alphabet is recommended by Sullivan as a pleasant means of forming a system of variation in thickness and direction of line, and is as good as anything else, because it necessarily brings in a complete range of straight lines and curves in various combinations and directions from the thick downstroke of the capital "I" to the thick and thin curves of the large "O."

It is the drawing which matters—the alphabet is merely something definite to talk about. The capital "O" is, after all, just our familiar friend the circle, and to draw a circle one need not think of an "O"; in fact, it is much better to get a penny or a plate and draw these in every possible position. Draw the penny first as a flat object, with a flat edge; it is simpler to commence with. Note well that when the penny is turned in such a way that it is represented on paper by an ellipse, the lines of its sides run sweetly into one another at the ends, suggesting the full circle even in the most foreshortened view. A child usually draws an ellipse with sharp points simply because the childish vision heeds only what it sees and is not influenced by the necessity to retain the impression of the whole object in its representation in perspective. From drawing the flat ellipse representing a piece of money to giving a right impression of the two or three ellipses necessary to show a plate, is a bigger step forward than it appears. It involves the correct placing of the interior ellipse determining the rim of the plate, also the fitting of the under part of the plate to correspond with this rim in positions where both are evident to the eye.

When the student can draw ellipses with the necessary understanding of their construction, and can give a convincing idea of a deep plate in any position, several vital facts in perspective have been acquired, together with an appreciation of sweetness in curves. In drawing an ellipse in ink, the natural way is to draw the top line first (when it is horizontal) from left to right, then half the lower line from the left and the other half from the right to meet it (when vertical), to draw two-thirds of the left side first, from the top downwards, then the top curve and half the right side, lastly the bottom curve and the rest of the right side, upwards, as shown in the drawing herewith (Fig. 21).

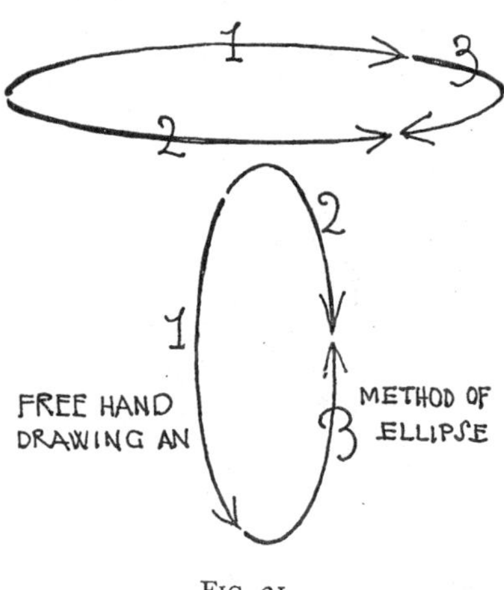

FIG. 21.

A good method of training the hand to execute sweeping, easy pen strokes, graduated or "swelled" at will from the finest line the pen will give, to its maximum yield in width of stroke, is to practise the old penmanship flourishes fashionable in "copperplate" days. These are beautiful in themselves, and design of a pleasing "bookish" quality is the inevitable result of devices built of a combination of several.

Pen lettering, which is drawing of letters in a style dictated by the pen, is also good training for decisive control of hands in more elaborate work. The deliberate curves with "swell" to be formed in exact position, the various directions and thicknesses of line, and the necessity for rhythm and flow in the entire work are formative of style.

There are many ways of approaching the production of finished work with the pen, and the kind of finish aimed at will determine the methods employed. It is absolutely necessary for the student who has attained a certain degree of proficiency in drawing and the mechanics of technique, to determine the kind of thing he wishes to do. The possibilities are so vast and diverse that the draughtsman who is not wedded to a certain range of expression is in constant temptation to flirt with methods that please at the moment, but have no root in his temperament.

A working method can be chosen from the rough division into eight definite categories herewith, each a formula for equally good work. Once chosen, the method must be pursued with the utmost loyalty until it fails to respond; an unlikely happening in actual practice, as devotion to a fixed idea eliminates waste effort, and progress is proportionately rapid.

No. 1. Pure outline drawing, unrelieved by solid blacks, tints, or light and shade, other than the thickening of lines to suggest shadow or accentuate parts. This sounds simple, but is actually the supreme test of the master hand. The French and German illustrators are its most successful exponents, and it can be studied in the work of Roubille, Grasset, Fabiano, and Paul Rieth.

No. 2. Pure outline with simply suggested tints and solid black spots to suggest colour. Newspaper illustration of the Phil May type.

No. 3. Chiefly depending on outline, but more freely treated. The outline supplemented by shading, and actually omitted in parts in deference to the determining qualities of masses of lines beginning or ending together. This classification includes the bulk of magazine and journalistic work dealing with grouped figures, generally in modern costume.

No. 4. Rich "colour" schemes, with full use of contrasts of light and shade, solid blacks and plain whites; with outline as a secondary consideration to general richness of pattern. Sullivan, Gibson, Cheney, Wilkinson, and S. E. Scott represent the wide range of work falling within this class.

No. 5. Deliberately designed illustrations to costume periods, imaginary fairy-tale lore, or beautiful landscape and architecture, including the work of Vierge, Abbey, Howard Pyle, H. R. Miller, etc., in figure, and Pennell, Peixotto, Rico, Griggs, and Railton in landscape.

No. 6. Decorative illustration in which nature is used as a basis for convention. The essentials of such work are pleasing arrangement of black and white, beautiful line, and harmony with the type page. There is scope for expression in vastly divergent styles within the limits of the classification, which includes the amazingly strong use of black and white space by Beardsley, the delicate line and fine drawing of Anning Bell, the strong fairy-tale illustrations of Maxfield Parrish and Garth Jones and the latter's decorative title pages, also the infinite play of fancy in the work of John Austin, the Robinsons, Annie French, and Harry Clarke, to mention only a few of the modern decorators of books.

No. 7. Architectural drawing as a distinct branch of pen work, with a wide range of usefulness, from the strictly mechanical elevation to the free and delightful rendering of proposed or existing buildings.

No. 8. Humorous drawing and caricature, the largest field for the artist in line at the present time, and certain to grow. Every one wants to be amused, and the artist who can make even a portion of the world laugh is not likely to lack appreciation.

Roughly, this list embraces all possible avenues to success as a pen draughtsman, with the exception of advertisement work, which is left out as a separate aim because it involves a nodding acquaintance with all the enumerated methods, plus a nice taste in lettering.

It is obvious that the method of attack to reach proficiency in these very diverse applications of the pen will differ. The exact moment when general training should give way to specialism is a movable quantity ; it depends on the individual and on circumstances. The stronger the personality, the stronger the determination to get down to brass tacks and tackle a branch with the definite intention of being identified with it.

As drawing will be the basis of all, the student cannot have too much of it, and his rendering of the simpler objects in nature will probably have considerable influence on future technique.

Some students will spend a whole term or even more in preparation of a set of pen drawings of leaves and flowers, while others will turn out the same quantity in a few hours ; both types excellent but entirely different, the odds being that the former will gravitate towards decorative work, the latter to realistic and illustrative.

FIRST METHOD (see Figs. 22, 23, 24).

Now to deal with the best means of getting to work in the various categories. The first may be dismissed in a very few words. It is the playground of genius, and genius will not need advice. But its characteristics may usefully be indicated for the benefit of the many who imagine that the absence of elaboration in result implies simplicity in working. It may be taken as an axiom that any drawing which is both simple and satisfying holds more than meets the eye, and this is decidedly the case in the German work of Paul Rieth (Fig. 23) and Karl Arnold (Fig. 22), and the French of Forain, Joseph Hemard, and Marc Carlègle (Fig. 24), to mention only a few of the many clever men who work towards the utmost simplification in the results actually submitted to the public. The methods of all these must necessarily vary to some extent, but one principle dominates them all—truth to a personal conception of nature based on acute observation and love of form. All are capable of perfect drawing in the academic sense, and each takes this cold perfection as a beginning rather than an end, and proceeds to search its accuracy for essential lines in which the rhythm of the whole can be conveyed, with additional interest and power, in the minimum number of strokes with the pen.

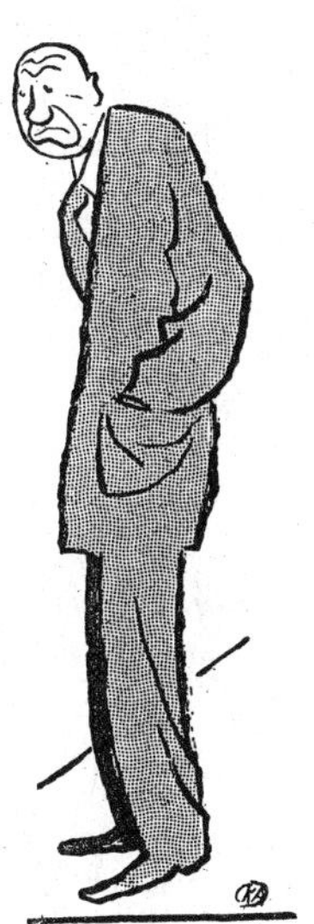

FIG. 22.—KARL ARNOLD.

Interest in this type of work in this country is mainly confined to artists who can appreciate its supreme cleverness. The English public rather likes its illustration without problems to solve, so the artists here who are capable of producing such work content themselves with the knowledge of reserves of

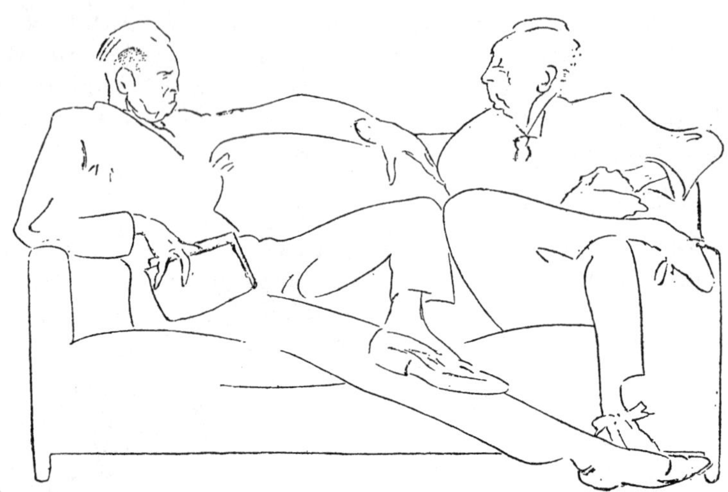

FIG. 23.—German. PAUL RIETH.

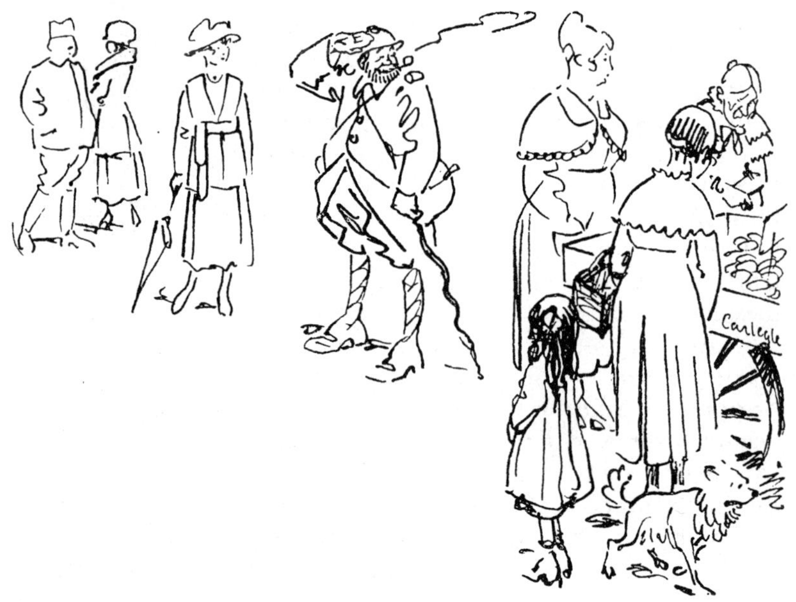

FIG. 24.—French. CARLÈGLE.

power, and give us work which is really in a preliminary stage.

In England two artists only have dared the final stage of selective line, and both, Edmund Dulac and Xavier Kapp, as Frenchmen, are hardly likely to knuckle down to the English point of view in these matters. Miss Fish, who is really in a category by herself, is the only English artist who approximates to the French in the strict economy of line she uses to present the exquisitely dainty little person standing for patrician femininity in the bud. The "Fish" girl has only an egg for a head, but the human expression that is put into that oval by the wonderful drawing and placing of eyes and mouth only is such that she has penetrated most civilised countries.

SECOND METHOD (see Fig. 25).

Newspaper illustration of the Phil May type indicates a similar aim to the first, but developed on different and more popular lines. The name of Phil May is associated with it merely to focus attention on a well-remembered technique that will help the student to appreciate the difference between the decorative and flowing simplification of Paul Rieth and Karl Boehmer and the much less rigorous elimination of tone in Phil May's work. In carrying on from the stage when drawing is sufficiently mastered to warrant experiments in technique, there are many ways of eliminating the superfluous. Some fortunate men are able to imagine or see in their model the lines which they know will give the desired result, putting them down in pencil in such a way that little alteration is needed in translation into ink; but this is perfection vouchsafed to the very few, and the student must reckon on making careful drawings of his subjects to use as scaffolding for the final efforts. There is much satisfaction in removing the scaffolding to reveal the work as it is to stand. The preliminary drawing or studies for this kind of work should be fully explanatory, with a definite intention of finding the building lines; the advantage of this being, that when these studies are used away from the model, that model is recalled in all essentials, and the simplifying process is undertaken with the assurance of definite information.

One very illuminating point is that it is much easier to see "what makes the drawing" in a careful drawing from nature than it is to detect the leading lines in actual figures, landscape,

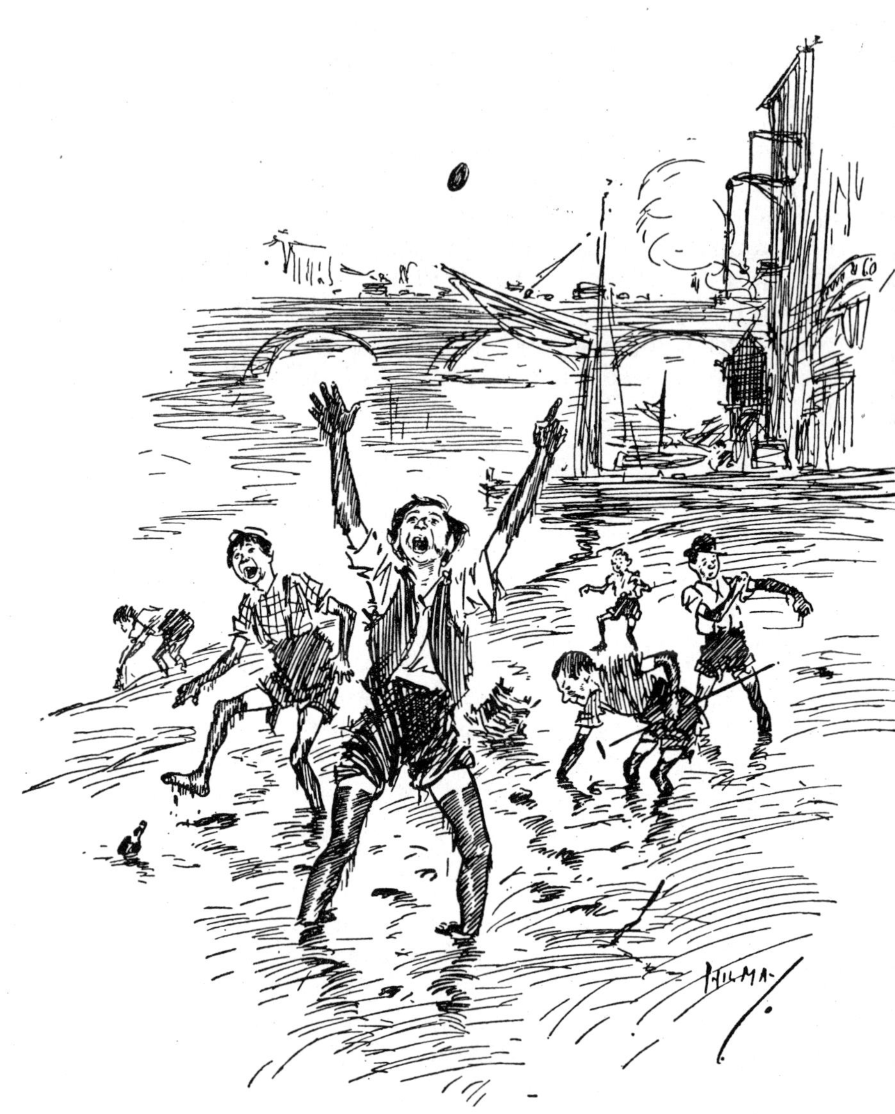

FIG. 25.—"Guttersnipes" by PHIL MAY.

or still life. With such fully explanatory sketches, the obvious way to rehearse the desired effect is to try it out on tracing paper, placed over the figure (or whatever is the principal object), roughly grouping accessories from separate studies, if necessary, by drawing them in scale with the central interest. Another method is to draw selectively on the actual card on which the finished drawing is to be made, grouping the preliminary studies in the process, as in drawing for methods Nos. 4 and 5. The disadvantage of the latter method is that the card is liable to lose its freshness in the course of many trials, and the very desirable effect of spontaneity may be jeopardised, to say nothing of the disadvantage of working on a disturbed surface.

Other methods, such as making preliminary semi-finished drawings on separate cards for final choice and redoing, necessitate much unnecessary work; so we come back to the tracing paper as the best way to get the necessary conviction that the element of safety has been respected in the cutting-out process.

The complete procedure for method No. 2 is, therefore: First, the idea and studies from nature to support its adequate carrying out. Second, the grouping and arrangement of these, and the reduction of their complex detail to an interesting and easily comprehended artistic shorthand by means of significant lines drawn over the studies on a transparent surface. Third, the transfer of this simplified plan of action to the card for finished drawing. Fourth, the finished drawing made with strict reference to the original sketches, but on the general outlines extracted by the experimental work on tracing paper.

THIRD METHOD (see Fig. 26).

The third method. Free, broken outline, supplemented by shading, is the timid version of the fourth method, which in the hands of the really strong draughtsman develops naturally from it in practice. Perhaps a good workable distinction between the two methods is that the former is always a little conscious; the effort is not entirely hidden; the drawing is still tentative and experimental, and the pen is treated with more respect than abandon, while the latter is the very essence of inevitability, giving the impression of mastery over materials and subject so certain and powerful that technique is merged in fine drawing, and incredibly difficult problems of lighting are tackled and conquered with evident joy in the victories.

Nearly all the illustrative work in English magazines and periodicals is in the third method, and it is as rare as it is refreshing to find work developed beyond its eminently safe level. Editors like it because it is safe, so it is the exceptionally

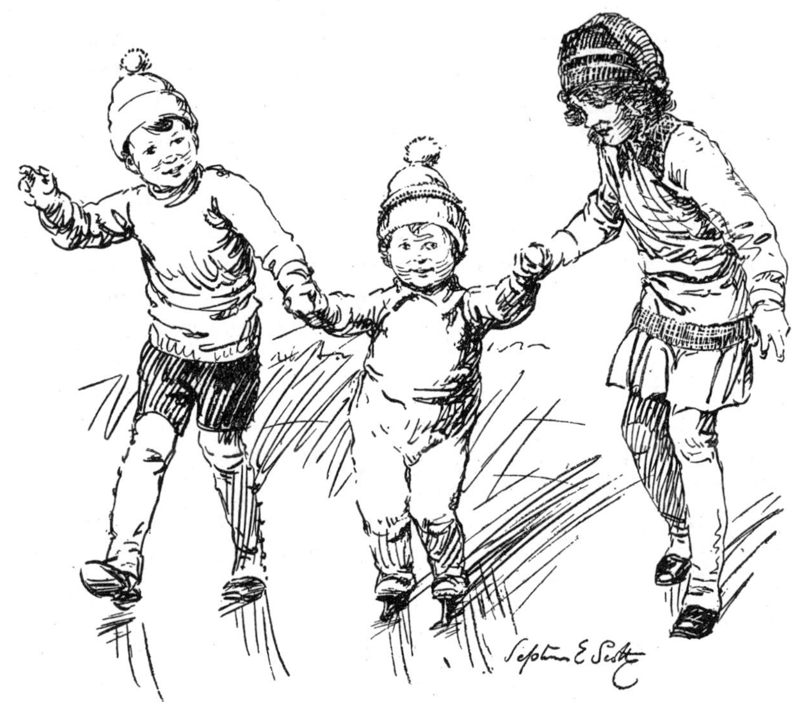

FIG. 26.—By S. E. SCOTT.

bold man who deliberately flouts their desire for it in reaching out for greater things.

The characteristic of the method is the employment of any and every device to make the result convincing and acceptable to the public. Townsend was perhaps its most complete and able exponent, which shows that it may give sufficient scope for a certain type of genius. Acquirement of the devices and technique necessary for success in it is so important that a complete section on magazine illustration will deal with this at length, supplemented by another on humorous illustration, with special reference to the *Punch* type of technique.

FOURTH METHOD (see Figs. 27 and 28).

Includes all work that is intensely personal in expression, in which materials and methods have been used with absolute mastery, the artist's attention focused on character and beauty of form, lighting, and composition. It resembles method No. 1, insomuch as it is possible for the genius alone, who must submit to the grind of accuracy of eye and hand as a preliminary to full freedom. This tends to limit the supply of artists in this category to a very determined and capable few.

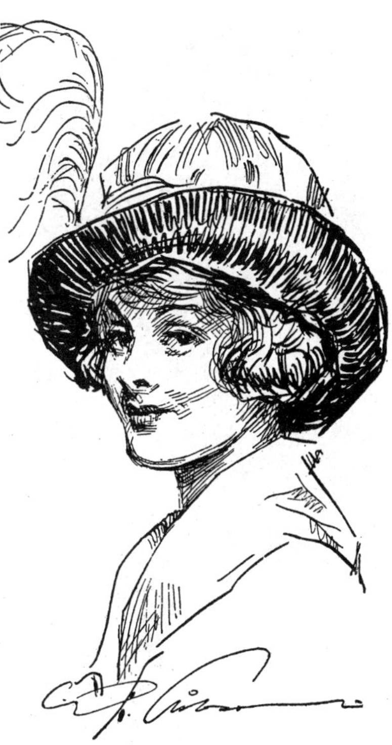

FIG. 27.—A Head by C. DANA GIBSON.

Drawing on a large scale is a useful habit peculiar to this type of artist. The usual way with illustrators is to make the original anything up to about four times (twice the width) the size of the reproduction; but these men, Gibson, for instance, frequently make their drawings approaching life-size, necessitating the use of very broad pens and clever management of modelling in tone obtained by variety in thickness and spacing of line. Many of the Gibson girl heads were drawn two-thirds life-size. But it is obviously impossible to work on this scale when dealing with whole figures or groups of people, and in his figure compositions the largest figures rarely exceed 15 in. in height.

FIFTH METHOD (see Figs. 12, 51, 98).

This is perhaps the most generally attractive field for students, offering on the figure side all the elements necessary for a lifelong revel in romance, and on the landscape side

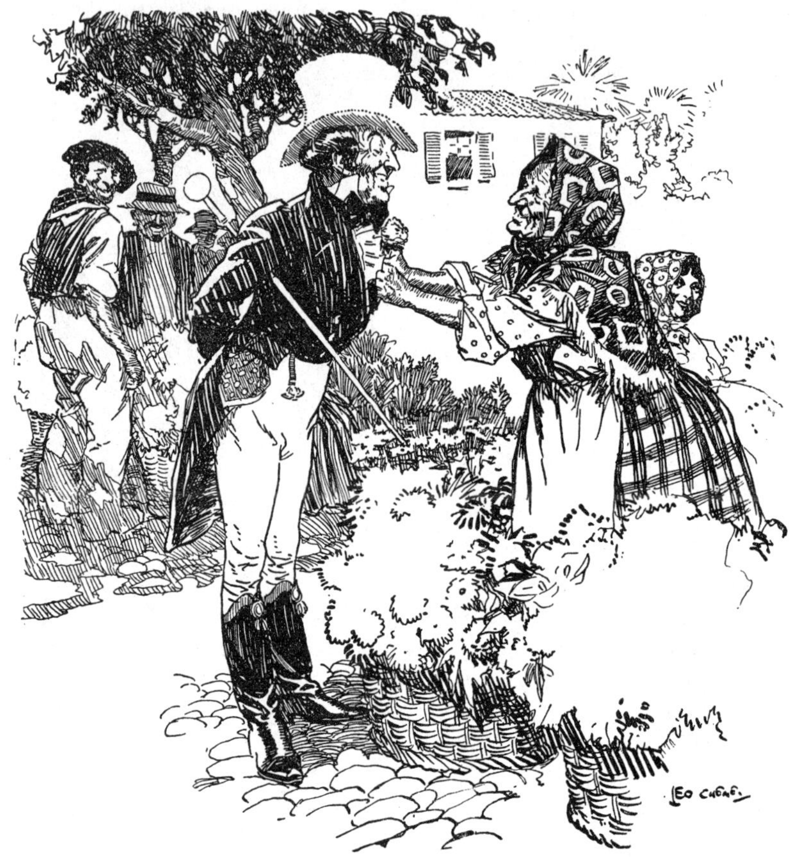

FIG. 28.—By LEO CHENEY.

constant association with the loveliest aspects of nature. The main characteristic is the placing of the various tones, from black to pure white, in such a way that their juxtaposition is in itself attractive to the eye as pattern. In Vierge this faculty of using the additional interest of colour pattern without losing the aspect of reality is wonderful, and both Howard Pyle and H. R. Millar owe much to him in the realistic side of their work, although each developed a "fairy-tale manner" entirely personal and imaginative, more akin to the sixth method.

The work of Menzel, Millais, Sandys, Boyd Houghton, and others of the 'sixties was in this fifth category of decorative realism, and there is much to be learned from them all, but especially from that prince of draughtsmen, Adolph Menzel, in his illustrations to "Frederic the Great"; in itself an education in costume illustration, and incidentally showing some of the most wonderful examples of facsimile wood-engraving extant.

E. A. Abbey's work in illustrations to Shakespeare and the old ballads of England shows what can be done with a mere pen; but it is an elaborate method which is as impervious to copyists as Phil May's simplicity. Alfred Parsons, in doing some flower and landscape illustrations to accompany the ballad drawings by Abbey, attempted the employment of a similar elaboration of line, merely demonstrating that it was not the elaboration of style that made the Abbey drawings pure joy to contemplate, but the exquisite sense of style and colour which the amazing technique "got across." The method is having some influence on modern magazine illustration; in the work of the late Warwick Reynolds and "Blam" for instances.

SIXTH METHOD (see Fig. 29).

Success in this depends on intensity of vision and feeling, together with fertility of imagination, supported by great resource in actual and theoretical knowledge of drawing. It is not an easy thing to get away from the actual, especially when the figures introduced are naturally drawn, as in Anning Bell's illustrations. In these every detail is recognisably founded on fact, yet the whole effect transcends earthly limitations in a beatific vision wholly in the spirit of poetry. Anning Bell's obviously sincere devotion to absolute beauty of form and line has inspired a generation of art students, and as with all who perfect a method or successfully adopt an old convention to their own handling, his copyists are legion, all unconscious of the fact that every element of his work depends on one personality for its creation and co-relation. Beardsley, with a manner as startling and bizarre as Bell's is calm, has influenced the same generation towards the free expression of personal views. The fact that his own personality was decidedly exotic had the useful effect of establishing at a stagnant moment the right of the artist to his own soul. Between the line of Bell and that of Beardsley there is a wide choice in the older forms of expres-

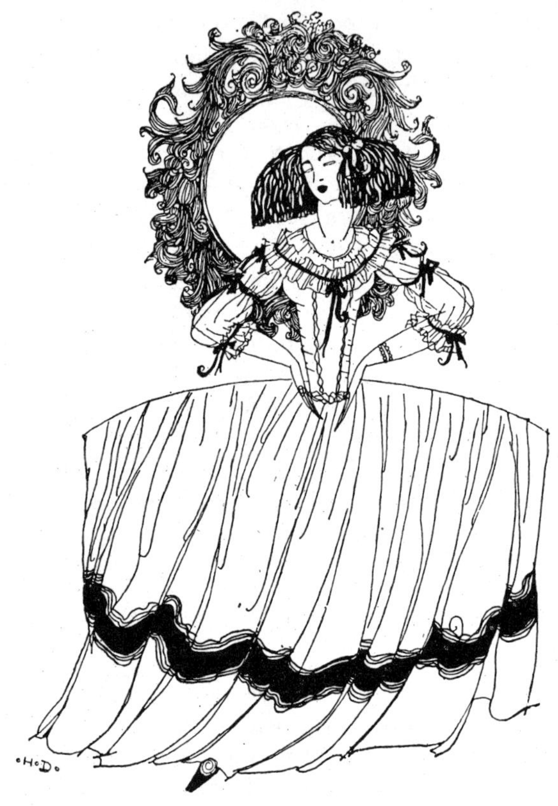

FIG. 29.—By HELEN DRYDEN.

sion, and beyond all this the naïveté of the moderns gradually coming to us from France and Italy via Germany and America.

In this sixth method there is much vitality; the trend is towards it, as beautifully decorated books are substituted for indifferently illustrated ones. Fine decoration is gradually creeping into commercial printing, and advertising literature promises much for decorative pen work. In America it is a commonplace to find articles with no artistic pretensions advertised with drawings by the best workers in this non-representational method. A few years hence it will be the usual thing here in England. We may see Albert Rutherston's work as an advertisement for a furniture house, infusing a little humour into a dull business.

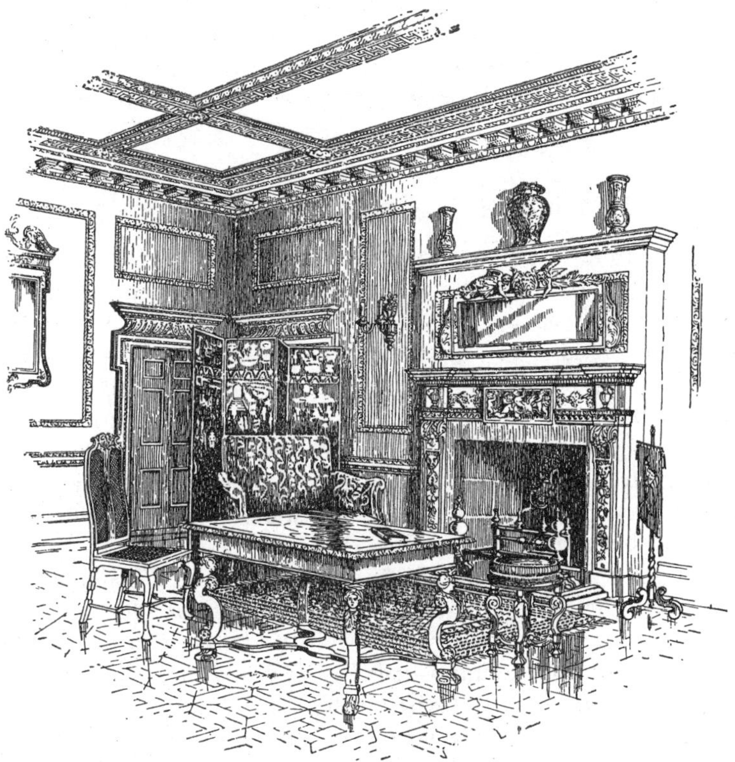

FIG. 30.—By H. CESZINSKI.

SEVENTH METHOD (see Fig. 30).

This architectural method includes the drawing of interiors and furniture both in elevation and perspective. It is an interesting and lucrative branch of pen work for those with leanings towards the exact and mechanical. It is certainly necessary for anyone contemplating it as a career to undergo some architectural training—even to the extent of becoming a qualified architect. From inside the profession the going is better, as commissions depend on the confidence of architectural clients in one's *knowledge* as well as draughtsmanship.

Although the drawing of actual buildings will form a considerable part of the architectural pen draughtsman's work, the names of Pennell, Railton, Griggs, Peixotto, Rico, etc., are left as practising in method No. 5, because their approach is entirely from the picturesque and pictorial angle, dealing entirely with existing work. The architectural draughtsman's *raison d'être* is in showing people what a building or room will be like, hence the need for knowledge of construction, style, and materials.

EIGHTH METHOD (see Fig. 31).

Humorous drawing suggests the rollicking artist, rubicund and mellow, to whom the quip is the natural method of expression in speech as in work; but, alas, it is not so really, and humorous artists are generally rather noticeably anxious to discover humorous items in the experiences of their friends. So students may take comfort from the fact that the humorous artist is not necessarily a humorist, and the conclusion that it is not even essential to possess a strong sense of humour to deal in the variations of the few basic jokes which have existed since the beginnings of things.

Horse sense is more useful than a sense of humour in making people laugh with you week in and week out for life, the power to register hits being safer with well-tried weapons.

To rely on producing a brilliant new joke for every drawing is simply absurd; so the wise professional humorist approaches his chief problem in a very business-like way, happy, indeed, if he can create a few types which "get over" and endear themselves to a grateful public who will love them and look for them for ever. The born humorist who sees the funny side of small things and the value of exaggerating their effect, has very little advantage over the business-like and energetic person who acquires humour at so much per joke—if accepted—from the professional joke factor.

These are wide generalities, but they are useful. We all know our Tom Webster, Bateman, and d'Egville as heaven-sent laughter providers, each with a personal laughter-provoking formula which is independent of the subject or joke, and is in cumulative effect a business in itself, with an extremely valuable stock in trade in the employment of a few lines which vary little in each drawing.

The student adopting humorous drawing as a profession should aim, therefore, at a little niche that he can occupy exclusively, and exhibit his small but lively collection of puppets in his own way, adding to the cast only when those already playing to crowded houses show signs of tiredness.

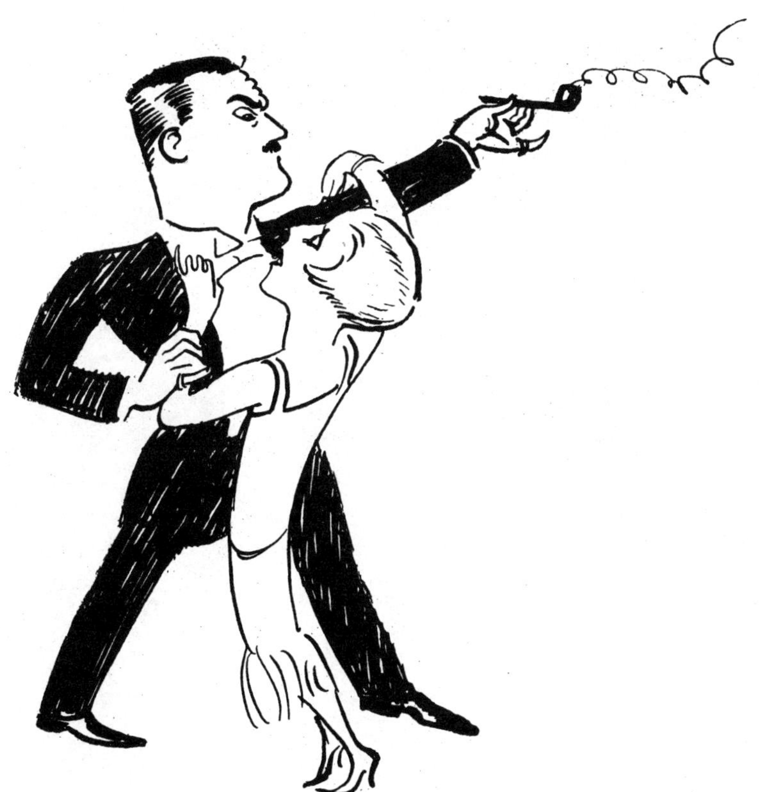

FIG. 31.—A Humorous Advertisement by BREABEY.

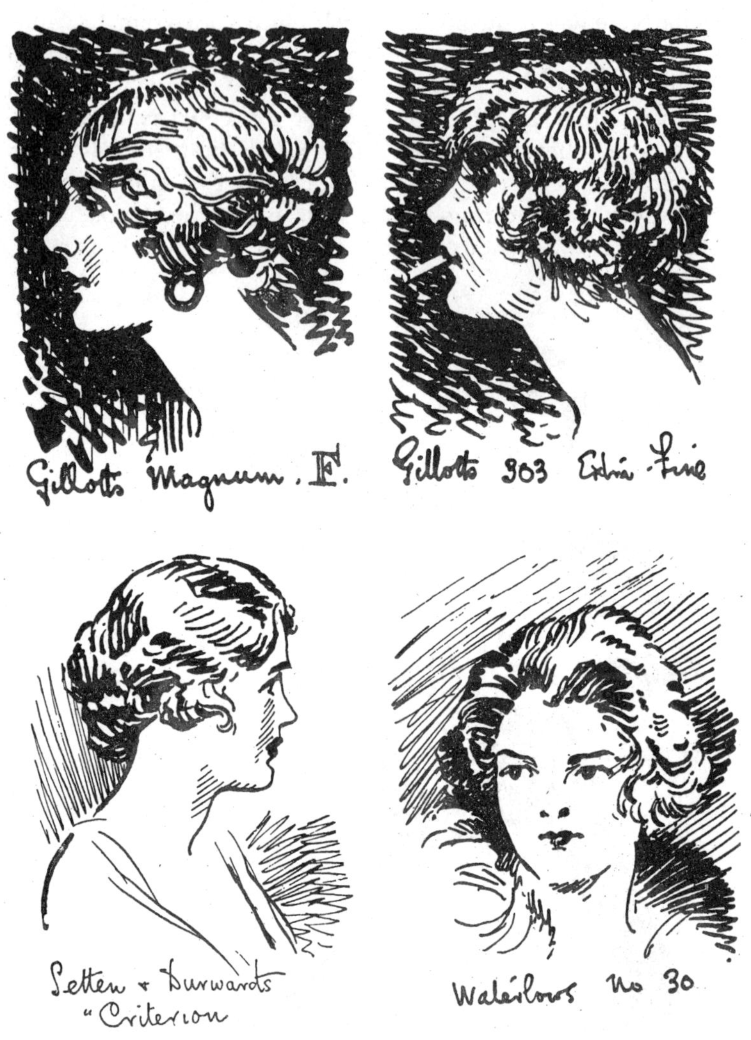

FIG. 32.—Comparative Results from Pens.

Gillott's "Magnum" will tend to give a line $\frac{1}{32}$ of an inch wide, or *without* pressure give lines as on cheek in drawing.

Gillott's 303 will offer a little more resistance to very heavy lines, and give finer ones under slight pressure.

Setten & Durward's "Criterion" is an absolutely delightful instrument on the lines of Gillott's 303, but a little finer in performance and build.

Waterlow's No. 30 is certainly the best pen encountered, and should be tried if still obtainable.

CHAPTER IV

MATERIALS

THE letters that used to reach me as editor of a technical paper, asking for advice on the materials to use in the practice of various branches of drawing and painting, persuade me that there must be a considerable number of workers and amateurs who really find it difficult to discover the right thing at the right moment, or having discovered it, fail to recognise that it is the right thing.

In the actual words of one puzzled inquirer: "How can I know that it is only perseverance that is necessary to overcome the cussedness of some materials, when it may well be that I am using something that is just wrong for what I am aiming at? The lack of a word of advice from some one who really knows from their own experience in practice or intimate acquaintance with the methods of practical men may leave me struggling for mastery over something that is not worth while; wasting time which is much too precious to squander in grappling with actual materials."

The professional artist is generally rather proud of his ability to get good results on any surface with any kind of tool; but this is the privilege of those whose hand and eye are trained to a point where the comparative value of experiment can be safely judged. The beginner is generally incapable of judging his own efforts, and is really helped by confidence in his materials.

Any undertaking is helped along by knowledge of the routine which renders progress smooth. No wise student will place reliance upon any formula which promises a short cut to proficiency in actual drawing; for the utmost that can be expected from pens, ink, and paper is that they obey you and place no obstacles in the way of your own expression. The help that good pens, ink, card, and paper can give is passive and largely a matter of individual preference and experience.

The preferences of the experienced are generally founded on basic facts which must be of value to the inexperienced, and it is these facts which are drawn upon for the information conveyed in this chapter. The range of variety in papers, cards, inks, and pens is so wide that the student may spend much time in unprofitable contemplation or expensive trial without striking the best in any direction.

The paper or board used for pen drawing should be pure

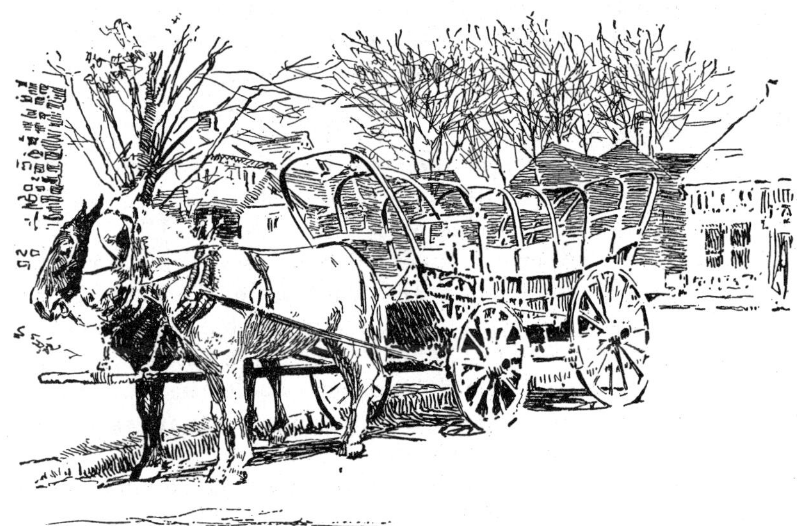

FIG. 33.—Distinctly shows use of two different Pens.

white. The charm of the method is in its contrasts, so the maximum effect is obtained by complete contrast between ground and lines. The use of tinted surfaces for pen work is bad from every point of view. Walter Crane used deep cream boards for many of his pen drawings for book illustration, thereby giving the engravers unnecessary trouble in photographing them, besides losing 50 per cent. of their charm as original drawings, the reproductions, printed on white paper, showing a much better effect.

Bristol board has an unassailable vogue as the most popular of all surfaces for pen drawing. It should be fully realised that the words are but a name used by many makers, and that its quality varies considerably. At its best it is certainly the finest surface for pure line work; its hard, glossy surface resists the scratch of the steel nib better than anything known. Many of Charles Keene's drawings were made on notepaper, and the right Bristol board should possess exactly the same surface as this old-fashioned notepaper with the additional advantage of greater thickness to permit the correction of mistakes. Pencil must be lightly used on it, as heavy marks are apt to become indelible and interfere with the subsequent pen lines. Extensive alterations to a drawing should be made with a sharp knife. It is possible to remove the surface of a properly made board and work on the erasure. Bristol board surgery is an art in itself, its greatest effort being the actual removal of the offending area in the drawing and inlaying a virgin piece of board which gives fresh hope of success. This operation is performed by cutting with a very sharp knife through the original board and another piece of the same thickness beneath it; if well done, with the knife held exactly upright, the lower piece should fit the space in the drawing so well as to be imperceptible when dropped into position.

Bristol board is made in foolscap, demy, medium, and royal sizes, and is built up in sheets. The thinnest sold is "two sheet," which is quite satisfactory for simple work. Three, four, five, or six sheet should be used for more elaborate work, according to its importance. The operation described above should not be attempted with boards thicker than three or four sheet. Before starting to "ink in" a drawing, some artists dust the board over with a "pounce" of fine chalk to give the ink a certain bite. If this is done, care must be taken to remove all trace of the chalk, or it will quickly choke the flow of ink from the pen by the formation of a minute but troublesome ball of chalk and ink mixture on its point.

Cheaper boards are made by covering cheap cardboard with sheets of white paper. These are quite satisfactory for many purposes, but alteration is practically impossible, as the covering paper used is generally too thin to stand disturbance and the inner card is far from white. For certain and direct work there is nothing against this kind of board, providing the covering is stout enough to stand the pen stroke and the inner filling has a smooth surface without the grain, which has a nasty habit of setting traps for the pen point.

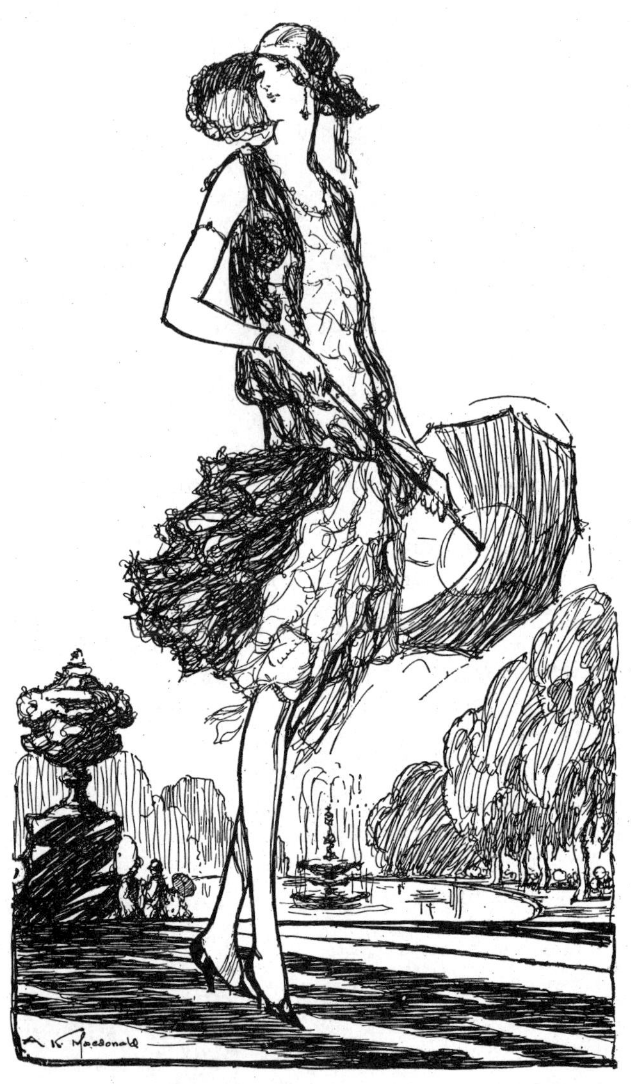

FIG. 34.—By A. K. MACDONALD.

The crispness of line shown is obtainable only on smooth, hard surface boards.

A surface possessing certain advantages over Bristol board is afforded by hot-pressed drawing paper, Whatman's, Arnold's, O.W.S., or other good makers, obtainable in sizes from demy, 20 by 15½, up to the huge double elephant, 40 by 26¾, beloved of the architects. The smaller sizes may be used pinned down to a board, but the larger need stretching to remain flat. The usual way to do this is to fold up about an inch of the edge of the sheet all round and place it on a board slightly larger than its full size. After moistening the paper thoroughly with very clean water and a very clean sponge, cover the turned-up edges with photo paste, or, better still, "shoemakers' paste," and turn them down to the board, taking the greatest care that there are no unstuck places. In turning the pasted edges down, pull outwards from centre in all directions to ensure even stretching; but do not stretch paper overmuch or it may burst as it contracts in drying.

The "bank" paper used in "press sketch books" combines transparency with a useful whiteness and hardness that makes it possible for pen drawing. Its particular quality is that a pencil sketch can be made on one page which can be selectively traced on the preceding page in ink, thereby saving the tiresome process of redrawing. Further, if the first attempt to render the sketch in ink is not entirely satisfactory, the necessary alterations can be made by repetition of the same process with the offending pen drawing.

Tracing paper can obviously be used in the same way, and good pen drawings can be made on it over photographs by those capable of selecting essentials. It is not easy to make a satisfactory drawing in this way, but it can be done. To lose the irritating effect of thin tracing paper, mount the drawing when finished on white card and cut a mount to cover the edges of it.

Although placed second in order of importance, the selection of the best pens to use is perhaps quite as vital as the finding of the best surfaces for them to travel over.

It is utterly impossible to indicate the "right" pen for general use; such an ideal instrument cannot exist; so we immediately arrive at the necessity for a range of pens covering individual needs. One of the first things the student will discover in connection with artists' pens is their extremely short life, due possibly to the action of drawing inks. To obviate this to some extent, the use of a bristle pen-wiper is recommended; such can be obtained in ordinary office stationers, a small china cup containing a bunch of fairly fine bristles tightly held at the base and less tightly held by the circum-

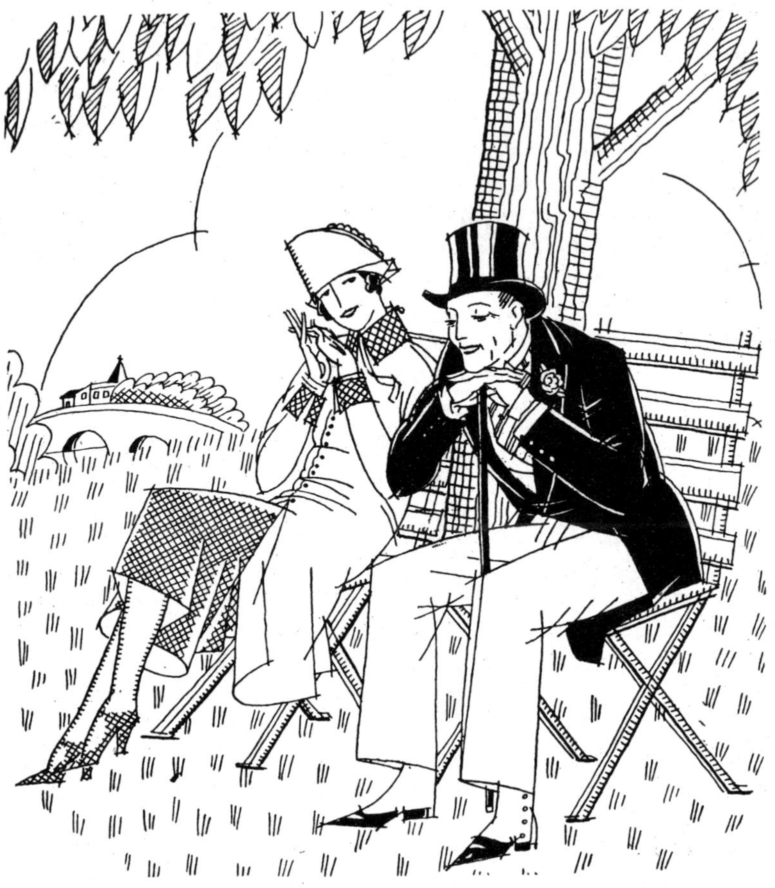

FIG. 35.—Part of a Circular Illustration by ASHLEY HAVINDEN.
A Gillott's 303 will give this type of line.

ference of the cup at the top. The pen should be frequently dipped into this while in use, and the deposit of ink removed before it hardens.

The pens most quoted by pen draughtsmen are "Gillott's crow quill" and "Gillott's mapping pen," both excellent instruments in their way, and for ordinary size work practically indispensable. The former is a nib with a normal line of extreme fineness, but so beautifully fashioned that it will easily respond to sweeping curves involving differences of thickness, though it should not be used for uniformly thick lines. The range of the mapping pen is greater, although its normal point width is equally delicate ; its life is short, especially if much advantage is taken of its astonishing flexibility ; it literally gives its life to the drawings it is used upon.

There are many useful pens of similar scope to the famous Gillott productions, but cheaper. The " Criterion," for instance, made by Messrs Setten & Durward, Birmingham, is a small mapping pen which gives good results in strength, endurance, and flexibility, and is sold on cards of twelve for one shilling. Waterlow & Sons' No. 30, a legal writer's pen, is a serious rival to Gillott's No. 303, giving even greater flexibility with rather less strength. The points are more liable to snap, owing to the daring arrangement of the ink-holding perforations, to which its extreme flexibility is due.

A stock of these four nibs will satisfy any artist's needs for the production of fine, flexible lines. The Gillott No. 303 will probably get most use. Next in size, the Gillott No. 404, is worth stocking for use on medium lines, which strain the finer pens.

For stronger work or drawings on a large scale for reduction by photographic processes, there is an immense choice of pens ; but it would be difficult to find a better than Gillott's "Magnum" barrel pen No. 227, which, although called " fine," will maintain a line one thirty-second of an inch wide with ease. The medium width nib of this same brand is not very good, from an artist's point of view, the main reason being that it parts with Indian ink rather too easily for safety. Both these pens are intended for purely writing purposes, but the fine-pointed variety certainly holds Indian ink as well as any artist's pen (see Fig. 32).

The " quill of our fathers," now used very seldom for writing, is still in favour with many illustrators for broad, effective work in foregrounds. Its flexibility is even greater than the softest steel nib, and it is delightfully responsive. Its " life " is indeed brief, especially if much use is made of its facility in spreading its points.

For drawings where it is intended to maintain an exactly similar width of line throughout, a " Stylus " is useful if it is kept very clean. Fixed inks should not be used, as they block the points immediately.

Fountain pens are lovely things to draw with ; but here, again, the difficulty of fixed inks is encountered. With unfixed Indian ink they work easily and dependably if washed out before each filling ; but it should be possible to get an ordinary black ink of sufficient density and obviate the necessity of this frequent cleaning, which is tiresome.

It is possible to get a " double-line pen," which has a certain limited usefulness. The name explains it as a two-pointed affair which makes two parallel lines at one stroke, and some interesting textures can be made with it. In private life it is intended for ordinary commercial " double ruling."

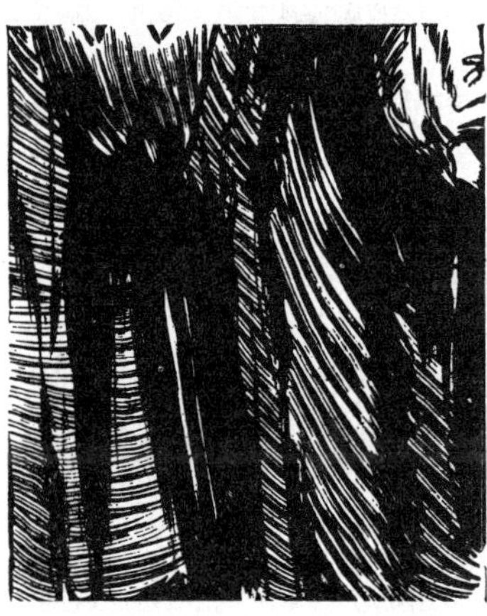

FIG. 36.

Wonderful effects can be obtained with a Japanese writing brush or ordinary water-colour Sable No. 2 or 3, cut away about half-way down the hair to leave a small point of hairs about equal to a No. 1 Sable. Brangwyn, Will Dyson, and Gordon Brown used this method in illustration with results entirely different in each case. The richness possible is shown in the square cut from a Dyson drawing herewith (Fig. 36) and in the drawing by " Tell " (Fig. 37).

With regard to inks, it is almost a foregone conclusion that the ready prepared variety in bottles will be used. The old custom of grinding one's own from stick Chinese is happily no longer necessary, for the result is not so good as that now available commercially. There are many varieties, and it will be found that one artist in his time likes many of them, and many artists like none of them at any time. The ideal drawing ink has yet to come ; of all artists' materials it is the least satisfactory at present. There are many preparations of the same stuff, and the " fixed " kinds all suffer

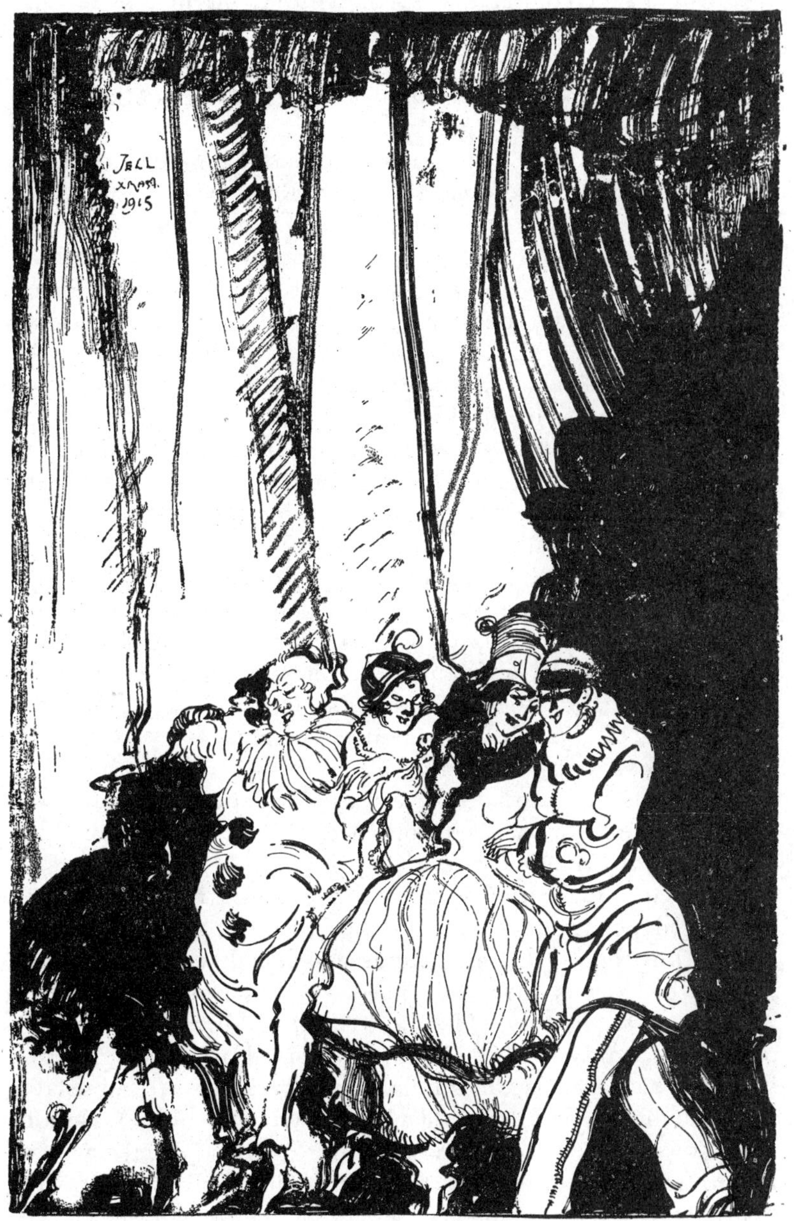

FIG. 37.—Pen and Brush Drawing by "TELL."

from the same complaints—accumulating on nibs, wrecking same, liability to thicken if exposed to air, necessity for distilled water for dilution—all due to the nature of the original materials which must be used to give the dead blackness essential before everything in pen drawing.

A list of the better known inks will perhaps be useful: there is very little to chose between them, but Rowney's "Kandahar" helps me to keep an even temper better than most, so I will place it first in order of service, merely on that account, without attempting to "place" the others. Higgins' (American), Bourgeois' "Encre de Chine Liquide" (French), Pelican (German), Winsor & Newton's, Reeve's, Madderton's, the last-named obtainable only from Madderton & Co., Loughton, direct. Maginnis, in his book on "Pen Drawing," mentions another American ink—Carter's; but I have not encountered it, and his only recommendation of it is that it is put up for sale in bottles which do not tip over on the slightest pretext.

Chinese white is the best corrective other than actual erasion, and is obtainable in bottles or tubes. In using this it will be found that it is always best to put a small quantity out on a very clean saucer and apply with a very clean and fairly new brush. It is a very unfortunate habit with many to take the white straight from the bottle or tube neck with any brush and run the risk of "graying" the entire contents.

White has many uses in addition to its corrective help, the most obvious being to add pattern to black surfaces by drawing over solid ink or massed line areas with a brush or pen charged with Chinese white.

The equipment necessary for successful practice in pen drawing depends much on the scope of the work to be undertaken; but there are many things additional to pens, ink, and paper which every artist will need. A table of some kind on which to draw is one. The old idea of this was a fairly large table with a drawing board tilted to a fixed angle resting upon it. The new idea is the studio drawing table with adjustable top and shelves at a lower level for materials. The table idea is discredited as not conducive to the greatest efficiency; the temptation it offers to load the space round the actual drawing board with irrelevant books, papers, and odd materials is too much for the average artist's power of resistance. The specially made table entirely kills this "collector" habit in any artist, forcing him for the good of his soul to concentrate on the drawing in hand, with no conflicting interests or worrying interference with the freedom of his hands. Books of reference,

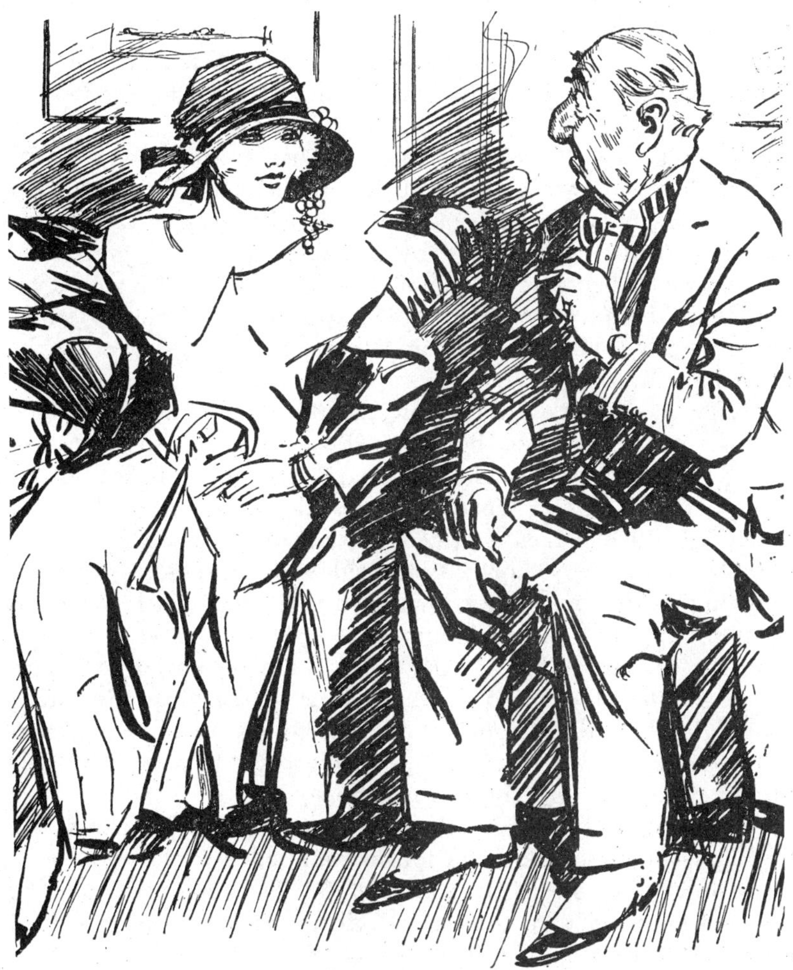

FIG. 38.—Part of a Drawing by GEORGE WHITELAW, showing the performance of a Pen under the Pressure of Quick, Sure Strokes to express Folds.

or anything else thicker than a photograph or rough sketch, *must* be arranged on a separate table drawn up beside the artist's desk and easily pushed out of the way when finished with. Unconscious of sufferings nobly borne under the old system of chaos, it is difficult for the experienced artist to realise the relief which the possession of one of these " desks " can give. The student who starts with one is fortunate. There are several makes on the market. Messrs J. Bryce Smith Ltd., 117 Hampstead Road, make one which in their own words is " roomy, rigid, simple, and cheap," and will take all the materials needed with drawing board, 31 by 23 in., for £4.

Failing the attainment of this most useful accessory, with its neat, trim, and workman-like appearance as a constant invitation to sit down and create masterpieces, it is necessary to have a drawing board at least 31 by 23 in. in size, and preferably with an attached rest on one of its longer edges, tilting it at an angle of about 15° with the table; if a greater angle is desired occasionally, this can be supplemented with wooden blocks at each end.

In choice of a board, the obvious advantage of a hard surface for drawing upon must be weighed together with the necessity of getting drawing pins into it and subsequently out of it. Very close grain in wood indicates slow growth, and has a tenacity which makes it difficult to pin drawings to it. Many old boards show a surface studded with steel—the driven-in remains of drawing pins which shed their heads in response to vain attempts to get them out.

The drawing table or desk should be placed at right angles to a window, facing north for preference, and in sitting at it the light should fall from the left side to obviate shadows from the hand falling on the drawing in progress. It is not advisable to face the light directly in working.

An outfit of mathematical instruments will be necessary. Compasses—a separate pair for ink and pencil work is advisable to avoid the waste of time and temper in changing the parts. Springbows (smaller compasses with spring outwards instead of screw hilt for opening)—a full set of three. Ruling pen with lifting side for cleaning.

A pair of proportional compasses is occasionally useful for exact reduction or enlargement of detail from sketches, etc. They are set with a screw so that all measurements taken by the points at one end are proportionally reduced and registered by another set of points at the opposite end.

A T-square with shifting head is useful, as it enables the

artist to get parallel lines in several directions. Its blade should be the same length or slightly less than that of the board it is to serve. Two celluloid (or transparent composition) set-squares, 45° and 60°, are needed for setting off lines at angles to the T-square.

Cut curves in the same material as the transparent set-

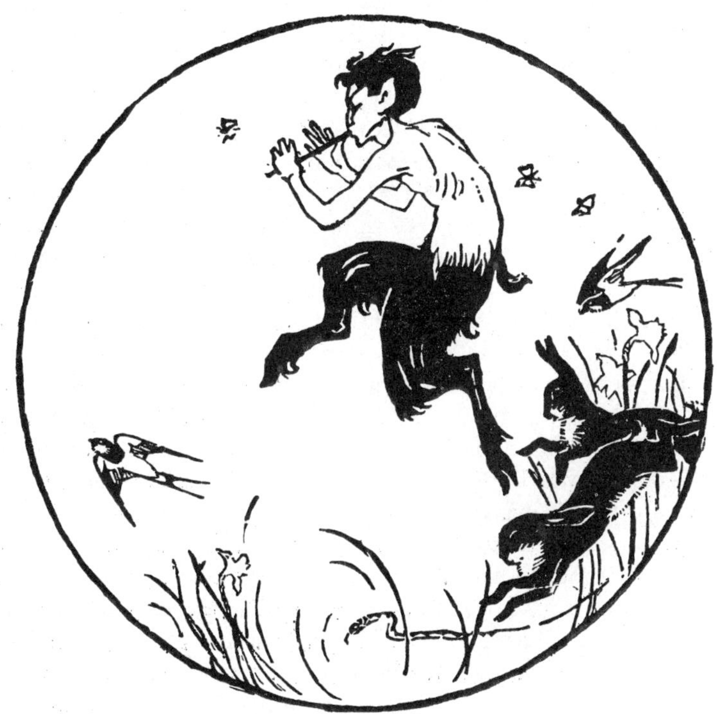

FIG. 39.—A "Woodcut" Technique for Decorative Work can be achieved with a Broad Nib.

squares are used for drawing exact curves with the ruling pen; they are splendid when the same curve has to be made in opposite directions. Balanced against the T-square and reversed to a marked point, they give the compensating curves with absolute accuracy, without effort on the part of the artist.

For measurements, a ruler marked in inches and a scale of centimetres and millimetres are required. They should be separate, as it is very annoying to find that when both are on one, the scale required is very seldom the first to turn up for use.

Drawing pins are usually employed to fasten the card to the board, which soon gets full of holes if constantly used for drawings of varying sizes. These holes do not matter if thick card only is used on the board ; but if paper is used, the pen has a trick of finding them through it, and it is wise to put card under the paper to get a safe surface. Some artists keep a piece of card on their drawing boards, and instead of drawing pins they use gummed paper to attach their working card or paper to this blank sheet, which is pinned at the extreme corners and needs renewing only at lengthy intervals.

When a glass " board " is used, this gum-paper method of attachment is the only one possible. Some artists distrust the power of wood to alter and get away from true angles, so for very accurate work they work on plate glass, which cannot alter very much and is also very pleasant to work on, the T-square running beautifully along its polished edge. A good method of working for those who habitually use the same size of boards is to glue to the glass a cardboard frame made from cuttings of these same boards, and large enough on the inside to admit of easily dropping in or taking out the boards for drawings ; very light gummed paper attachments only are needed when this is done, and they may be cut through with a penknife for removing the drawings.

India-rubber is rather a worry to the user of surface boards ; the ideal rubber is another of the things that are very hard to find. It is always best to use soft white rubber for removing pencil marks. The right way to use rubber is very lightly on the drawing and more heavily on a spare piece of paper, which means that the unwanted pencil is gently lifted out of the way instead of distributed over the surface in a fine film of grey. Soiled rubber may be washed in soap and water if care is taken that it is thoroughly dry before it is put into use again. An ordinary typewriter eraser is employable for taking out light ink lines, but the disturbed surface must be made smooth before working upon it once more. This may be done with an illuminator's agate burnisher, which must be absolutely clean and dry, or it will crush dirt into the grain of the board. A safer method is to keep sheets of thin, smooth bank paper to put over these roughened places while they are pressed smooth by rubbing with the handle or blade-back of a penknife.

A reducing glass, giving a greatly reduced version of the

drawing seen through it, is a necessity. It gives an approximate idea of how the work will come in the size it is to appear

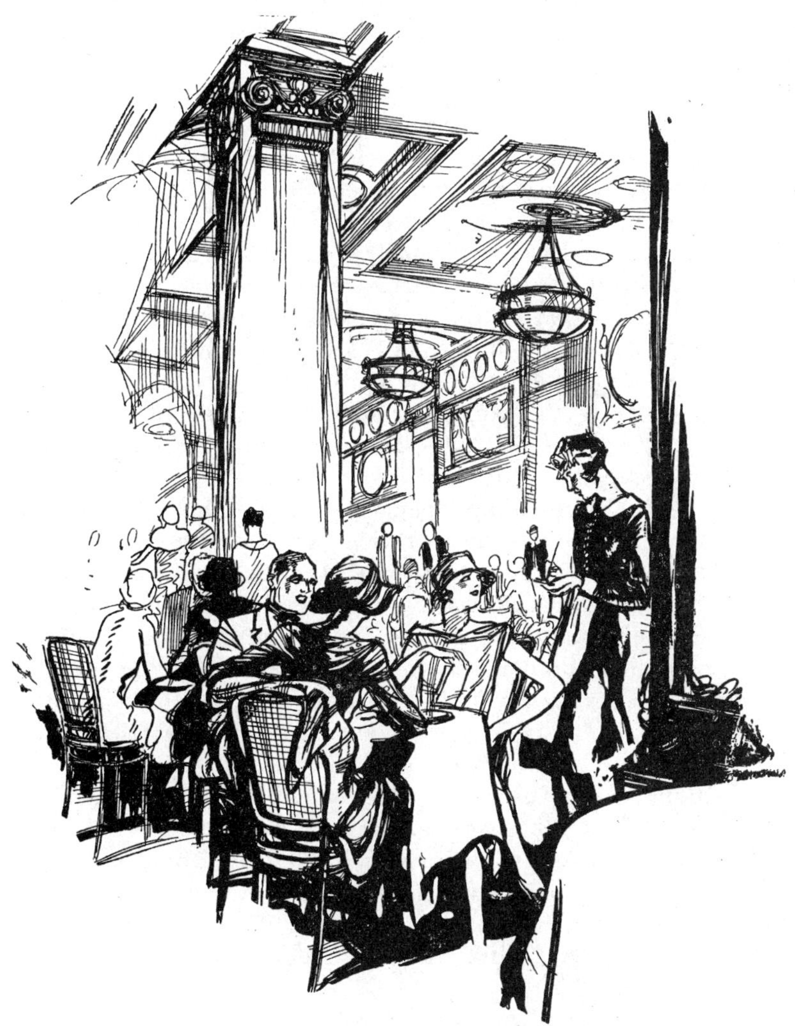

FIG. 40.—By JOHN PIMLOTT.
Clever contrasts in line by employment of two or more nibs.

when reproduced. By it every line is reduced in exact proportional thickness to its original. In photo reproduction some thickening in the lines usually happens, so it is not a bad fault if some of the thin lines in drawing appear over-fine under the reducing glass. It is practically impossible to get a line so thin that the camera will not reproduce it in printable form. A rectangular unmounted lens is the most useful, but the usual circular kind is cheaper and should not be less than 2½ in. in diameter.

Pencils are extremely important to the pen draughtsman. A responsive pencil assists ideas as much as a refractory one hinders their flow. Badly made pencils behave badly under the sharpening process, and a fairly good test of the grade is its ability to stand cutting sharply away from the holder as in the act of whittling a stick, which is the cleanest way to sharpen, as it sends the black powder away from the hand instead of distributing it over the thumb and forefinger, which happens in the case of cutting towards the body. A pencil which breaks repeatedly under the whittling method is generally unfit for artists' use; but the test must be conducted with a very sharp knife; any pencil will break if it is pushed off instead of cut.

The finding of a suitable pencil is therefore a serious matter to the student. Some can work best with hard pencils, others with soft; some do everything with the medium grade, H.B., or writing pencil. The best way is to keep a range available, ready sharpened, and including every grade that is likely to be useful. For preliminary studies all will probably be needed in various ways, but for actual work on the board that is to be inked in, an H. or H.B. is generally best, and should be used very lightly. F. H. Townsend's pencil drawings from his first studies, when finished on Bristol board and ready for working over in ink, were models of what should be done, having the appearance of highly finished silver-point drawings. They must have given him pure joy in the actual translation into pen and ink, for with every detail of drawing and composition settled, he could concentrate on technique and fine tone effects.

The pencil "grades" range from 6 B. to 6 H., very soft to very hard. The B. grades include 1, 2, 3, 4, and 6 B., and are mainly for sketching and preliminary studies on paper. F. and H.B., the medium grades, contain leads of firm texture useful on either rough or smooth surfaces; both are suitable for drawing on Bristol board. The harder varieties, H. and H.H., are also useful for work on drawings to be afterwards inked,

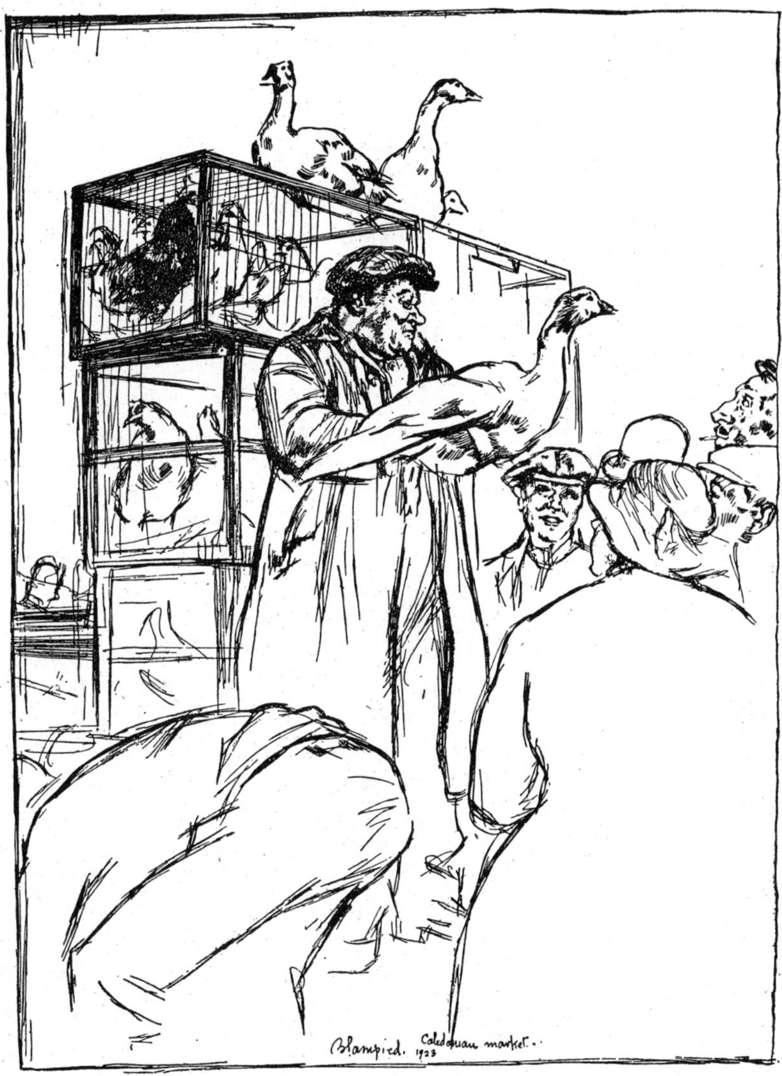

FIG. 41.—The use of a very fine line gives this drawing almost the quality of an etching.

By E. H. BLAMPIED.

but great care must be exercised that they do not indent the surface and spoil it. The 3, 4, and 6 H. grades are mainly for mechanical and architectural drawing, but all can be used on Bristol board for very precise work if the above precaution is observed. It is not easy to get a good cheap pencil, and there are several makes of reliable quality such as "Venus" and "Koh-i-noor," which guarantee care in their production and render the search for cheapness hardly worth the candle.

It is often essential to transfer a preliminary sketch to the final card, necessitating transfer paper of some kind. One method is to cover the back of the sketch with pencil, rubbed to form a solid mass surface, and trace the sketch through on to the card; this is quite useful, but also wasteful in time, so most artists make a sheet of thin transfer paper by covering very thin bank paper with powdered black or blue pencil, thoroughly rubbed in to its surface on one side. Carbon transfer paper must not be used, as it gives a line which is liable to photograph as well as ink, and is almost indelible.

Tracing paper is necessary for transferring parts from rough sketches, duplicating detail, and tracing drawings which have gone wrong to the extent of making a new start advisable. The best way to trace from thin paper is to hold it up to a window and apply the tracing paper to the back, thereby tracing the drawing on its face in reverse. The advantage of this is that the tracing can then be rubbed down direct on to the drawing card by pressure on the back of the tracing and appears in its correct form.

Finished pen drawings may be made on good tracing paper. The older kinds were too greasy to hold ink properly; it would either spread or refuse to make continuous lines, but good modern tracings give a perfectly clean, reproducible line. It is possible, therefore, to make pen drawings direct from photographs or rough sketches by superimposing tracing paper and working on it, a method which is much appreciated in commercial work. When using a photograph in this way, it is best to have a duplicate copy, as visibility is low under the tracing paper, and the extra copy is wonderfully explanatory.

A finished drawing on tracing paper should be either cut to the exact size and mounted on stout white card, or a mount should be cut to this size and used to cover the edges of the tracing paper left beyond the actual size required. In mounting, some clear mountant is essential, otherwise stripes show unpleasantly and detract from the effect.

It is best to get tracing paper in rolls of 50 yards, which should be hung on wire or string through the centre so that the required quantity can be cut as needed. Pure white or bluish-white tracing is best; the yellowish varieties are apt to deepen in colour, and are in every way unsuitable for artists' use.

Pen Drawing on a Photographic Basis

The use of photography as a basis for any kind of drawing is quite legitimate. In pen drawing it happens to be specially useful, as the ink used, being waterproof, makes the bleach print process possible.

In this process, which is much used by commercial and press artists, the actual drawing is made on a photographic print which is subsequently removed by "bleaching," leaving the pen lines on perfectly clean and undisturbed card.

Numerous examples will be found in the trade papers of the various applications of the process, which is almost indispensable in engineering, motoring, cycling, and kindred types of illustration demanding great accuracy to enable interested parties to distinguish vital points in make. The advertisement for a commodity or article is generally illustrated by what appears to the uninitiated as a marvellous pen drawing, with every mechanical detail in place and important points duly stressed in a way that would be practically impossible without the photographic basis.

The bleach print method is very simple in working. A light print of the photograph to be used is made on paper suitable for pen work. Any small print can be enlarged to a workable size by the ordinary enlarging apparatus. The drawing is then made over this print in any medium that is quite waterproof, and when finished the photographic basis is removed. If the paper is not flat enough for working in comfort it can be mounted on cardboard and unmounted by soaking in water before it is submitted to the baths necessary in the bleaching process.

Any photographic firm will make a bleach print to any desired size from a photo or snap, and will do the bleaching out after the drawing is completed; but the process is fairly simple, especially to those familiar with photographic developing and printing. It is just possible to draw over an ordinary print if fuller's earth is first dusted on to give a bite for the pen and ink on the polished surface; but it is rather difficult to see how the drawing is going over such a strong ground, and the result when this is removed is apt to be very disappointing. Therefore it is best to get specially light prints on thick paper, as this saves mounting and facilitates the work of selection from the abundant detail.

The actual bleaching-out process is simple, according to the formula given by Bernard Foster Stokes in "Drawing," and chemical or photographic knowledge is not necessary in carrying it out:—

Two developing dishes must be obtained large enough to take the largest drawing contemplated; one pound of hyposulphite of soda, commonly known as hypo, and an ounce of potassium ferrocyanide, which is generally in a small glass bottle. Both chemicals are in the form of crystals, and the total cost is about a shilling.

Take a pint dish and half-fill it with water; into this put about two teaspoonfuls of hypo. When this has dissolved, add potassium crystals until the solution becomes a deep yellow colour. This gives the bleach, which must be mixed fresh and used immediately. Place the print in it, face downwards; it can afterwards be reversed and the disappearance of the photograph observed. The dish should be gently rocked to assist the operation, and the print allowed to remain in the solution for a few minutes after this is apparently completed to ensure against future trouble from stains not immediately apparent.

When all signs of the photograph have disappeared, the process is complete. Transfer the sketch (as it now is) to a second dish, which should be filled with clean water for washing. This should be carried out by several changes of water for from twenty to thirty minutes, and must be conscientiously done, otherwise stains will appear and discoloration take place in the near future.

Drying can be done by hanging up or by laying the sketch face up on a clean blotting pad. It can afterwards be mounted and the drawing touched up, if necessary. To mount, place on a piece of glass, face down; damp the back, remove surplus moisture, and apply a good paste mountant, working from the centre to the edges. Remove from the glass to the mount, again place the glass over the sketch, and apply even pressure for a few moments.

The success of the drawing thus obtained depends on the technical skill of the draughtsman; but the commercial advantages of the process are obvious in great saving of time and the possibility of showing elaborate things adequately in papers where tone blocks are unprintable.

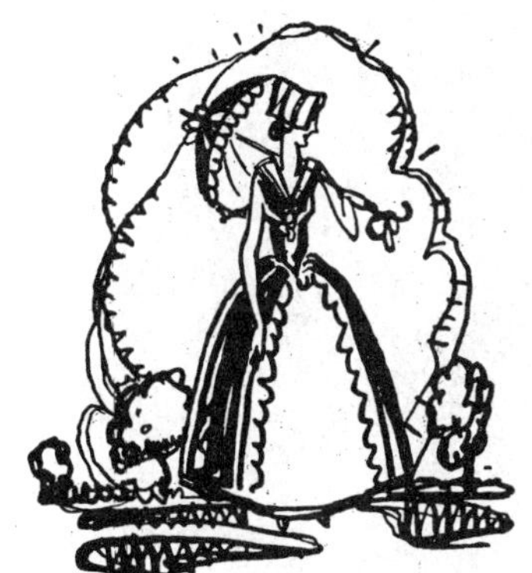

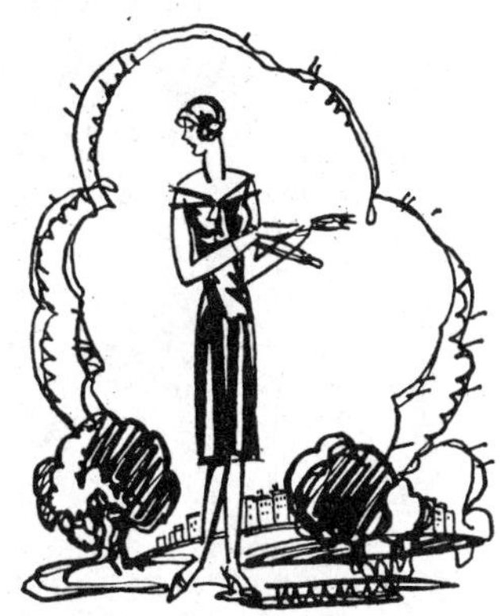

FIGS. 42 and 43.—Pen Decorations by MILNER GRAY.

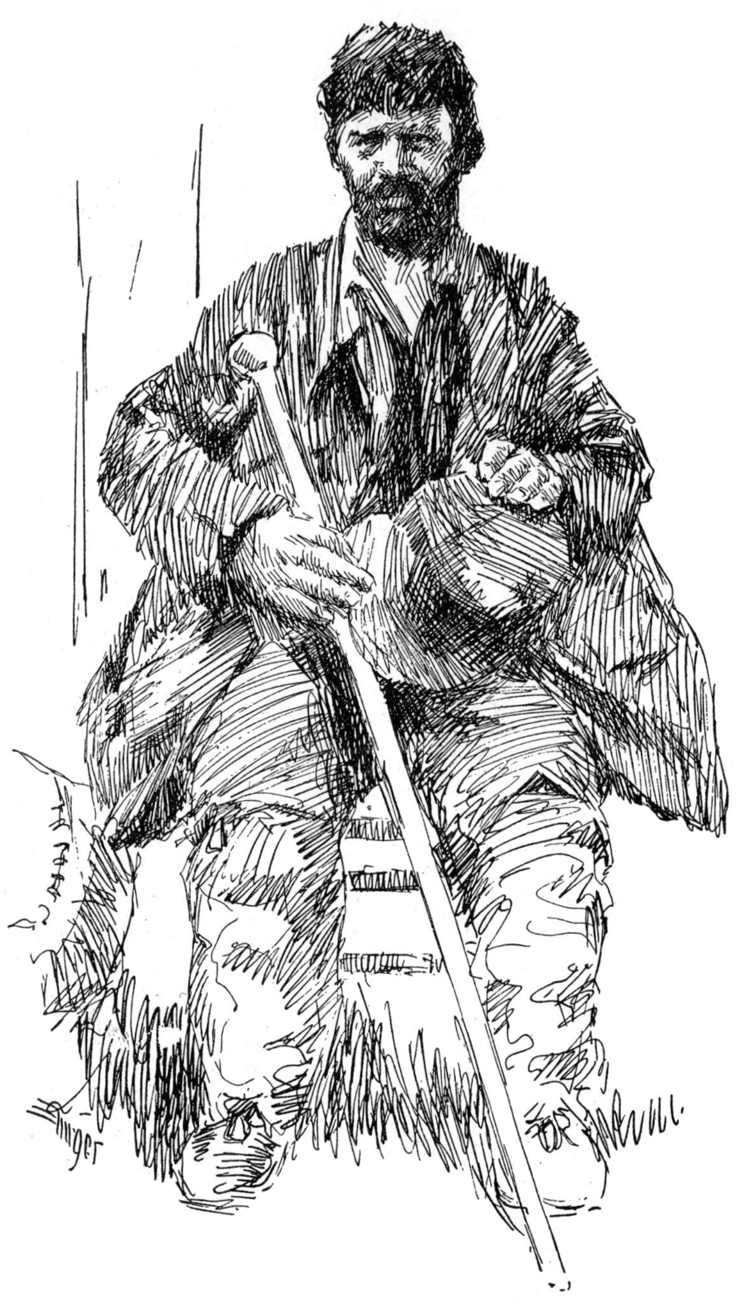

FIG. 44.—Pen Drawing direct from Model without Conscious Outline by EARL SINGER.

CHAPTER V

STYLE IN PEN DRAWING

THE desirable qualities implied in the word " style " in pen drawing are those closely connected with the right expression of one's ideas within the strict limitations of the medium.

The folly of reaching out for marked characteristics to develop an exotic style is demonstrated by understanding study of the work of acknowledged masters. The sense of style is in all sincere work simply because it is sincere, and every student who is strong enough to rely entirely upon his own conceptions has already the assurance of impressing upon others that sense of personal authority which underlies style.

Style may be defined as immediate evidence that the drawing is executed with a pen by some one understanding the use of pens to convey personal impressions or abstract ideas.

Artists speak of the " style " of other artists as their " handwriting " because, like handwriting, it is a recognisable expression of personality. The precise moment when style degenerates into mannerism is when the artist is consciously seeking the blatancy of " *a* style " instead of developing unconsciously the subtlety of " style " from the art of selection.

A child exercises selection in showing us things as they appear to the unsophisticated mind. Consequently a child's drawing has style, while that of a sophisticated and incapable artist has not.

The whole art of pen drawing is selection ; the recognition and separation of essential stimulants to the imagination of the audience. The work of the artist presents vast spaces, great buildings, masses of figures, accurate characterisation and beautiful form, humour—in fact, the whole aspect of the world, actual and potential, in a few instinctive lines, with " style," because he alone sees instinctively where the interest is concentrated that "makes" the picture, and is literally able to bring things home to us by the supreme skill which enables him to erect a slight but magical scaffolding for our imagination to build upon.

The pen draughtsman who would excel must remain a student, using his pen in the most direct and workmanlike manner as a means to a definite end, which is the record of an impression or an idea. It is well to realise that the pen is an excellent servant, working faithfully and well under a control capable of restraining the tendency to exhibit its paces and become master.

The usual convention of pen drawing is a treatment of selective outline accentuated by massed lines to indicate the infinite tone gradations in nature. It is, of course, possible to dispense with perceptible outline and rely entirely upon planes indicated by gradations of tone; but the method is obviously less satisfactory because the best characteristic of pen drawing is missing, and the sense of effort to do without something which should be used will be evident in the result.

The main reason for the employment of outline is the great reduction in size the various planes which constitute a picture must undergo in translation to card or paper of manageable proportions. The strengths and varieties of line that may be used to build this outline are inexhaustible, as new men who seriously adopt the pen as a means of expression are constantly showing us.

It cannot be too strongly insisted upon that a pen line which requires consideration for its own sake is a handicap to expression. A workmanlike and therefore good line must be the direct result of an artist's search for the easiest way to convey his meaning; nothing good will result from misguided efforts to invent an interesting line as such, apart from this, its obvious, mission.

Mannerisms, even original mannerisms, are tiresome; but at second hand they become blatant and unbearable. For example, the wonderful architectural work of Herbert Railton (see Fig. 81) suffered very much from his own amazing facility in handling, the result of a huge output of similar drawings. Railton was an extremely rapid executant, and his passion for "texture" led him to reduce the various elements composing his drawings to a kind of shorthand which fascinated by its very cleverness. The making of a drawing by Railton in his later years was comparable to the effort of an expert compositor, putting together with the utmost ease and sureness a set of symbols selected automatically. This fatal facility, unfortunately, attracted lesser men to try the same methods, and a school of imitators arose, led by Holland Tringham, copying with the utmost faithfulness everything that was obvious in Railton's work, and producing thereby soulless drawings which the great vogue enjoyed by Railton enabled them to sell to editors who felt it better to have a bad Railton than be out of the running altogether.

An amusing instance of the blind confidence reposed by these copyists in the infallibility of their inspiration is to be found in their wholesale use of Railton's "dot" mannerism; so marked that it became the unofficial signature of all these disciples. In the original instance it was the actual result of speedy execution: Railton would rush lines at a terrific rate and in terminating the stroke his pen would strike the paper somewhere and make a distinct dot; this was seized as easy and effective by the copyists, and dots became an integral feature of sham "Railtons."

For the greatest exponent of "style" in pen drawing we must go to the Spanish genius Daniel Vierge, born in 1851, and trained in the art schools of Madrid, having Madrayo, the painter, as a master, and showing outstanding ability from the first in the school competitions. He illustrated his first book, "Madrid by Night," in 1867, and journeyed to Paris to study painting two years later. He did not study painting, for the simple reason that the Franco-Prussian War created a demand for neatly efficient pen draughtsmen on the Paris papers, and Vierge was launched on his life-long connection with the *Monde Illustré* and *Vie Moderne*. Books illustrated by Vierge include Poe's "Tales," Michelet's "History of France," some of Victor Hugo's books, and Quevado's "Le Grand Toscagno."

Vierge used a curious staccato line that grew directly from an intense desire to convey an impression of actuality. It succeeds in this, its first duty to the multitude, and in addition is a source of delight and inspiration to artists and connoisseurs for all time. The patient analysis of a series of Vierge drawings will impress upon a student the invaluable lesson that is to be found in all superlative work—the hard fact that achievement is built upon effort ; in Vierge's case, stupendous industry and bravery (see Fig. 45).

Among the modern school of landscape men Joseph Pennell is a stylist near to Vierge in actuality and brevity of expression. Like the earlier master, he shows the uncanny power to tear

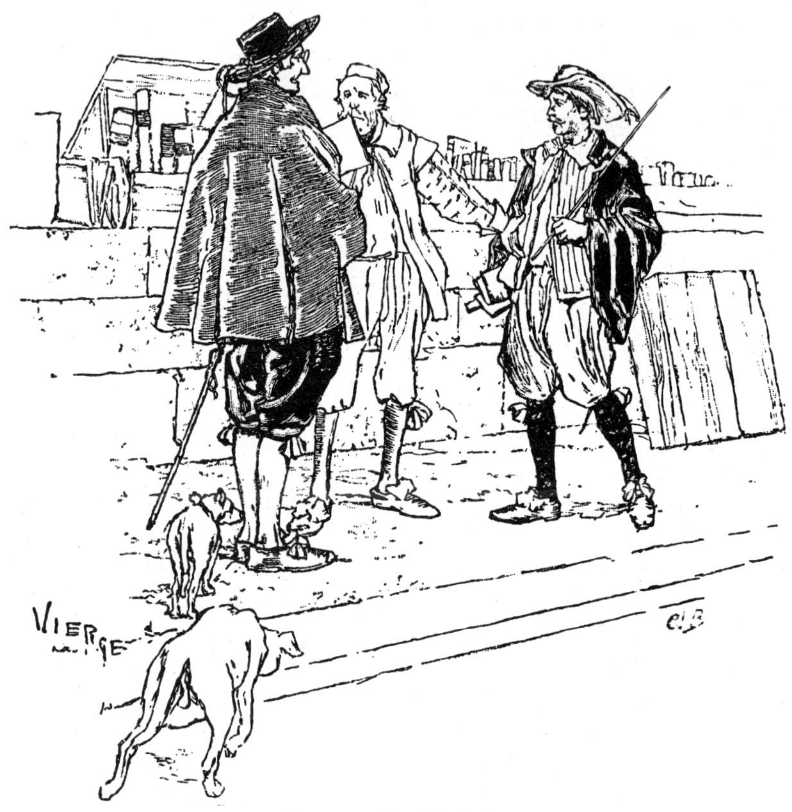

FIG. 45.—By VIERGE.
The Spanish master whose work has influenced most illustrators.

out of a complicated composition everything that can be spared and reveal to us the essentials of its loveliness. It looks so simple as Pennell does it ; all his experience, his intense interest in nature, and desire to bring beauty to others, unite in unique clarity of vision and a superb power of presentation that is the very epitome of style (see Fig. 72).

John Fothergill, writing on "The Teaching of Drawing

at the Slade School," says on this very controversial subject: "There are drawings which make us feel that the draughtsman has been learning at every touch, or if they be not direct from nature they will show a constant effort to represent observations previously made from nature. To the eye accustomed to stylised forms in art and formal style, these drawings may appear other than beautiful. But they have beauty. So long as the artist is making discoveries his work, though it may puzzle or irritate some, will be eloquent to others who have experienced the emotion of form. Now, the only forms we know are those of nature; therefore, if nature is beautiful, this work of research is the only kind of drawing which *can* be beautiful. To determine which forms are beautiful in nature and which are not is a work for the theorist and novelist. The lover of natural form knows no such distinction. The painter is not judged by his selection of this or that effect of light, but only by the truth of his representation. Nor, I think, can the draughtsman be logically judged by the forms he selects, but by his representation of them.

"It often occurs that a draughtsman becomes content after a time with what he has learnt from nature, perhaps feeling that he can learn no more; he proceeds to work with better confidence after an arbitrary manner of his own. He confessedly sacrifices the learned and truthful representation of the forms of nature to the attainment of a 'style'; is praised for what is called a sense of line, penmanship, and other peculiarities. Each stylist has his 'style' which is peculiar to himself. Their forms do not relate to nature but to the stylist who did them, so the searching student cannot find in them an explanation of his own difficulties or aspirations. If stylists be not over-scrupulous in their renderings of nature, by what feelings or experiences of our own can they be judged or appreciated, since we know of no other forms than those of nature? Is the student to acquire style from nature or from the work of a previous stylist? Are we to get our ideas of life from life itself, or from what has been written about it? Plainly from nature and from life. Style, then, cannot be acquired by the student in imitating the habits and mannerisms of stylists.

"If the capricious and ignorant representations of nature do not seem to deserve the term style, what is style in drawing, and how can the student hope to attain it? There have been

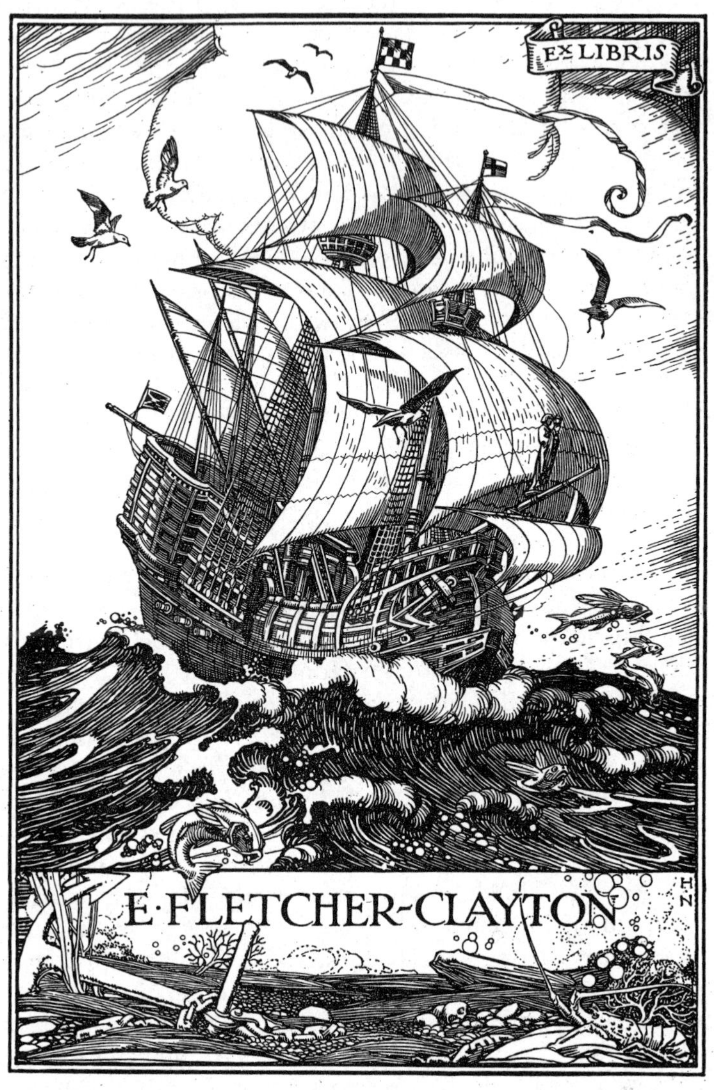

FIG. 46.—A Decorative Book-plate by HAROLD NELSON.

master draughtsmen of every time and country who by their own words, as well as their works, are known to have been infinitely respectful to the form of every detail in nature. Their drawings always recall to our minds reality as we, ourselves, have seen it, *i.e.*, if we have studied form from nature and not from pictures. The drawing of a hand, for instance, by Hokusai, Rembrandt, or Ingres revives in us our own impressions of the forms and aspects of real hands. In a word, there is manifest in all these drawings, whatever the difference of medium or superficial appearance, an entire dependence on the forms of nature. Hence it is impossible for us to imagine they were conceived and executed with the conscious effort to obtain some independent and formal 'style.' The style they plainly have can spring only from this common quality, their truthful and well understood representation of the forms of nature. *Style, then, is the expression of a clear understanding of the raw material from which the artist makes his creation. In drawing, this is the forms of nature. Without this clear understanding no style is possible.* Now, as there is only one way of understanding one thing, there can be, therefore, only one manner by which it can be rightly expressed. But it does not follow from this that, because the manner of Michelangelo is different from that of Dürer, one or both show a lack of understanding. The understanding of no two people, by reason of their different temperaments and constitution, lies in exactly the same direction. Nature, being so much raw material, is inexhaustible in the conceptions and moods she gives; hence there are as many manners as there are individuals. No two masters will draw even a finger with the same interpretation of what they understand in it; how much farther must they diverge in the drawing of a whole figure or landscape! The simplest incident in life will be so full of varied import that no two people will give the same account of it, yet each account will be, and also sound, true, so long as the narrator limits himself to telling the truth as he understands it.

"Therefore, to attempt to employ the manner of another would be to presuppose in yourself a perfect coincidence of temperament (*i.e.*, understanding of things), which, especially if you were not under his immediate influence, would be inconceivable. Your work would be quickly esteemed unspontaneous and false by those who know nature and the truth of your original. Style, as understanding, cannot be imitated; it is one and the same thing in all the manifestations of art, thought, and action, and whenever there is a manner of expressing things (the forms and colours of nature, or the spiritual and intellectual events of life) which does not show a spontaneous and immediate understanding of them, that manner is artificial and spurious, and by its pretence is misleading to the student. So long as a work is created within the limits of the understanding, however narrow, and no further, it will have style. To act beyond your understanding is to pose, and such conduct is openly lacking in style to those who know better. Whether this or that manner does show understanding let each man judge according to his own knowledge and personal experience of the events expressed. By this reasoning we can determine what style is, and how alone it can be attained; but owing to the varied interests, and often the perversity of people, style can never be universally recognised.

"But there are many so-called principles that profess to teach the student style. There are inculcated into the bewildered student terms such as 'the ideal,' 'classical severity,' 'selection,' 'purity of line,' 'tradition,' 'the grand manner,' 'good penmanship,' 'Greek,' and so on. These are qualities which are found not in nature but in finished works of art; they are discovered second hand, so to speak; and they who preach them to students do not regard the fact that the artists who were first in the field with such qualities, however gradually they were developed, could not have had before them any examples or teaching of this kind. For instance, there are some who recommend the student to assume an archaic or primitive simplicity, etc. They little consider that archaic and primitive art was without the teaching of a foregoing advanced art and critical formulæ, and that therefore whatever qualities we admire in it must have been drawn from, and developed solely from, the observation of nature. So to teach the inquisitive and ingenuous observation and understanding of nature would be the only principle by which the student might be brought to acquire archaic qualities. Moreover, it must be borne in mind that the student, however much he may be persuaded of the importance of æsthetic and critical notions (the ideal, the essential, etc.), when he sits face to face with nature cannot apply them if he would, that is, if he desires to make use of his model and cares for it at that moment more than for works of art."

This short extract from a lengthy and carefully developed thesis is given because it emphasises the warning that "style" is the triumphal arch at the top of the steps of achievement and mastery in pen work; it is not the slightest use trying to get to it without first climbing.

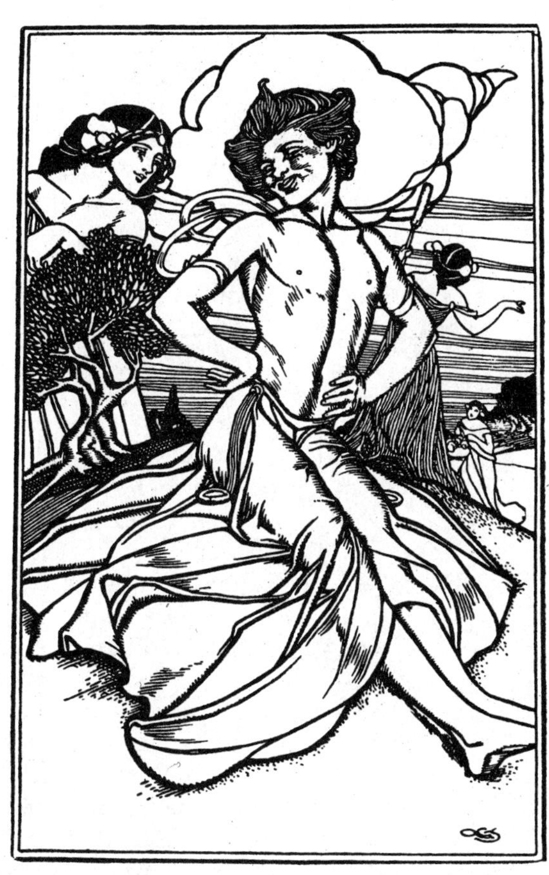

FIG. 47.—Book Illustration by GARTH JONES.

The later trend of Mr Fothergill's article develops the theory of three-dimensional drawing as taught at the Slade, where ordinary methods of measurement and the use of the plumb line are discouraged as dealing with two dimensions only, students being taught to estimate by unaided vision the true relation of length, breadth, and depth (thickness), and express them in true relationship.

The old two-dimensional method is at the Slade called "copying," and Mr Fothergill gives as an illustration of the method and its inevitable results, a parallel from music: "If a man born deaf were taught to read music on the piano, he would never be able to give an individual interpretation or expression to a piece, because he could have no idea of sounds and tones and their values. His playing would be, to those who are musical, utterly insignificant. He is playing by sight and not by sound. If it were possible to instruct him where to give 'expression,' the interpretation would not be his own but his master's. This man could never be a musician. For the same reason the man who draws by sight and abstract measurements, and not instinctively and wholly by touch, is drawing like a parrot, and can never be a draughtsman. . . . The individuality shown in the works of great draughtsmen is due to their very different ideas of touch. Words will not, of course, express the subtler differences between one draughtsman's work and another's. But such phrases as 'delicate touch,' 'rough handling,' 'nervous feeling,' etc., as applied to drawings, must be understood in their literal sense. They tell us the manner in which the artist visually touches or handles form. Both the detail as well as the entire character of a master's work is determined by his temperament: that is, his peculiar understanding of the forms of nature. . . . The construction of any object or scene in nature, indescribable in words, and vague enough, maybe, in our minds if we try to recollect it, is yet the first thing that strikes us, and the first and only cause of any appreciation that we may have of it. Therefore, if the draughtsman's work is adequately to represent what he appreciates, he must not occupy himself with giving numerous striking properties, but he must give a single conception of the object's character, viz., its construction."

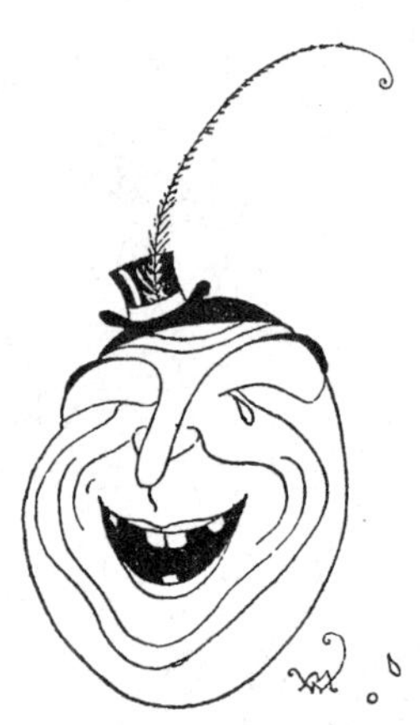

FIG. 48.—Mask by M. WATSON WILLIAMS.

Style may be evident in the simplest device and is not killed by fun.

Mr Fothergill's is the clearest explanation possible of the great principle of expressionism as opposed to the futility of making maps of things seen at a given moment. The striving to get understanding of the figure as a corporate whole is made clear as the right end and aim of the would-be figure draughtsman in a few words: "A drawing of a human figure must express one conception, viz., the conception of its character or construction, which must be as single in conception and expression as a drawing of a square box."

The old admonition to "look before you leap" may be translated into "think before you draw," for art is a matter of intellectual selection rather than accurate transcription, and a drawing of a figure must be a blend of attitude, action, and proportion, the concentration of the raw material which nature offers in three dimensions into one, if it is to stand as a work of art.

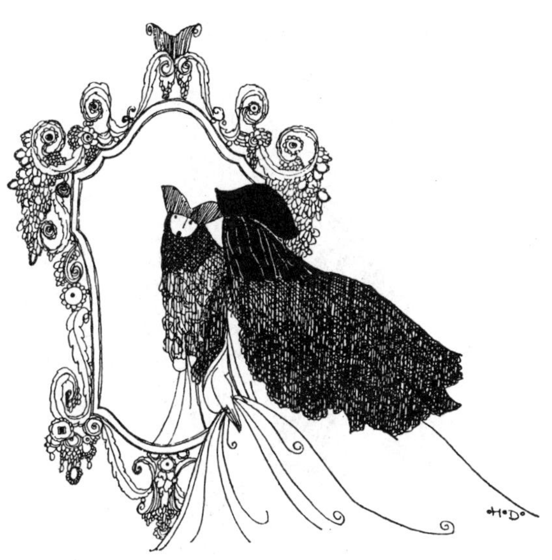

FIG. 49.—Art is a matter of intellectual selection. Drawing by HELEN DRYDEN.

The student, therefore, in drawing a model or any living object, must force his intellect to form a definite conception of the "attitude, action, and proportion" of the model, which is in itself a complex, rather than a unity, of form. "In a word, if it be by the corporeous construction of an entire form that we know and appreciate it, is it not by presenting this in its complete isolation that the slightest sketch of a master is of high value, whilst the elaborately finished work of the student without a conception is of no value at all?"

One final quote must be made from the end of Mr Fothergill's article as it sums up the whole question of "style" in a definite and inspiring instruction: "In drawing, the matter is a corporeous unity; hold this, and the line and shading will follow without you or your critics being conscious of it; they will follow only in correspondence with the fullness of your conception."

This apparently simple instruction contains the secret of great achievement in drawing of every kind. But in giving the last short extract, much preliminary qualification has been omitted which anticipates the inevitable inquiry as to how the student is to reach that happy state of ability to visualise a subject and mentally subdue its complications into a completely satisfying unity which he can convey to others by drawing.

Inevitably we come again to the word "selection." The student's mind must be selective and cultivated. The selective power will be determined by contact with nature and concentrated effort to tear from her profusion the elements of beauty, using her as the designer uses flowers—selecting and simplifying to the requirements of a preconceived and precious effect of pattern. The cultivated mind in art is achieved by storing right impressions both from nature and the rendering of nature by great masters. Intensive analysis of the outlook which results in masterly work is better than the study of mere technique from the actual work; but there is nothing against the student's efforts to understand how the conceptions of these men were simplified in actual rendering into line drawings. The adoption of actual technique is even permissible, providing it be not allowed to influence the individuality of the complete synthesis.

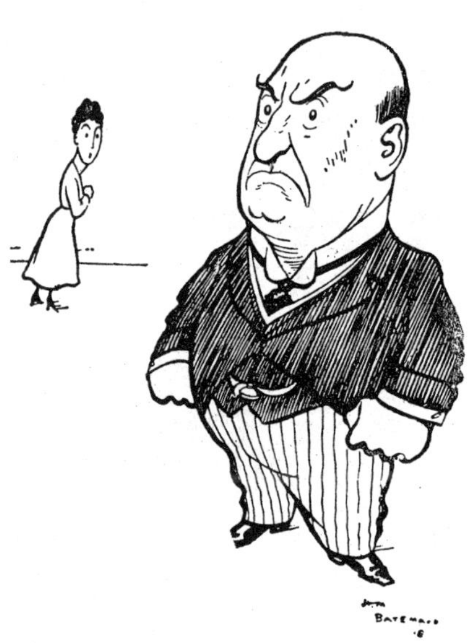

FIG. 50.—By H. M. BATEMAN.

A new and peculiarly English technique which is always close to nature.

In pen drawing technical problems are chiefly concerned with the representation of light and shade. Nature's scale of colour, when represented as tone and not left for the imagination to fill in to expressive outline, is suggested by lines of varying thickness, drawn more or less closely together, or crossed in various directions on white paper.

Outline is non-existent in nature; but as a convention in drawing, especially with the pen, the necessity for it is so apparent that it is almost universally used either for the entire construction of the drawing, or to put the necessary definition into light areas left in full tone drawings, with the least possible disturbance of these as white patches in the scheme of pattern.

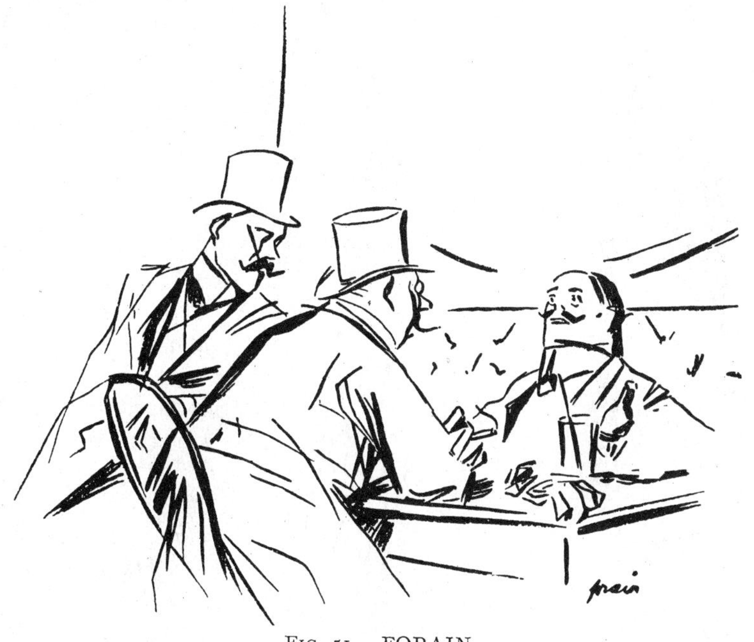

FIG. 51.—FORAIN.

It is generally a mistake to attempt the elaborate division of tone in pen work; but there are notable exceptions in the landscape work of F. L. Griggs and the wonderful figure compositions of Gilbert Wilkinson, which shout defiance at the dictum of Mr Charles Maginnis that "the chief element of style is economy of means." Maxime Lalanne is given as an example of this economy carried to its extreme in landscape, and Forain occurs to one as a parallel illustration in figure-work (see Fig. 51). Both are excellent; but the success of each depends entirely on splendid drawing and almost uncanny selective power attained by experiment over a long period of drawing from nature. Without immense power such drawing is impossible, and the student must realise that extreme simplicity is reached by methods anything but simple.

A definition more immediately useful than Mr Maginnis's is suggested to students in a development of the familiar *artis est celere artem* into "the chief element of style is the concealment of effort." This leads to the same place, but points out the safer road on which all the great men have travelled, Phil May being, perhaps, the most conspicuous.

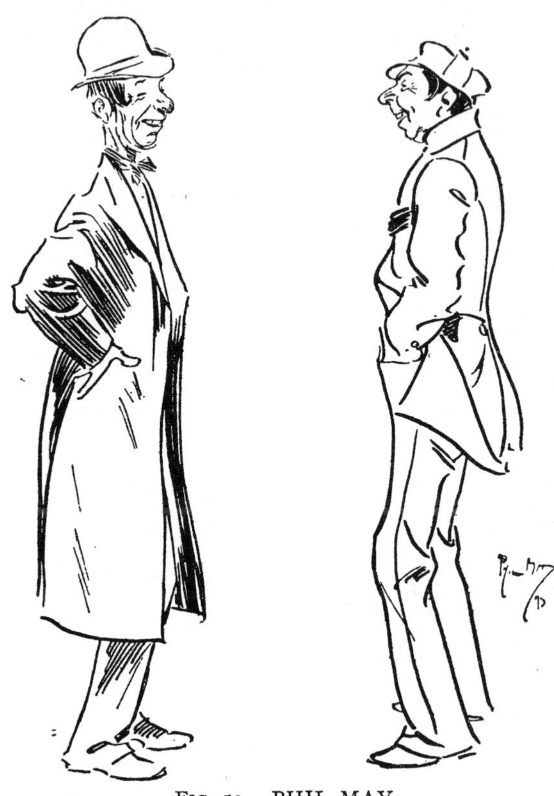

FIG. 52.—PHIL MAY.

First of the modern school of humorous pen draughtsmen, Phil May became famous as a caricaturist; but he is much better described as a laughing philosopher.

A humorist with a strange insight into humanity, his estimate of its frailty was shrewd but ever kindly, expressed for a grateful public to laugh at, yet sympathise with. He was lovable, and his quaint subjects became lovable in turn.

The extreme economy of line by which his effects were produced covered much preparatory work (see Fig. 52). Phil May was a slow and desperately serious worker, building up his drawings from innumerable sketches and notes as carefully as if the design was for a great historical painting.

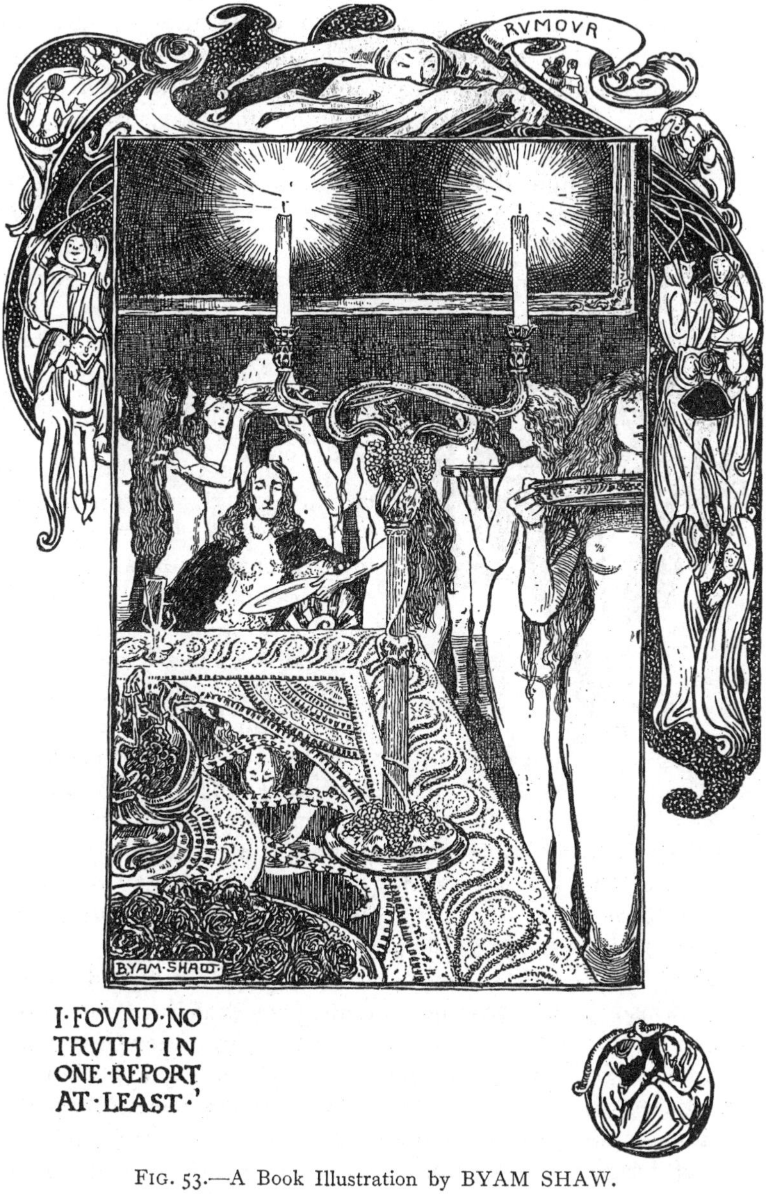

RVMOVR

BYAM·SHAW

I·FOVND·NO
TRVTH·IN
ONE·REPORT
AT·LEAST·'

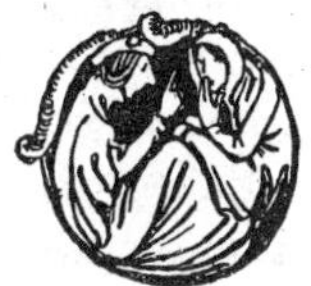

Fig. 53.—A Book Illustration by BYAM SHAW.

Preliminary to the actual execution in ink, he had before him a pencil drawing of considerable elaboration, worked up from these studies of people and things jotted down in sketch books, on odd scraps of paper, or more elaborately in black chalk on brown paper, with high lights in white, or as studio studies in red chalk.

On this pencil drawing he began a drastic process of elimination; every touch that could be spared, went; the elaborate scaffolding had served its purpose in building a perfect thing, and could be taken away to reveal a drawing wonderfully simple, yet completely satisfying to both connoisseur and layman.

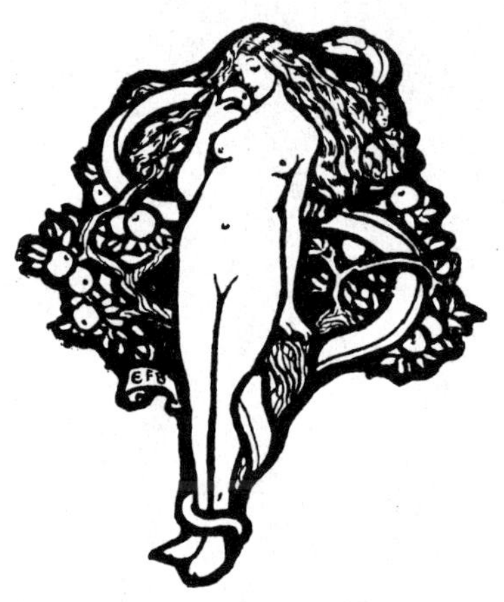

FIG. 54.—ELEANOR FORTESCUE BRICKDALE.

The two figures herewith (Fig. 52) are typical examples of his genius in the delineation of character, and show his method of suggesting clothes in a few lines of surpassing significance.

Between the extremes of simplicity and elaboration of method there is a wide choice of individual expression. Joseph Pennell, in his landscapes and architecture, strikes a very happy medium, and Gilbert Wilkinson in his extremely clever story and joke drawings, also shows a happy blend of fine drawing with a deceptively easy looking pen technique, so fresh, clean cut, and crisp that it has the pleasing quality of playfulness as an element in a style of obviously rare distinction.

Study of the work of Lalanne or Pennell, Townsend, Forain, or Wilkinson will repay the student, providing it is undertaken in a spirit of investigation and not with the intention of mimicry. It is never worth while to mimic the style of anybody, however fine their work. See first how others found themselves, then set about the great adventure of discovering yourself. It is perfectly right to take hints, one or many, from other men's methods, but neither right nor politic to adopt the particular combination of methods employed by any one man and constituting his style.

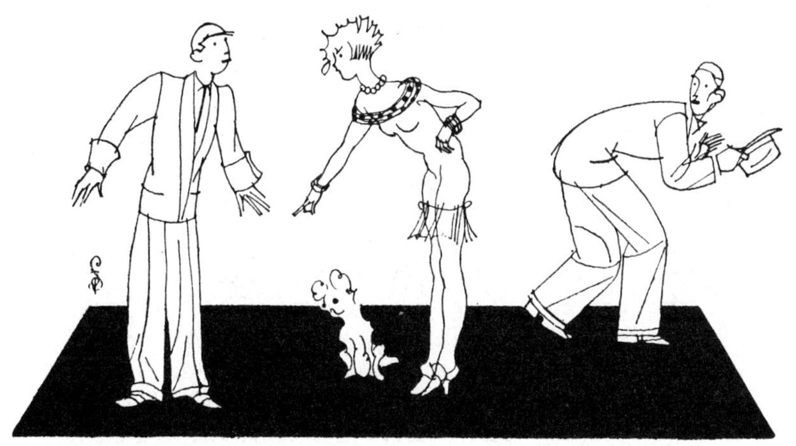

FIG. 57.—The Figure in Illustration.

CHAPTER VI

THE FIGURE, FACES, AND HANDS

VERY few English artists have seriously exploited the treatment of the nude in pen drawing, and if we exclude those who have used an outline convention for more or less decorative drawings, the number is reduced almost to vanishing point in English work.

It is no simple matter to deal with the subtleties of the human form in pen line, and this fact is mainly responsible for the apparent surrender to the quaint English prejudice against such drawings appearing in the press. In France the artist is more free to exercise his art, for there exists a more enlightened public opinion on the æsthetics of the human form translated into terms of print. A distinct school of life draughtsmen has flourished in Paris since the latter half of the nineteenth century, their talents almost exclusively devoted to the representation of beautiful women exquisitely drawn and amusingly presented.

Prominent names among these witty and accomplished Frenchmen whose work compels admiration for its complete artistry, are Auguste Roubille, Carlègle, Jean Veber, Jehan Testeraide, Louis Morin, Forain, Edouard Bourgeois, Jacques

Nam, Ferdinand Misti, Louis Icart, Gil Baer, Cheret, Préjélan, Fabiano, A. Vallée, and Leonnec, all of whom are well worth study for their sympathetic line in dealing with the female form. Maxime Dethomas is another master, but in a different and stronger technique which emphasises anatomy and is therefore doubly interesting to the student.

Some of the best figure drawing in the world is to be found among the avowed humorous draughtsmen of the Continent. Félicien Rops and Heinrich Kley are examples of men whose knowledge of the figure is so complete that it presents no difficulties to them. Kley's anatomical knowledge is so copious that structure flows from his pen, and every drawing is a *tour de force* that holds other artists breathless at the skill and knowledge displayed. He is also an expert in drawing complicated machinery, and delights in combining his accomplishments by representing the spirit of power controlling big machines, and even turning actual machinery into human forms which are often menacing, weird, and titanic, but on occasions quaintly amusing and fantastic. Kley's work may be found in old numbers of "Jugend" in colour, wash, pen and ink, and combined line and wash, and may be usefully analysed by the student in search of methods of indicating structure.

In an essay on "Painting and Drawing," Max Klinger wrote: "The pivot upon which all art turns, and the centre to which all its parts bear relation, is the human body. Every elaboration of style must in the end rest solely and alone upon the conception of the nude, for everything imaginable in sculpture as well as in painting, in architecture as well as in the applied arts, can be measured only in so far as it bears relationship to the human form."

Heinrich Kley, more perhaps than any other artist of our time, demonstrates the truth of this dictum. To Kley the human body is paramount indeed, and the tremendous determination that must have driven him in search of knowledge in the early stages of his career has resulted in a glorious efficiency that enables him to treat great problems with consummate ease. His imagination can soar to any height because he is sure of the technical accomplishment to interpret it adequately to the world.

The strongest recommendation is offered to the student to follow Kley's example and get familiar with structure, simply because it makes things so much easier afterwards to know the why and wherefore of surface movements. It is an axiom of pen drawing that the less work put into an actual drawing, the more knowledge is required to know what to omit, so the student should not be deluded by the apparent simplicity of the work of men like those mentioned above into thinking that it is a simple matter because it looks slight and playful. That is the whole matter in a word, with the requisite knowledge the whole of one's work can be playful and the killing effect of doubt eliminated from effort.

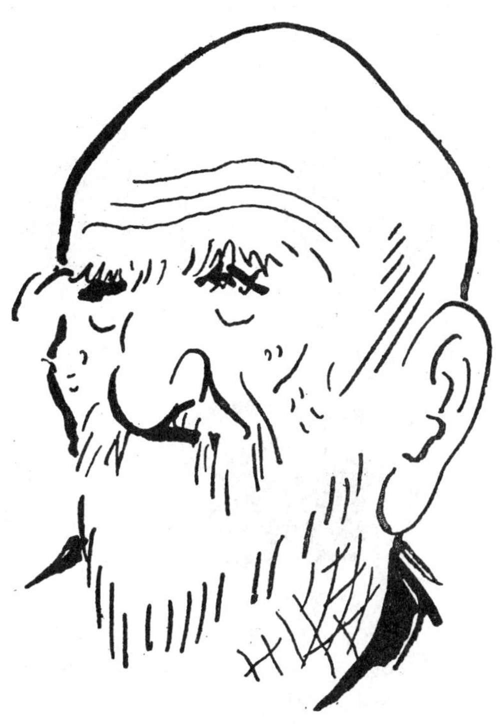

Fig. 58.—"Direct" Pen Portrait by ART YOUNG.

The anatomical knowledge of the surgeon is not essential to the artist who needs knowledge of outer form and central support only. It is perhaps better to know the names of bones and muscles, but it is not vital. Artistic anatomy is best mastered by repeatedly drawing first the skeleton from actuality in all kinds of positions, and then adding the muscles as they appear in these positions; afterwards testing one's knowledge by anatomising direct from the model or from photographs.

Fig. 56 shows a direct pen rendering by E. J. Sullivan from a photograph of a posed model (Fig. 55), and reveals the work of a master hand in seizing on the essentials of the figure and adapting them to a very personal pen technique. Most students are scared of the direct use of pen in drawing from life, yet many will use the pencil with exactly the same precision of line, perfectly happy in feeling that corrections *can* be made, although they would despise themselves if their hand failed to respond to their vision. Such brilliant draughtsmen have seen fit to substitute the pen for their pencil, and to find it even more responsive to the nervous work of following and interpolating in line the elusive contours of the human form.

Direct portraiture and caricature in pen and ink is the

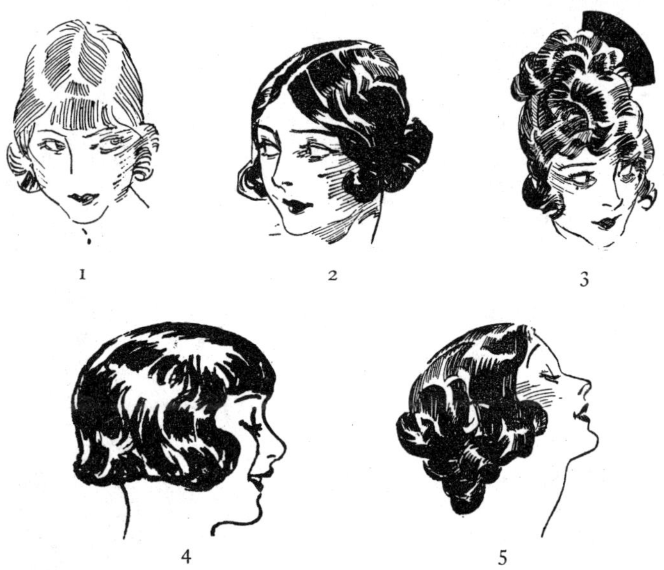

FIG. 59.—Some Pen Methods of dealing with the Feminine Head.
1, 2, 3, and 5 by GILBERT WILKINSON. 4 by WILTON WILLIAMS.

most compelling route to acute observation and analysis of essential lines. The basis on which the successful portrait or caricature depends is the power to seize these essential lines without hesitation, in knowing exactly what it is that separates the individual countenance from every other. If this faculty is missing, it is indeed difficult to make portraits and absolutely hopeless to attempt caricature.

In working with such an unyielding and indelible instrument as a pen, the habit of searching observation is acquired more rapidly than by careful tone sketching, in which the student waits and hopes for the planes to emerge

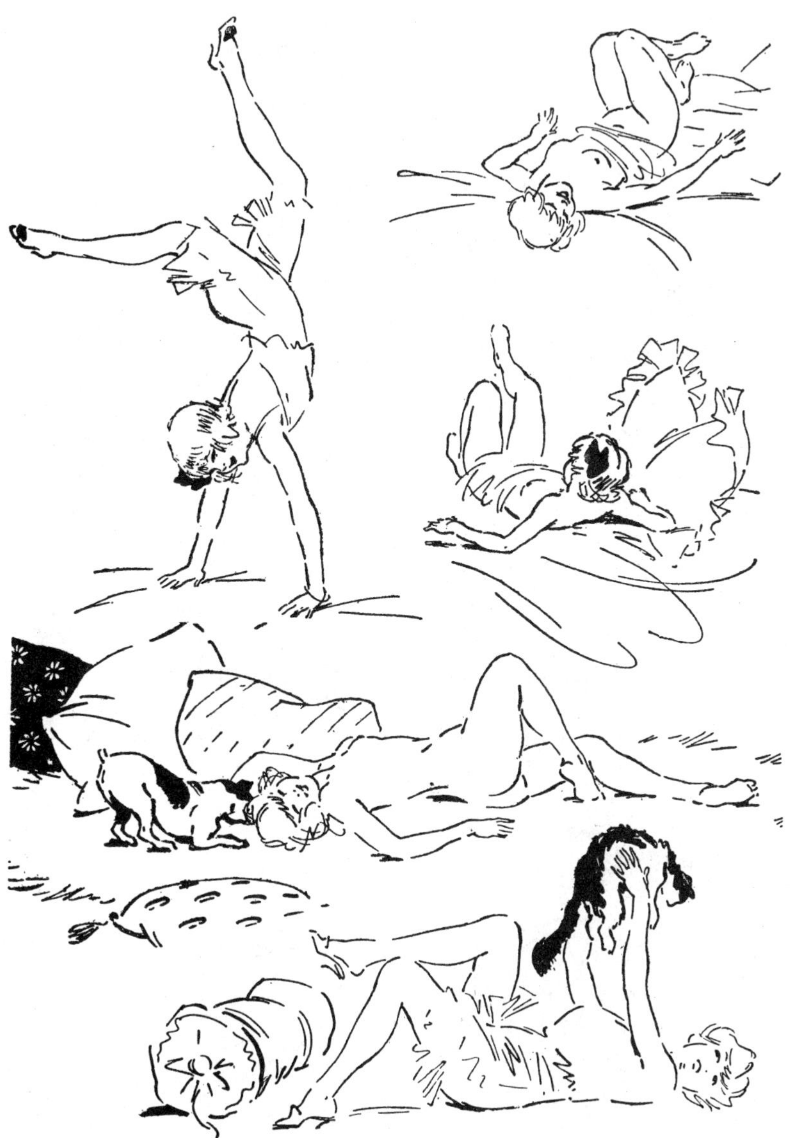

FIG. 60.—Studies by PRÉJÉLAN, possibly the greatest master of line in dealing with femininity.

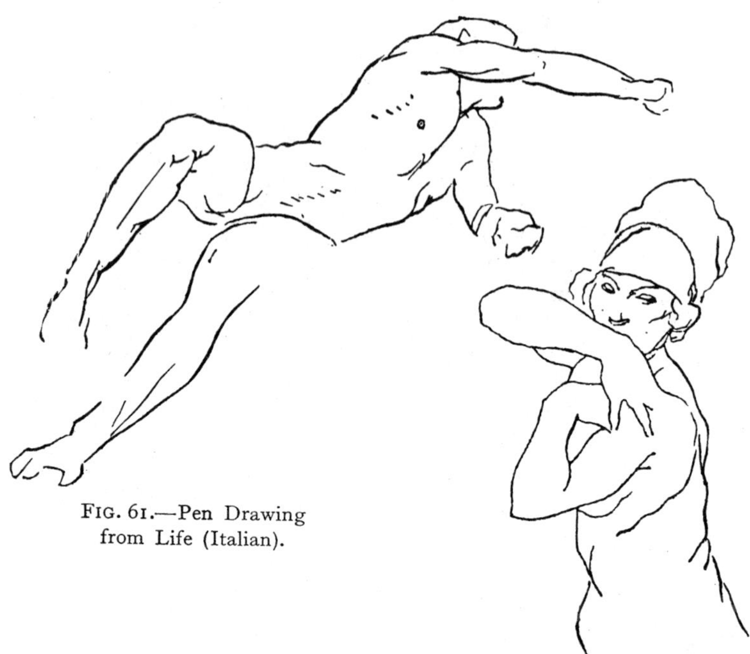

FIG. 61.—Pen Drawing from Life (Italian).

FIG. 62.—Pen Drawing from Life by RUPERT C. W. BUNNEY.

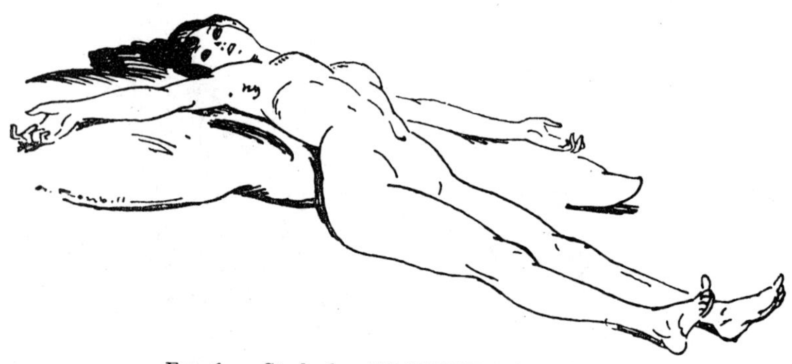

FIG. 63.—Study by AUGUSTE ROUBILLE.

in such relativity that they at length reveal a likeness on the principle of the "physical map" of geographers.

The student's aim should be to get the portrait with the maximum of thought and the minimum of work, its every line the definite sum of acute mental analysis and consequently charged with meaning. At first it will involve perseverance in the face of disappointing results, for it is almost certain that preliminary drawing will fail to hang together. Concentration on parts will result in faulty placing and relationship until practice determines a mode of progression leading to unconscious accuracy in this vital matter. For it is the relation of rightly placed features to the containing line of the face which determines a portrait.

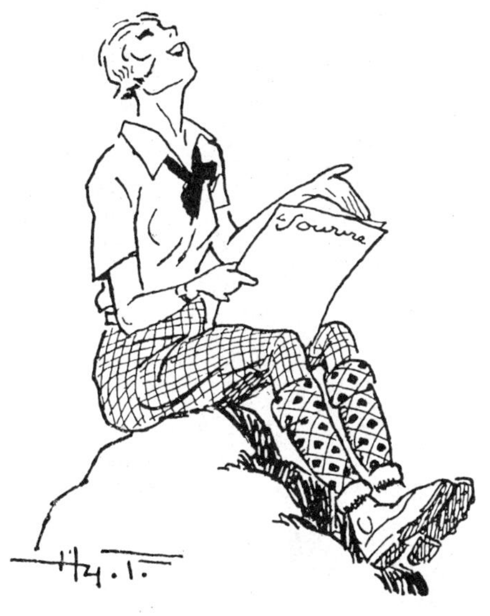

FIG. 64.—A French Drawing which plainly shows the ability to draw to figure. The clothes are built on to the convincing model.

Vivid expression is attained in the merest sketch if understanding is in its few actual strokes. Notice the economy of means used to obtain different expressions in the sketches of heads shown in Fig. 59.

Hands are a difficulty to most novices in any medium, but especially so in pen drawings, where so many make the mistake of treating them as minor accessories because they usually appear small in reproduction. Well drawn or rightly suggested hands are important if only for one reason—badly drawn, they immediately attract attention from the good qualities of the whole drawing. A faulty hand is a magnet to the eye, because every one has such a clear conception of the appearance normal hands should take in any and every position by constant association with their own.

There is little excuse for badly drawn hands, as the artist

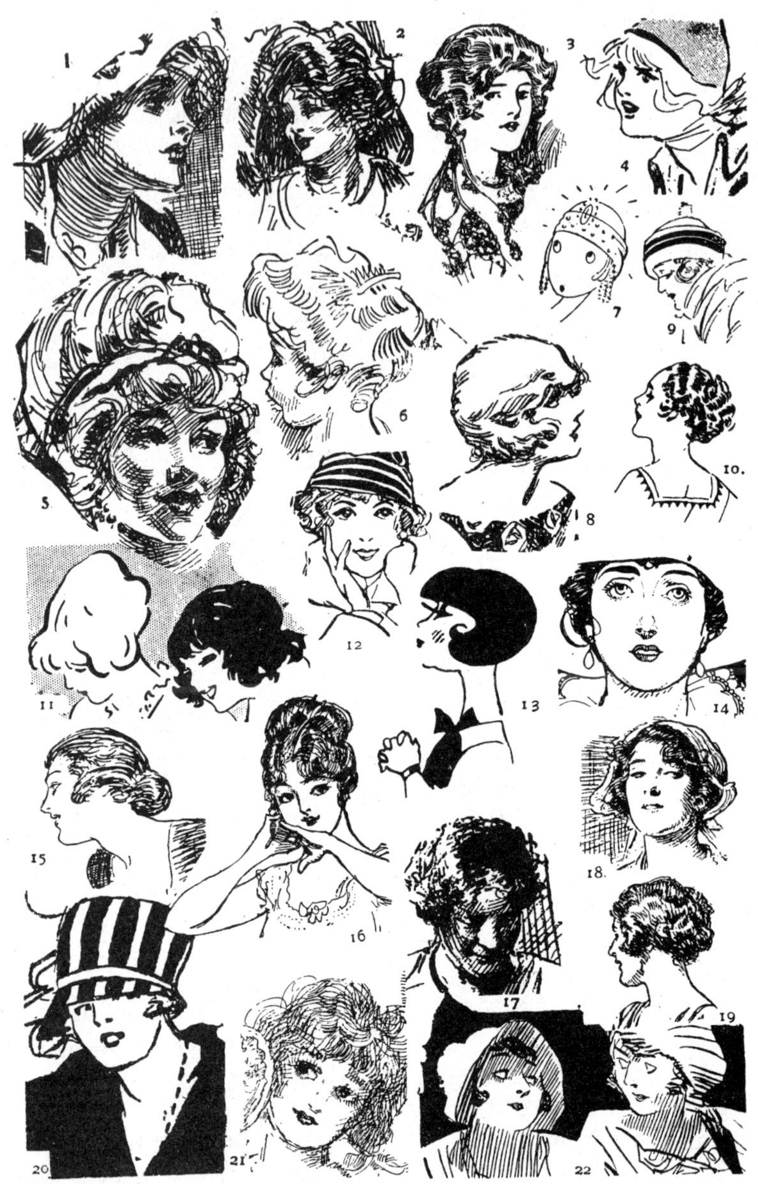

FIG. 65.—FACES.

1. C. D. GIBSON.
2. C. D. GIBSON.
3. A. K. MACDONALD.
4. PRÉJÉLAN.
5. C. D. GIBSON.
6. JAMES MONTGOMERY FLAGG.
7. FISH.
8. ARTHUR FERRIER.
9. HELEN M'KIE.
10. A. K. MACDONALD.
11. NAM (2 Heads).
12. FABIANO.
13. NERMAN.
14. POPINI.
15. FRANK R. GRAY.
16. AMERICAN.
17. S. E. SCOTT.
18. F. PEGRAM.
19. F. PEGRAM.
20. HIGGINS.
21. BLAM.
22. GILBERT WILKINSON (2 Heads).

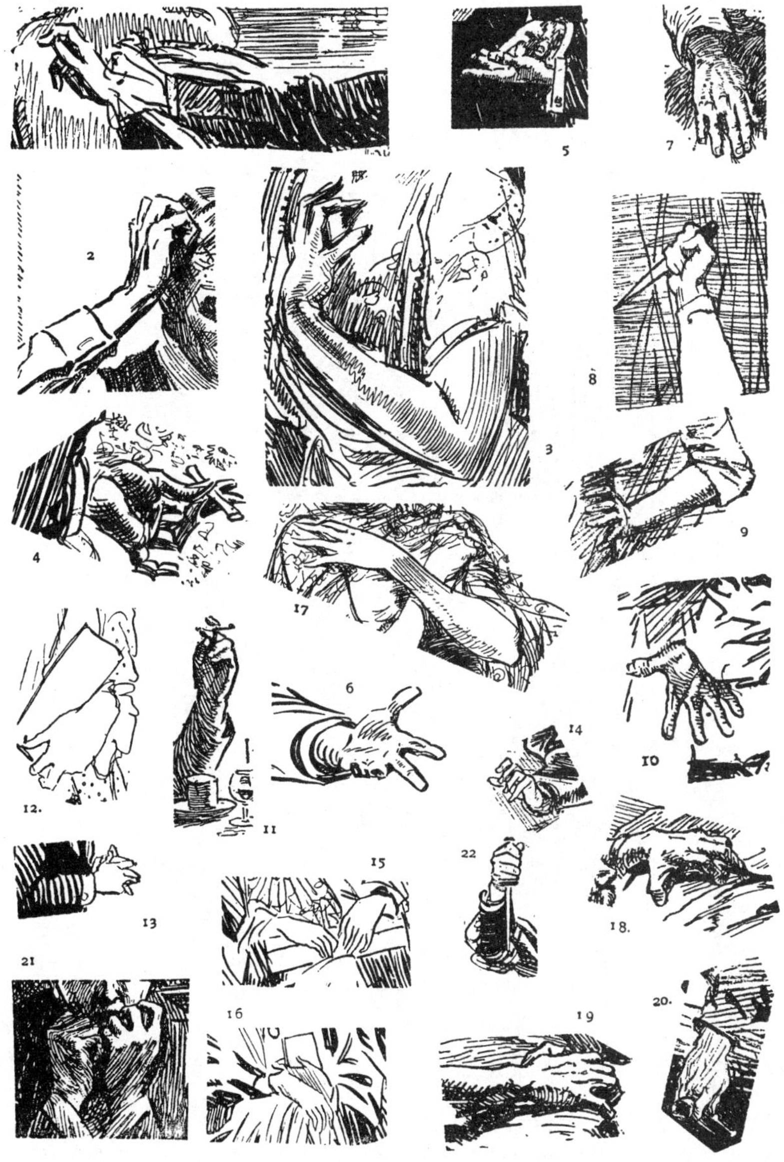

Fig. 66.—HANDS.

1. C. D. GIBSON.
2. R. F. SCHABLITZ.
3. C. D. GIBSON.
4. C. D. GIBSON.
5. LEO CHENEY.
6. ALFRED LEETE.
7. H. R. MILLAR.
8. WARWICK REYNOLDS.
9. S. E. SCOTT.
10. LEO CHENEY.
11. F. PEGRAM.
12. POPINI.
13. ARTHUR WATTS.
14. H. M. BROCK.
15. GILBERT WILKINSON.
16. GILBERT WILKINSON.
17. SOULIÉ.
18. BERNARD PARTRIDGE.
19. BERNARD PARTRIDGE.
20. S. E. SCOTT.
21. GORDON BROWNE.
22. H. M. BROCK.

has a model constantly available in his own left hand, which can be studied as a right hand also by an ingenious arrangement of one or two mirrors.

The anatomy essential to drawing hands with authority can be mastered in an hour or two. After this it is merely a

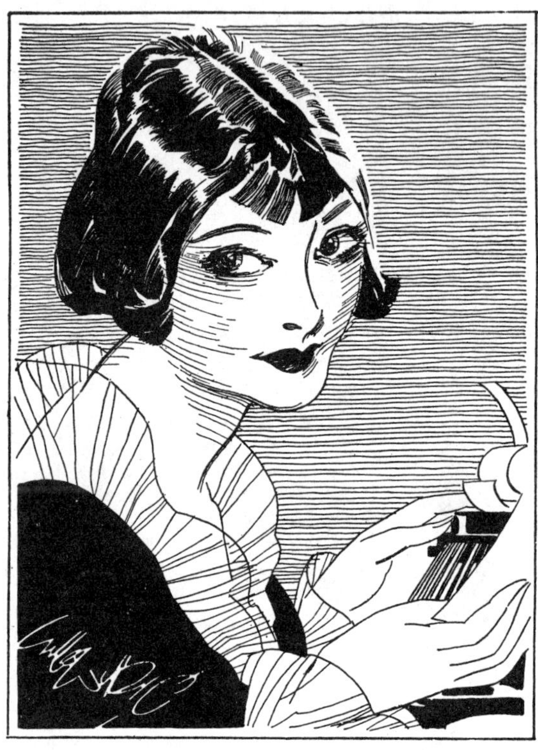

FIG. 67.—Head of the Modern Girl wonderfully interpreted by GILBERT WILKINSON.

matter of determined practice to find the necessary pen shorthand to suggest them in all positions.

The first tendency is to get too much detail, especially in dealing with the fingers as a series of hooks in hanging, grasping, or pulling; but this is a good fault in helping the student to discover by elimination just how much is necessary to convey an adequate impression of graceful tapering roundness in female and square muscular grip in male fingers.

Once the power to work direct from the model in ink is acquired, it is quite usual for artists to revert to pencil as an indication of where the principal lines are to fall. There is no sanctity in any method, and the direct has only been so strongly advocated as the greatest incentive to decision of

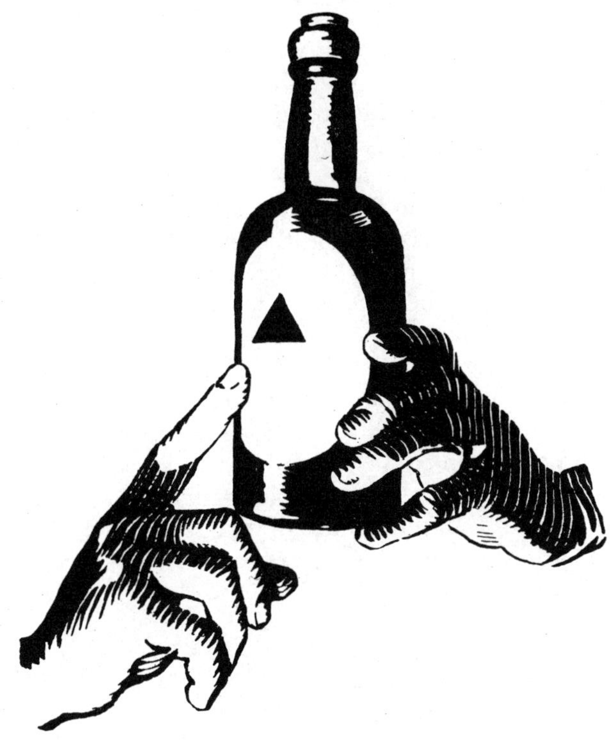

FIG. 68.—HANDS.
Drawn by JOHN AUSTEN in the woodcut manner for an advertisement.
The demand for well-drawn hands to show goods is constant with advertisers.

drawing. Many artists prefer to work in pencil first and make a final selection and modification of their impressions in "inking in."

In planning "figure compositions" it is usual roughly to pencil the figures and accessories, alter their disposition until satisfactory, then proceed to draw laboriously from sketches (again in pencil) until the whole thing is ready to turn into black and white, the whole process tending to induce that tired feeling long before the vital work begins.

For the student who finds joy in the virility of studies direct from life, there is another method, which is to scheme the composition roughly in charcoal, pose the models and make good pen drawings from them, then place these drawings under a sheet of thin but good white paper, arrange them exactly as they are to be and draw *over* them, filling in the accessories afterwards. The result is a much more vital affair than the usual slow progression gives on any but the most expert hands.

The best preparation for any artistic career is to be able to draw the figure with ease and authority; everything is possible to those who can. It helps in everything, and in most careers in art means simply the difference between failure and success.

There is a certain vogue among dealers for excellent life drawings, and some artists have held exhibitions mainly composed of such in various mediums and found purchasers. A life study by Meninsky or Schwabe is certainly desirable, and of greater interest framed in the house of an appreciative connoisseur than buried in the portfolio of its creator. It is good news that there is a public for drawings as such, and a new interest is promised in the range of exhibitions.

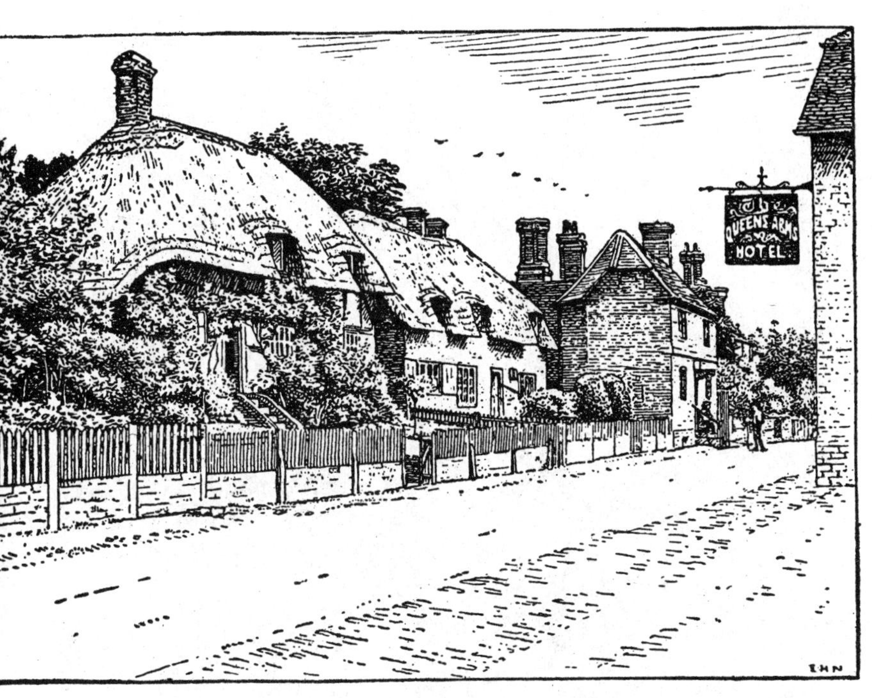

FIG. 68A.—Drawing of Old Cottages by E. H. NEW.
A simple and direct technique appropriate to the subject.

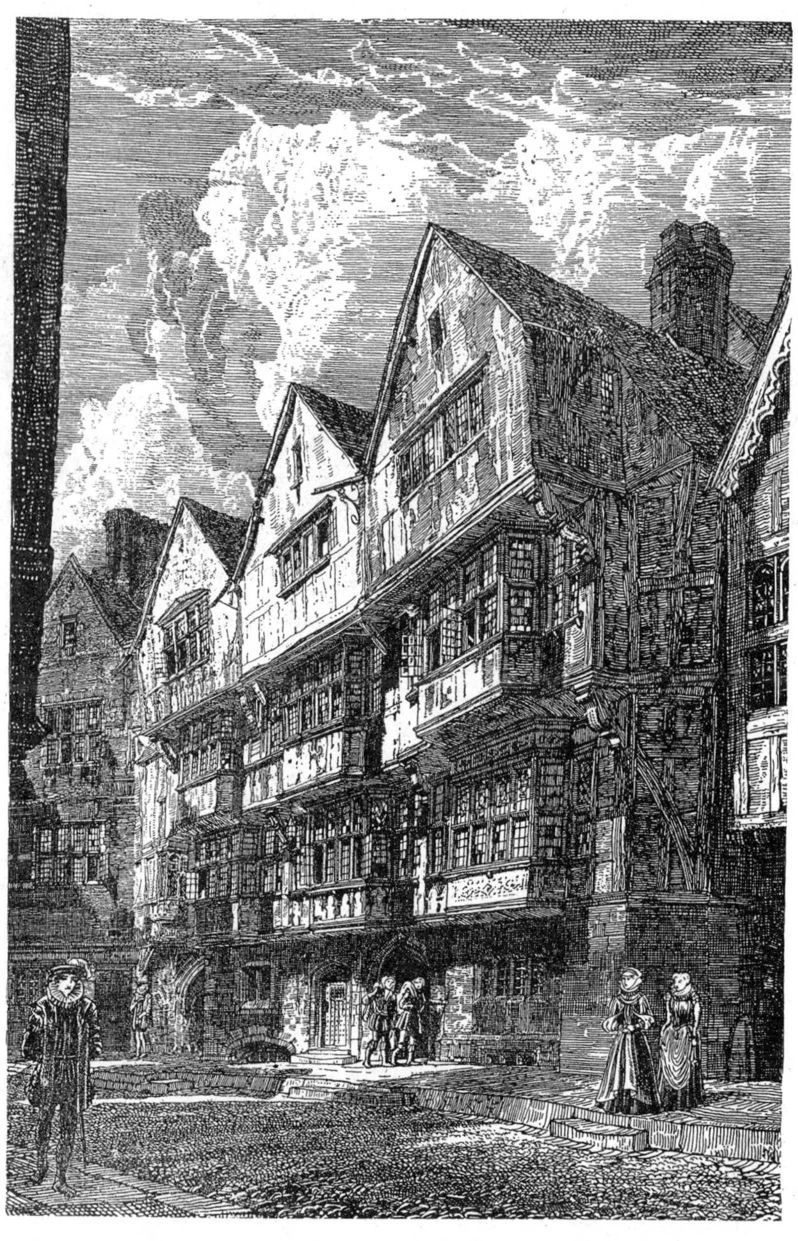

FIG. 69.—Cloth Fair. Portion of Drawing by F. L. GRIGGS, A.R.A.

CHAPTER VII

LANDSCAPE AND ARCHITECTURAL ILLUSTRATION

THIS is an occupation quite distinct from professional architects' work, and as a branch of illustration has suffered more than any other from the competition of photography.

Editors of thirty years ago were in competition for drawings by H. Railton, J. Pennell, Holland Tringham, R. Randall, Burke Downing, etc., showing places of immediate "news" value, as when royalty or distinguished people visited a provincial town or country house. This work has been almost entirely taken over by the press photographer, who is considerably cheaper and gives "actuality" ready for block-making in an hour or two.

The demand for landscape and architectural illustration at present is for books of travel, such as Macmillan's "Highways and Byways" series; and in advertising, for showing premises or location of factories, although there may be possibilities in the weekly papers of standing, the *Sunday Times* having published several series of Hanslip Fletcher's artistic and convincing drawings of London streets and buildings.

There are a few journals dealing with automobiles, cycles, and travel which use pen drawings of landscape. F. Patterson's work on "Cycling," for example, is well known, and a newer man, Sydney R. Jones, contributes good work to many technical papers, though making the almost inevitable plunge into etching. His style is exemplified in Fig. 77.

F. L. Griggs, A.R.A., is our most distinguished exponent of landscape pen drawing, with an almost incredible range of tones and variety of line, involving infinite labour and skill, which is amply repaid in the "quality" of his lighting and atmospheric effects. Griggs is now interested in etching, and treats his plates exactly like his pen drawings, which are pre-

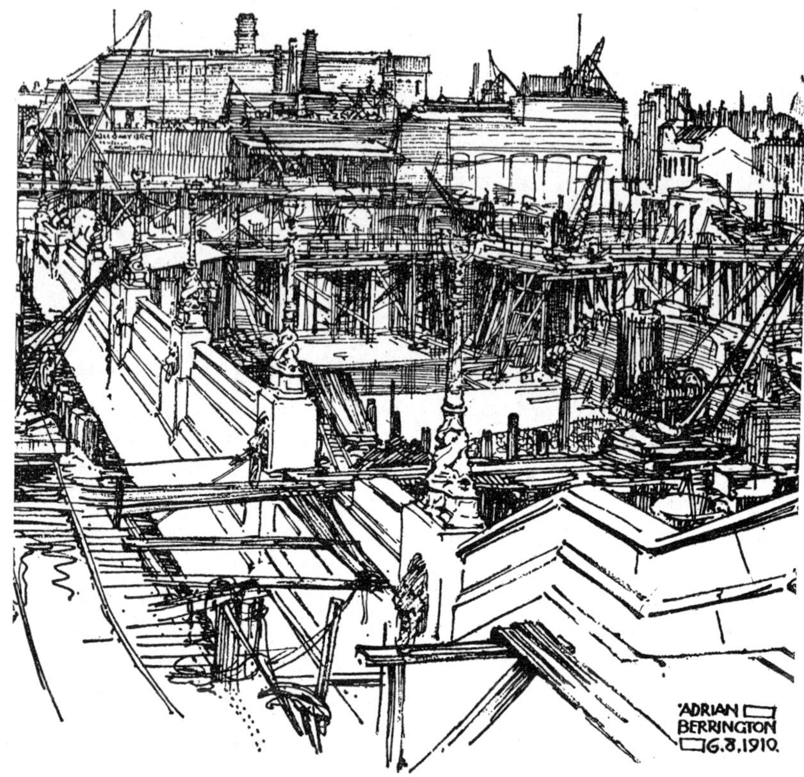

FIG. 70.—By ADRIAN BERRINGTON.

An architect's sketch, " Building the County Hall," showing clever simplification of a complicated subject in pen and ink direct from nature.

ferable to the etchings, as the line is more free and the black ink gives a quality not equalled in the plate impressions.

Students can learn much from Griggs's work in its sheer triumph over the resistance of materials. The impression given by his technique is that of reduction from large originals ; but this is not so, for his drawings are seldom large, and it is the extremely fine and clear pen work in them which creates the impression.

The " Griggs " here given (Fig. 69) is a portion only of a monumental drawing of " Cloth Fair " made some years ago. It shows meticulous care for detail maintained without loss of breadth and atmosphere ; in fact, it is all study and calculation ; nothing is left to chance or accidental effects.

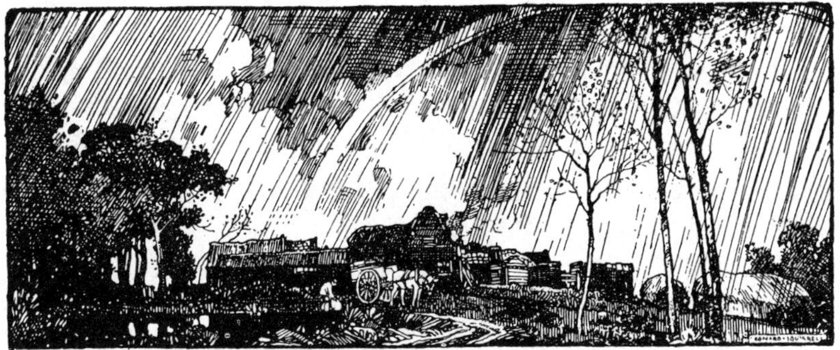

FIG. 71.—RAIN. By LEONARD SQUIRREL, A.R.E.

His treatment of white stone buildings against dark trees or graduated sky tones is very characteristic; but the "St Albans Abbey" and "St Peter's Church, St Albans," in the Hertfordshire "Highways and Byways," are equally successful with the towers toned against clear white light. The possibilities of cast shadows are shown in the "Hoo End Kimpton" drawing, and brilliant hot sunshine in that "At Aspenden." Contrasted dramatic effect as in "St Ippolyt's Church" and the peaceful evening light in "Farm at Knebworth" show the range of expression, and in "A Hertfordshire Lane," "Minsden Ruins," "Wymondley Magna—Morning," and "Near Ayot St Peter," the various ways of dealing with foliage and light and shade in trees may be compared.

Architecture, magnificent or simple, lives in his work. No one can get the spirit of its conception and materials as he can, or realise so fully its strength and subtlety.

His early experiences in construction and professional "perspectives" for architects have given such thorough understanding, that, in throwing off the restraints of the latter, he can and does revel in elaborate pen drawings of beautiful buildings, such as "Hatfield House" or "Stansteadbury Manor," and quaint streets, as the "Honey Lane, Hertford," or "High Street, Hemel Hempstead."

Leonard Squirrel, A.R.E., etcher, painter, and pastellist, has a sympathetic pen technique, and is perhaps next to Griggs in sincere treatment of nature. His buildings are entirely lacking in the architectural qualities of Griggs, but his skies are well rendered, and he can get quality, convincing perspective, and fine colour into landscape which he keeps typically English (see Fig. 71).

Herbert Railton and Joseph Pennell have been held up as examples to students for more than thirty years, and there is something to learn from both. The young admirer of the

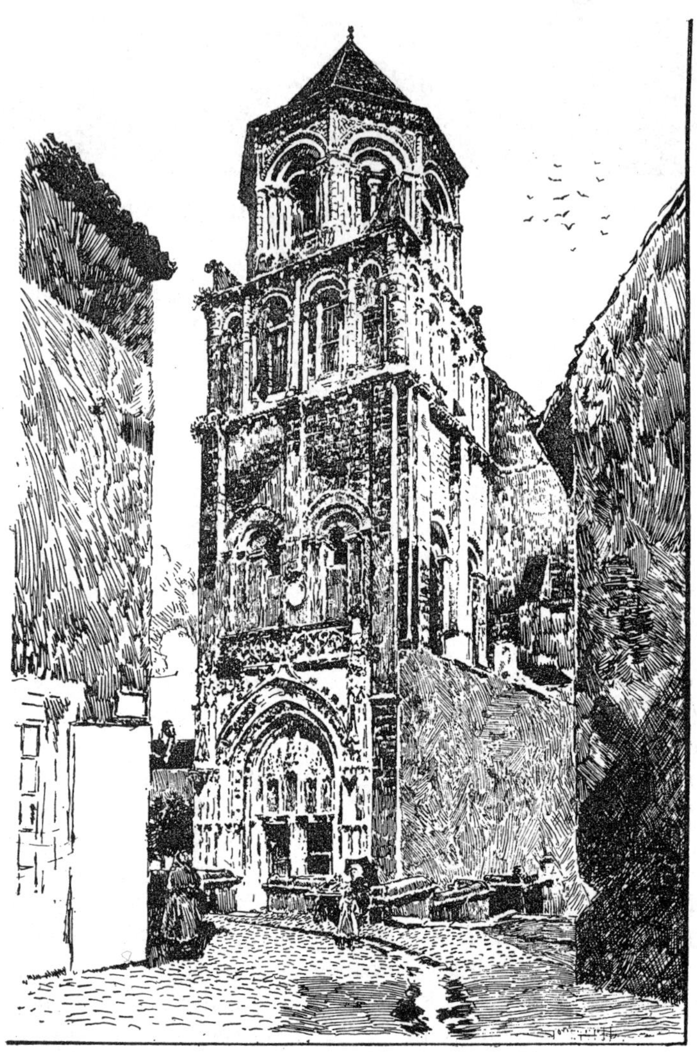

FIG. 72.—JOSEPH PENNELL.

A drawing probably photographic in inspiration, but with much spirit, colour, and suggestion of weather-worn textures.

former is generally attracted to his worst faults—the wild alteration in direction in his shading, and the habit of breaking lines

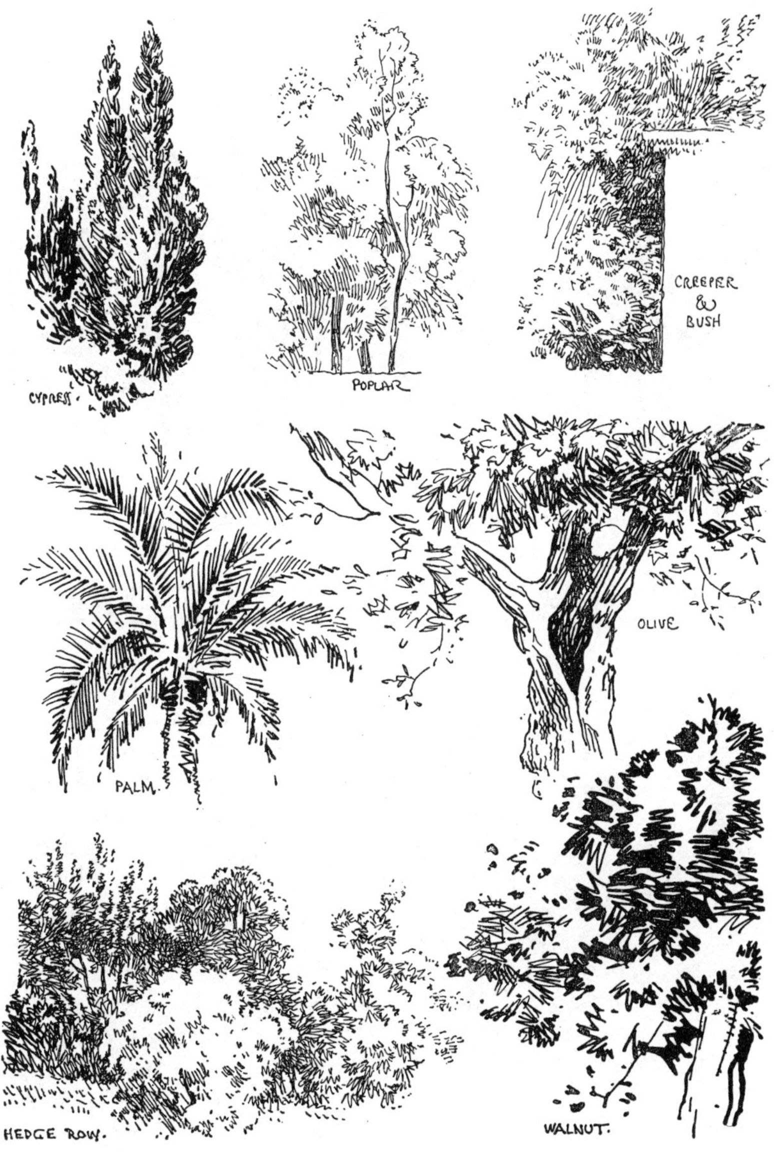

FIG. 73.—Some Examples of Tree Technique based on Drawings by JOSEPH PENNELL.

and placing inconsequent dots (see Fig. 81). Railton has only one message for the student—his drawing excused his technique, and if the student will draw as understandingly, his method of

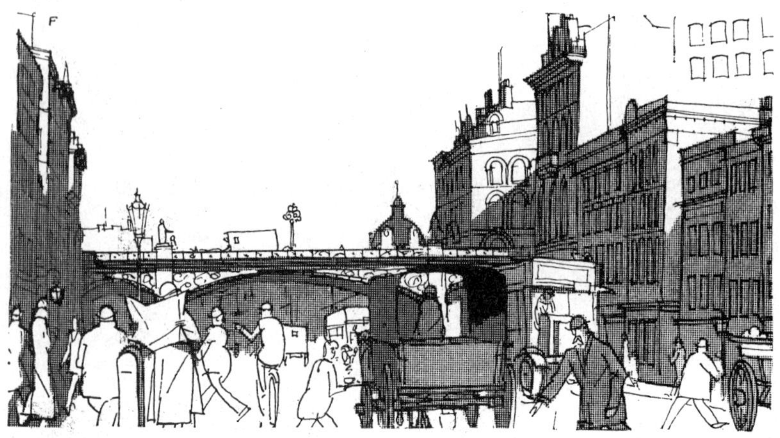

FIG. 74.—A Modern Rendering of the Prout Tradition in Architectural Perspective. Used as an advertisement. By ALEC FRASER.

expression can be what he likes. Pennell's technique is similar to that of another American, Ernest Peixotto, but he developed more variety and colour. His pen drawings invariably show a distinct "etching" quality due to a wonderful sense of design. He "tears the heart out of a landscape," and so fills a given space with it that it is a joy to the eye apart from topographical interest. Pennell's use to the student is mainly as an example of actual use of line to express foliage, shadows, architecture in relation to landscape, immense distance, great height, etc., in which he

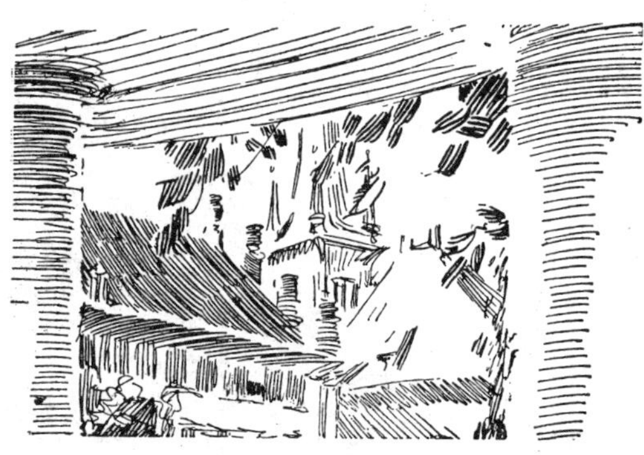

FIG. 75.—By JAMES MONTGOMERY FLAGG.

excelled with a daintiness concealing infinite strength and resource (see Fig. 72).

If there is danger of confusing the mind with many masters in holding up three such different men as examples, it is more apparent than real, for it hurts no student to know the methods by which others have achieved success.

There is a decided tendency among the "advanced" artists to revert to the Prout tradition of pure line drawings of landscape and architecture, entirely without shading. It is a very difficult technique, but decidedly interesting both to do and to see. The secret of success lies in suggesting enough for the spectator's eye unconsciously to fill in the rest, and the execution of such drawings is an education in avoiding the crime of superfluous lines.

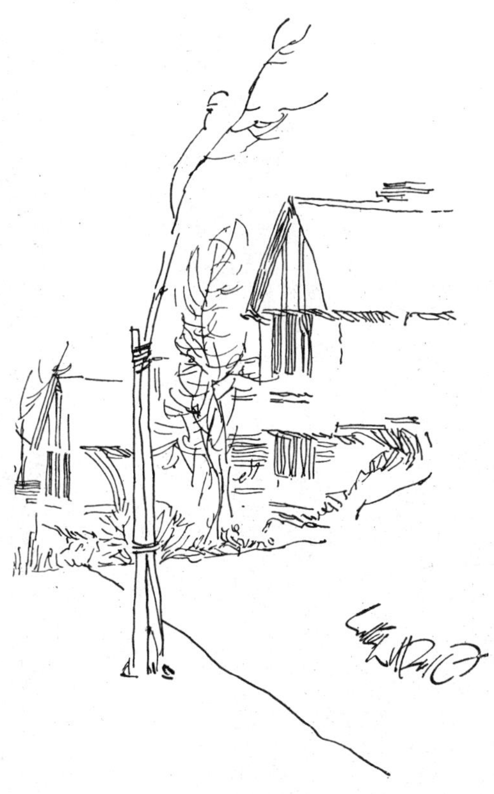

FIG. 76.—By GILBERT WILKINSON.
Something may be learned from the light touch employed by professional illustrators in suggesting architectural backgrounds.

E. H. New, working somewhat in the old woodcut manner, evolved an interesting pen technique for topographical illustration which goes extremely well with the printed page in well-printed books, but fights with ordinary magazine type-setting.

New revived the idea of accurate but decoratively rendered panoramic views of towns and groups of buildings, and his drawings of Oxford Colleges are widely appreciated and treasured by Oxonians in memory of their college days. The

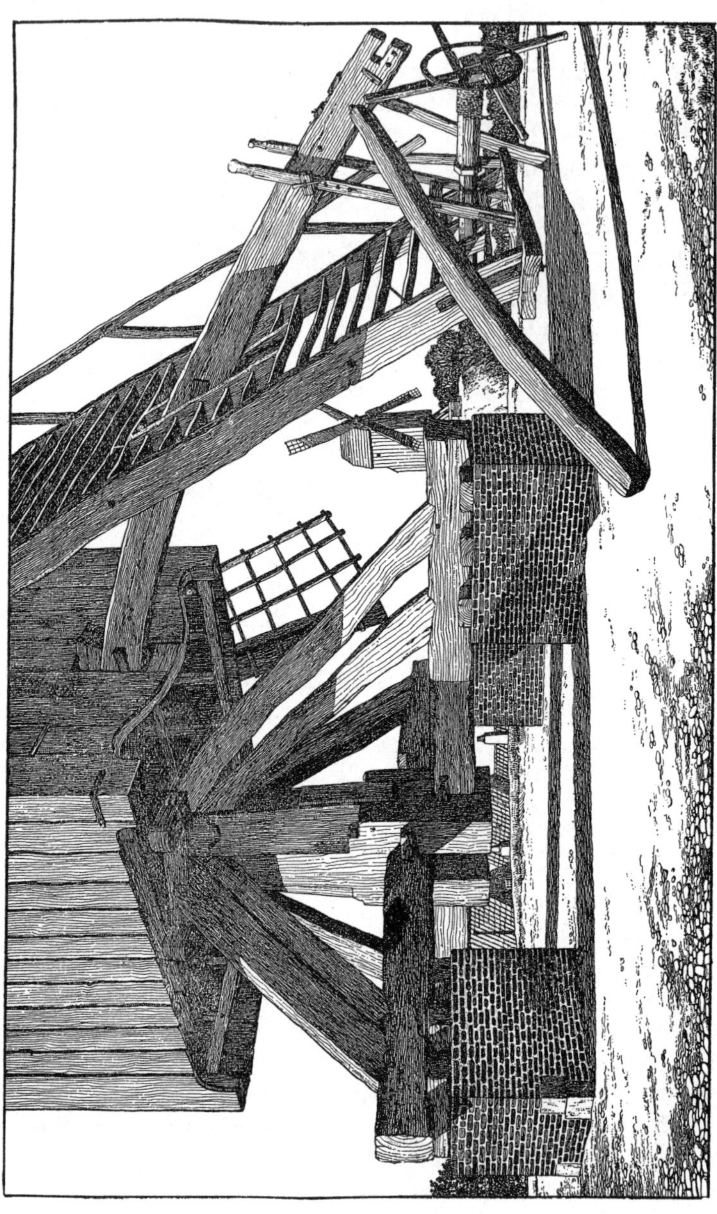

Fig. 76a.—Elaboration of Tone in a Drawing by CHARLES WADE.

idea is a good one and worthy of extension, especially in these days of aerial photography when data is available without the hard work which older drawings entailed.

A satisfactory topographical drawing entails loving care in preparation ; the hasty sketch, unless it is something instinct with genius, is quite out of place in view of the bigness and permanence of one's subjects. A fairly good test of composition and general placing in such pen drawings is to consider them as works of art intended to stand alone ; to ask oneself if they are good enough for translation to the copper as etched plates, and reconsider them if they fail in the test, which is applicable to both the elaborate and simple methods.

There is a certain monumental quality which fits a drawing for the permanence of biting on metal. Railton seems to have missed this ; Pennell, on the other hand, thought naturally in terms of bitten copper, and his pen drawings were always potential etchings. The line of demarcation between drawings possible and impossible as etchings is perhaps fine, but it is there, and can be made useful in self-criticism.

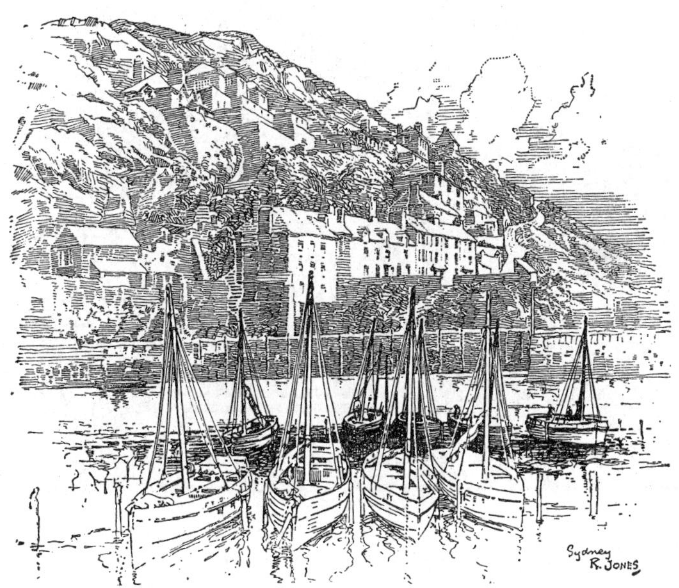

FIG. 77.—Combination of " Colour " and Delicate Line in a Landscape Drawing by SYDNEY R. JONES.

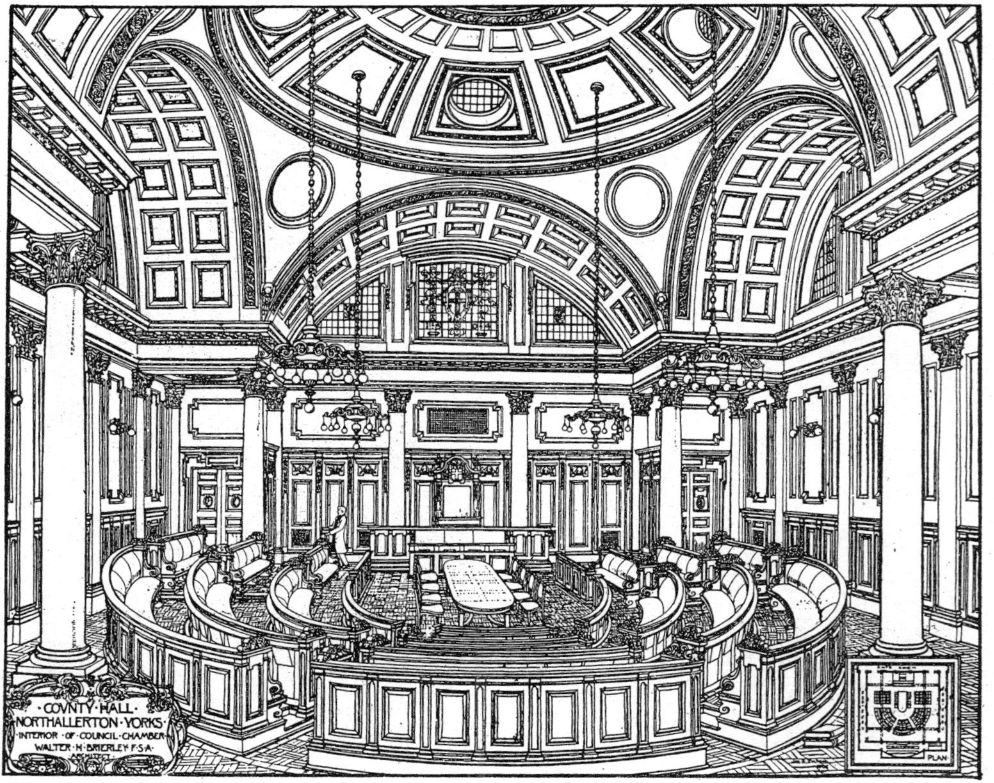

FIG. 78.—Architectural Drawing by J. B. FULTON.
An example of the painstaking accuracy necessary in this style of work.

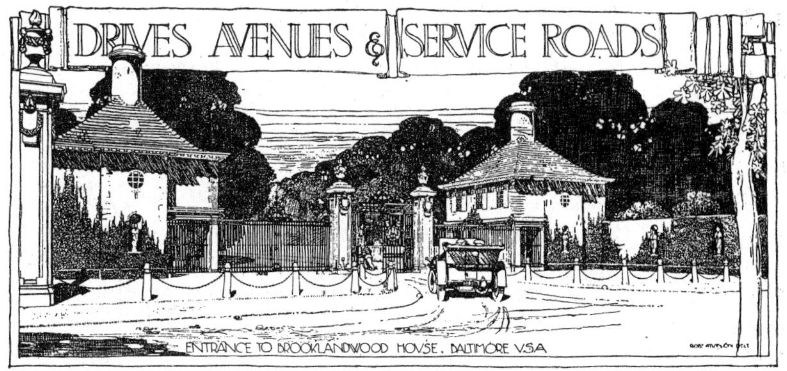

FIG. 79.—Use of Architectural Forms in Book Decoration by ROBERT ATKINSON.

CHAPTER VIII

ARCHITECTURAL DRAWING

STRICTLY speaking, this title should embrace all drawings of architecture ; but by long usage it is associated with the profession, and implies the sketches made to show clients their buildings as they are to look in the built state.

The clean, brittle effect obtainable with the pen is peculiarly fitted for this purpose, and pen drawing, therefore, is a favourite method in use for those enticing imaginative efforts, which share with railway posters the distinction of flattering the place they represent without being traceably unlike it in any way.

Architectural drawing tends more and more towards simplicity and suggestion—more thought and fewer lines. The vogue of hard, exact perspectives and elevations, showing every joint and brick to scale, is dead, and for the student interesting only as history.

It is difficult to talk about architectural drawing without mention of Railton and Griggs, whose work is classified with that of Pennell, Rico, and Peixotto in method No. 5, simply because they elected to work as book illustrators and adapted their methods to that end. Railton was trained as an architect, and F. L. Griggs was intimately associated with the technical side of architecture in doing perspectives before he turned first to book illustration and later to etching, the method which sooner or later attracts every architectural draughtsman of genius.

Railton's name persists in association with a very definite standard of style which has influenced professional draughtsmanship more than the manner of any other artist, and laid the foundation of the complete freedom now enjoyed.

F. L. Griggs, A.R.A., interprets the poetry and mystery of old buildings in a technique of monumental quality which gets as near perfection as is possible in this world. It is precise and almost geometrically correct, often intricate in line and tone, yet the effect is invariably one of superlative strength.

Peixotto, Rico, and Pennell are interpreters of the picturesque in landscape. Architecture is incidental to their aims, and treated entirely from the pictorial angle, with no passionate interest in it as structure. This gives their work a unity which is generally absent from the avowed architectural drawing, where the building is stressed at the expense of complete unison between foreground, trees, and sky.

An architect who is busy with actual building has little time to make drawings other than the working designs for these buildings, and so employs specialists whose business it is to interpret rough notes and scale drawings into fine perspectives, easily understood by clients and assessors in competitions. It must be conceded to the glory of these men that they often do much with very unpromising material, and many architects owe much of their reputation to the sea change which their ideas undergo in pen and ink by a brilliant draughtsman.

Life would be considerably sweeter for the perspective man if all the buildings he was called upon to visualise and present in realistic form were within measurable distance of beauty; but, alas, they are generally pretty tough propositions to invest with charm of any kind, and it is easy to forgive the somewhat violent pen work sometimes used, in sheer desperation, to infuse a little life into Regent Street classic, the eternal shop elevations which form the bulk of modern practice.

Architectural perspectives are business propositions and seldom made for fun, hence the necessity to subordinate picturesque accessories to the building, unless the placing of this in beautiful country or garden setting will help it commercially.

It is a good notion for the student to first get ideas for

the rendering of the various details, surfaces, and textures that comprise entire drawings; in other words, to get a "vocabulary." Railton's work is of the utmost value at this

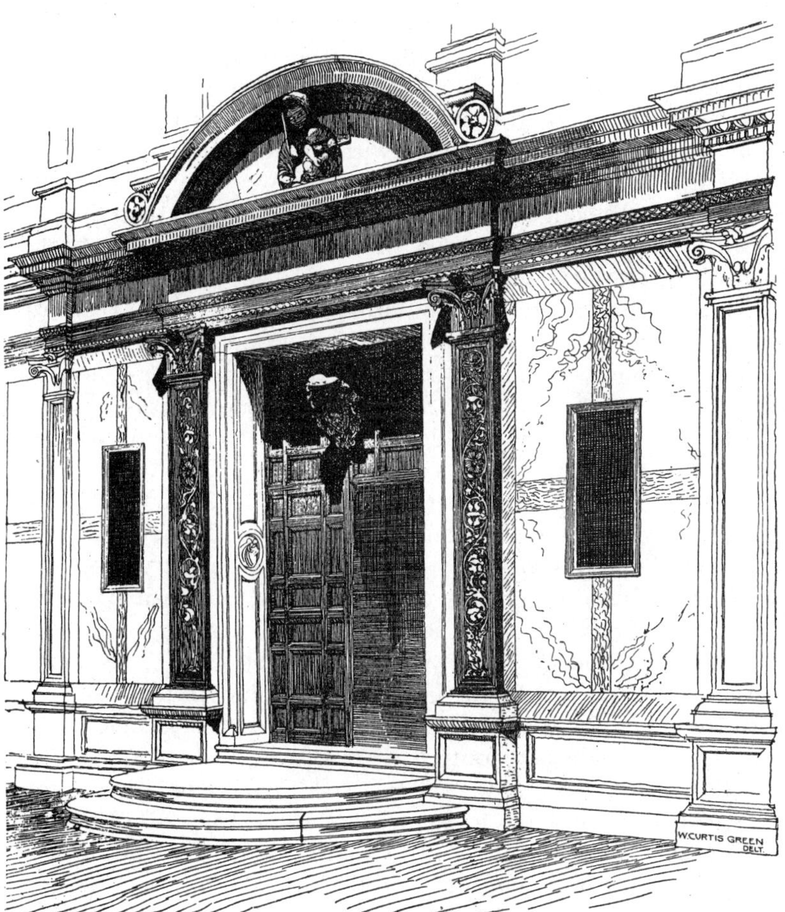

FIG. 80.—W. CURTIS GREEN, A.R.A. A Masterly Drawing in the best Architectural Tradition.

stage; his "vocabulary" contains every possible expression for architecture in line. The fact that he worked this overmuch is no detriment if his drawings are studied with the sole idea of finding equivalents to their richness of colour variations, picturesque light and shade, and clean shorthand method of indicating stone joints, brickwork, doors, windows, and mouldings. Most students will derive confidence from actually copying parts of his drawings and analysing the marvellous dexterity of hand by which they were put together.

Railton was an extremely rapid worker. His pencil lay-out for working on in ink was merely the roughest indication in soft lines of where he intended the big masses to fall in the finished state. For this he used soft pencils, some round and some of the "Carpenter" type with broad chisel surface, which evidently suggested his curious technique in dealing with trees. His pencil drawings were even more mannered than his pen work in their exaggerations of the picturesque and broken aspects of old buildings.

He revelled in the Tudor period, and in Hood's "Haunted House," which he illustrated in his second and best period. His imagination could run riot in a very delightful conception of a gabled ruin with its features well enough preserved to show the effectiveness of his touch in all the useful tricks of architectural drawing.

The drawing, "For over all there hung a cloud of fear" (Fig. 91A), is one of several illustrations in the book in which variety of tone is carried to the excess of rivalry with steel engraving, but it is valuable as showing what is possible in range of colour obtainable with pen line. The contrast of the dark balustrading and gate-post against the dark grey of the distant gable, and the wonderful gradation of tone from behind the broken gate up to the light on the ruined roof, are useful exercises for the student in pen control.

For richness in gradation of line in an altogether lighter key, the "Porch" on p. 77 of Loftie's "Inns of Court and Chancery" would be difficult to beat as an example of masterly facility and much suggestion with little definition. Railton's transgression into wanton curliness is almost absent, and the slight but adequate touches representing stonework and windows are informative. To copy this drawing on the same scale as Railton usually worked—about 18 in. high—will test the student's power over his pen and give a certain stock in trade of handling on which to found an individual style.

Railton's first period, altogether harder, is represented by his illustrations to "Coaching Days and Coaching Ways," published in the long defunct *English Illustrated Magazine*, and his later over-florid style, with mannerisms exaggerated beyond toleration, is shown in some of his published drawings of Westminster.

Useful work by Railton will be found in the "Inns of Court and Chancery," by W. J. Loftie, and in the volumes of *Good Words* for the 'nineties, obtainable at the old booksellers.

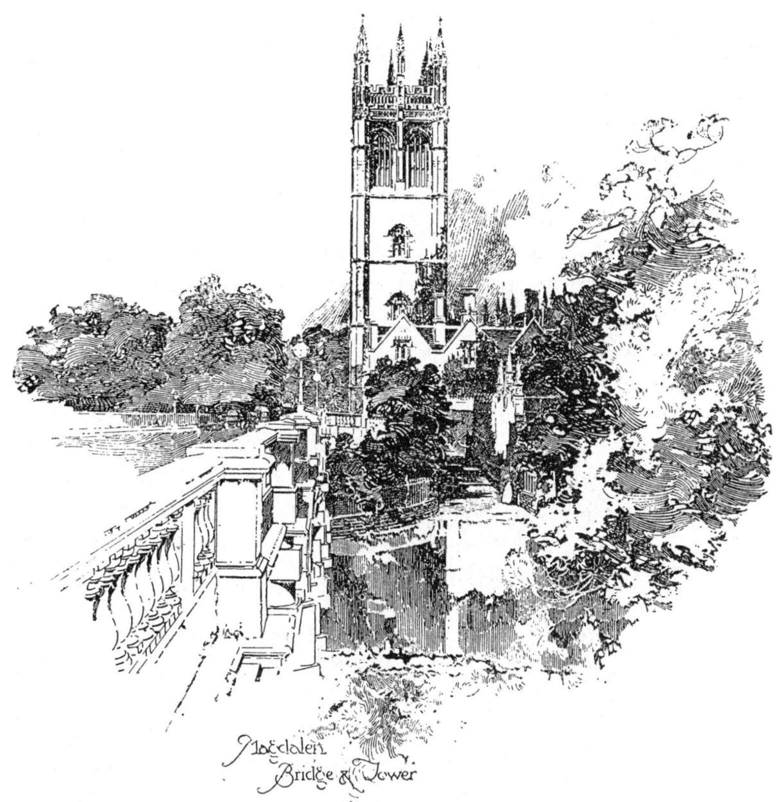

FIG. 81.—A Typical "RAILTON."

It must not be concluded that Railton is the ideal model for students; but in a style which is so definite and compendious there is much that can be studied and usefully adapted to modern usage. Briefly, his good points are such that they atone for the meretricious picturesqueness which is his chief fault.

It is wise to study the work of many master draughtsmen in the intervals of making independent efforts to render such simple subjects as parts of buildings. Something is gained when the average door, window, cornice, and chimney-stack can be made interesting by some personal touch which lifts them out of their "builders' catalogue" plainness. In drawing windows, for instance, there are many points which it is wise to think about and evolve standard methods of dealing with. The fact that glass reflects, altering from dark to light as the cloud shadows flit across a building, gives a valuable hint to use them in getting variety and interest.

The treatment of detail depends on its size in the drawing so much that it is impossible to lay down fixed rules; but some hints generally applicable may be useful. In dealing with Norman, Gothic, and Tudor shapes in doors and windows, the important thing is to get the drawing right. If this is successful, the pen work will look after itself, as the slightest suggestion of the beautiful old work, convincingly drawn, is infinitely preferable to the most elaborate pen work on drawing which is fundamentally wrong. The best proof of this is in the work of W. Walcot, in which elaborate architectural detail is invariably reduced to the utmost simplicity of statement, with entire success, because there are no sins of omission or commission in the drawing on which the few surviving lines depend. The fact that Walcot seldom deals with buildings other than classic does not alter the application of this reference to his thoroughness in preparation.

The late fifteenth-century doorway to Eastington Hall, reproduced herewith (Fig. 83), is a good example for the student to attempt as a pen drawing. The first thing to do is to make an enlarged pencil drawing at least 6 in. high (but preferably larger), searching for the construction and endeavouring to think out in pencil the subsequent treatment in ink. The formation of the various elements should be carefully studied and understood. The cornice moulding, for instance, shows its true section at the extreme corner; this should be carefully drawn and the lines defining its members taken back in perspective from a point determined by the intersection of its top line with the line of the edge of the lowest step, produced to meet on the right of the photograph. This point will give all the horizontals and keep the drawing true. Next, put in all the vertical lines and the trusses supporting the cornice, and finally the door interior and steps.

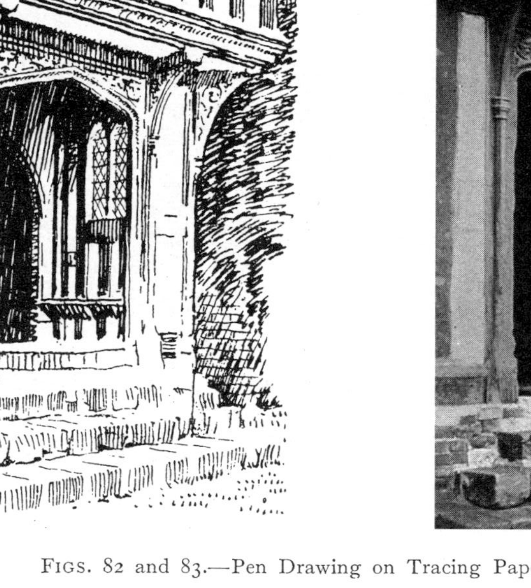

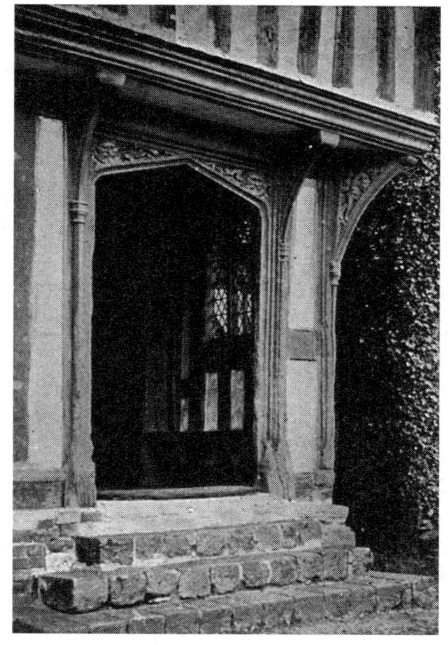

FIGS. 82 and 83.—Pen Drawing on Tracing Paper over a Photograph.

[*To face p.* 112.

In proceeding to ink, decide which is to be the darkest part, and leave this blank until the whole surrounding portion is put in as lightly as possible. The necessary weight of dark can then be judged in relation to the whole effect desired. In this subject the darkest part will be the interior of the entry, the equal weight of the foliage at right hand in photo being reduced, but still left strong enough to balance the drawing, the composition of which will be upset if the projecting corner of the building is not supported by considerable weight of colour. It will be advisable to break the stiff corner in this foliage, which coincides too exactly with the line of the upper story of the building, and the general direction of the lines indicating it should be upwards away from the house to counter the strong downward thrust of the cornice and door head.

The sketch herewith (Fig. 82), made on a rough tracing of the photograph, gives an indication of a possible result from the treatment described. Owing to the small scale on which the drawing was made, the difficulty of showing the cornice properly is apparent; with an enlarged drawing it would be easier to show the corner and to get the right proportions of the members. It will be noticed that the soffit under cornice is left white, a forced value which relies for justification on reflection from below and gives an effect of strong light. The whole of the surround to door opening was drawn with the back of a Gillott's crow quill, and the actual interior with the right side of the same pen. In working on tracing paper the back of the pen will often give better results than its usual side owing to the sharpness of its "bite" on a surface which eludes the yield of the easily opened points.

Next try later doorways, especially some of the beautiful Renaissance and Georgian varieties, which make excellent subjects. Do these from the actual doors, if possible; if not, from photographs.

These exercises all deal with doorways which are in themselves picturesque, and the resulting drawings should at least maintain that quality, and in execution give the student considerable knowledge of the various problems that arise in dealing with mouldings, shadows, textures, etc., and indicating stone and brickwork, ornament and timberwork.

In dealing with mouldings, as already mentioned, there is generally a point where they terminate or intersect, at which their nature can be clearly shown, otherwise they must be suggested by line and shadow, which is not easy, and should not be laboured. It is best to leave much to the imagination.

Shadows are an interesting study in themselves. It will be found that in short shadows, cast by slight projections, the accentuation of the lower edge of shadow will give an additionally sunny effect. This is difficult to explain, but it is true. Also it is best to let the lines forming a shadow follow the direction in which it is falling. Shadows are the only means of indicating projection in many cases, so their importance in the scheme of things is apparent. A method of showing the shadow accentuated at the lower edge is shown on Fig. 14, "Shadow and Shade," where quickly made strokes, roughly parallel and at an angle of about 45°, run together at the base owing to a slightly harder pressure as the pen leaves the paper.

The expert pen draughtsman generally develops a passion for textures, which certainly are tempting, especially in interior work. It is a hobby which can very easily be overdone, for the indication must be subtle and the differences felt rather than seen in the drawing. Some materials, such as brickwork and tiles, become texture in small scale drawings, and a method of indicating both must be found. Bricks are generally dealt with by getting the prevailing tone and indicating the bond in places, sometimes by filling the whole space with bond lines in black or tiny bricks irregularly drawn, both very obvious methods which are very seldom resorted to by the great Dutch interpreter of architecture, J. W. R. Wenckenbach, whose employment of tones and contrasts expresses not only materials, but materials seen through atmosphere (see Fig. 84). Griggs is the only man approaching him in sympathetic accord with the spirit of fine building, and his perfection lacks the warmth of these wonderfully intimate renderings of old Holland, masterly in their variety of colour and texture, the absence of shadows suggesting the prevailing greyness of the climate.

Time spent in the preliminary stages of a pen drawing is time well expended. The student is naturally impatient to get to grips with the actual pen and ink, but experience teaches that the best results are obtained when the entire subject is very definitely planned in pencil first, the drawing quite convincing and the " values " thought out in pencil with full allowance for translation.

In the making of a pen drawing it is well to remember that things are not always what they seem, and success does not depend on accurate rendering of parts, or their relations to adjacent parts, but on the relation of each part to the entire scheme. A window, by contrast with the stone wall containing it, may appear black; but in the whole scheme a pattern of

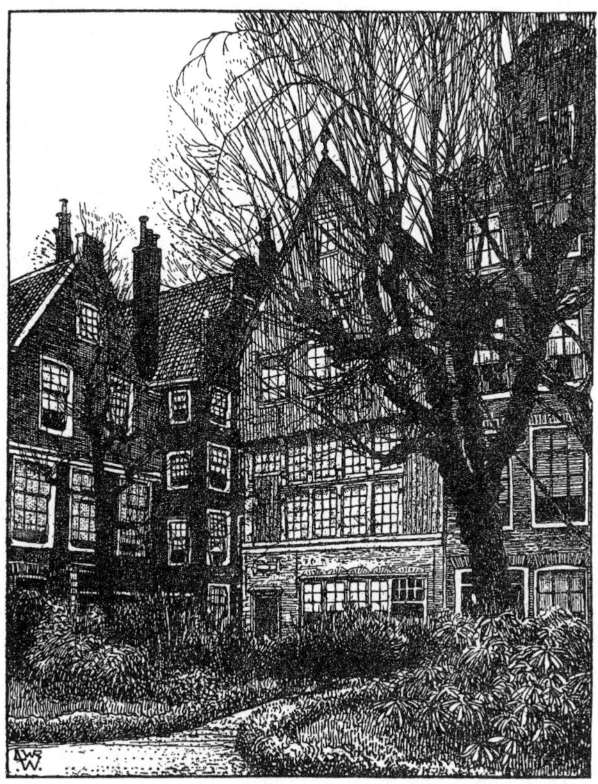

FIG. 84.—J. W. R. WENCKENBACH. Old Holland.

black windows may be very disturbing and obviously wrong. Such things are found out in a careful preliminary plan or scaffolding for the ultimate building of the satisfactory drawing.

A student who has experienced the delight of working with pen and ink on a thoroughly well-prepared foundation drawing, seeing it grow inevitably and in order towards significance, will not grudge the effort necessary to produce such useful groundwork for subsequent drawings.

It is *possible* to produce fine pen drawings of architecture or landscape with only the merest pencil indication of what is to be—or even with none; but it involves genius and experience beyond the ordinary. Railton's preliminaries were slight indeed, but his formula was so definite that the method of attack was instantly decided upon and the drawing built up according

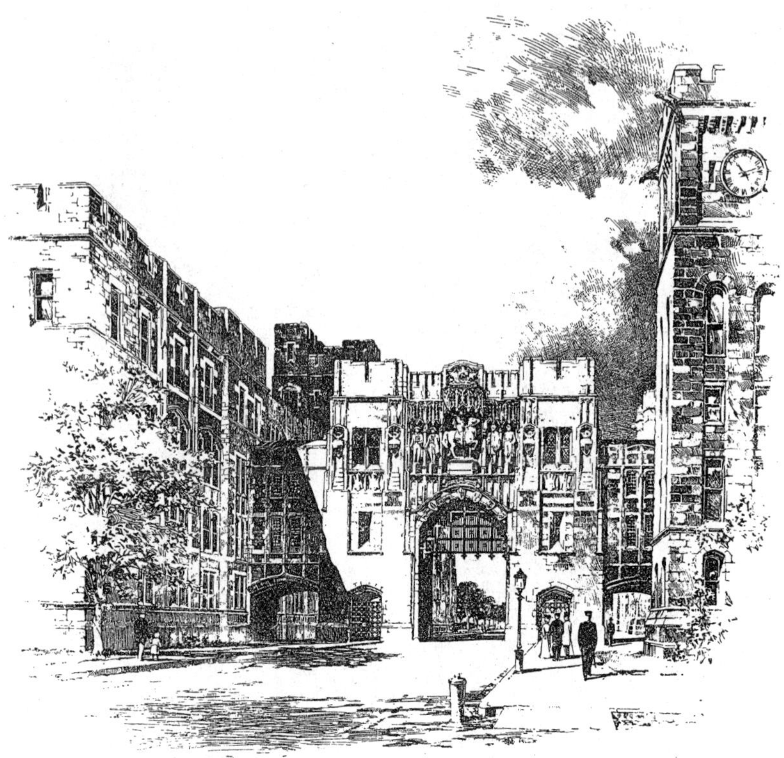

FIG. 85.—Drawing by BERTRAM GROSVENOR GOODHUE.
A preliminary rendering in pen and ink of one of his own designs.

to plans retained in the artist's inner consciousness from former battles with similar problems.

Of all the men inspired by Railton's methods, Bertram Grosvenor Goodhue, the great American architect and decorative artist, was most successful in adapting the good points to his own use and escaping the pitfalls which the apparent ease of Railton's work holds for the unwary. In Goodhue's case the influence of Railton is most apparent in drawings executed about 1895-96, at which period he had evidently assimilated all he needed for the formation of a sound and interesting personal style, giving perhaps a safer source of inspiration for the student than Railton. The drawing on Fig. 85 shows a mellowed return to his own style, previously hard and accomplished in the accepted architectural manner of the period, but here made interesting by his excursions into Railton technique, although adhering with uncanny fidelity to the actual photographic detail and colouring.

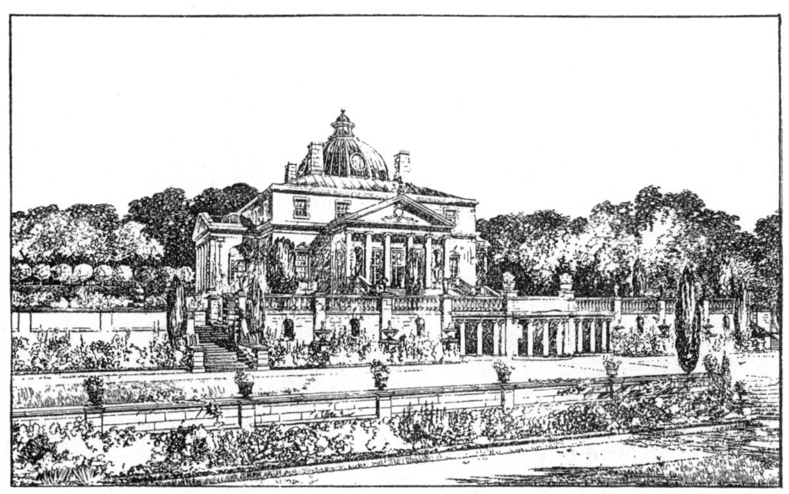

FIG. 86.—Drawing by C. E. MALLOWS.
The typically workmanlike architectural style.

"A Book of Architectural and Decorative Drawings," by Goodhue, published by the Architectural Publishing Co. of New York, and in England by B. T. Batsford Ltd., contains various solutions of all the problems an architectural draughtsman is likely to encounter. The monumental drawings of his own churches and cathedrals are inspiring in their breadth and actuality, and the whole collection is an education in the use of the pen for purely professional architectural drawings. Goodhue's work is also illustrated in a fine record volume by Dr Cram and others.

Beauty in an architectural drawing is frequently discounted by indifferent figures introduced because they are believed to lend animation. It is a golden rule to leave figures out unless they can be well done; badly drawn, they attract attention and detract from the dignity of the architecture. Goodhue has spoiled many of his best drawings by hasty and unconvincing figures, and Railton enlisted the help of his friend Jellico to put in "human interest" where he thought it necessary, with the unfortunate result that the figures always look conscious interlopers with no real connection or use in the scheme.

The method of William Walcot, the greatest living master of architectural suggestion, is to indicate figures just sufficiently to give scale without attracting attention to themselves: a very sound idea, but the figure must be understood thoroughly to be able to treat it thus playfully and keep it within the picture. The main characteristic of Walcot's treatment of architecture is that there is so much more in it than actually meets the casual glance. A basis of superb drawing, the salient points of which are emphasised with a wizard's touch in the handling of the etching needle or brush, accounts for the complete impression of accuracy and actuality.

Modern architectural training wisely includes life drawing, and an architectural draughtsman should supplement this by cultivating the art of sketching figures in everyday costume with vitality and movement. The facility thus attained will react on the treatment of entire compositions, bringing architecture and figures into the harmonious relationship evident in the architectural etchings of Brangwyn and Walcot.

With the confidence born of knowledge, much can be done with figures and vehicles in bringing drawings together. In a tall office building or block of shops, for instance, a certain dullness obtains unless some definite connection with everyday life is given by the bustle and interest of pedestrians and traffic, which can be manipulated to give interesting lights and darks where needed, and break the monotony of angles and straight lines by free contrast. An excellent method is to draw one's "human interest" from good photographs of crowds in movement, such as are often given in the illustrated papers, selecting from these groups and single figures to fit the situation, and giving very free and suggestive renderings in which swing and vitality are more in mind than detail and solidity.

The lazy habit of putting in figures from memory because they are small is the basis of most failures. Few people have visual memory capable of dealing with figures in action, and the slight extra trouble involved in basing them on actual sketches from life or photographic data will certainly pay.

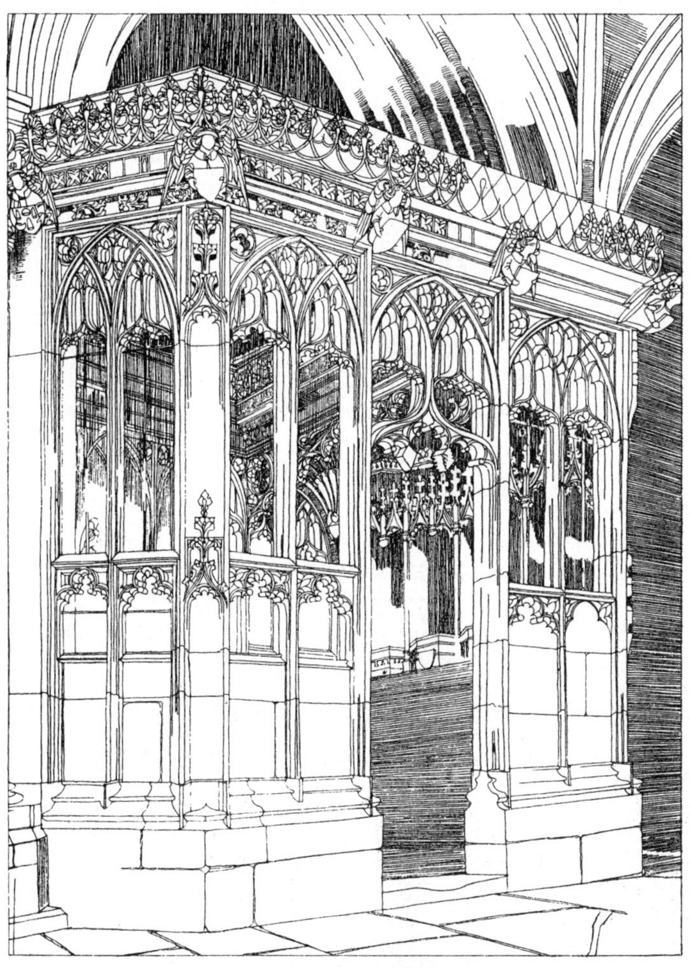

FIG. 87.—A Delicate Rendering of the Difficult Details of Gothic Tracery by W. S. A. GORDON.

Muirhead Bone and Henry Rushbury are examples of perfect technique in the relation of figures and architecture, and should be studied by those in search of a high ideal, admitting no compromise with effort.

Muirhead Bone's pencil drawing of the Pincian Gardens, Rome, shows very clearly the decisive yet slight means employed to give the effect of figures in strong sunlight, all obviously intent on their own business and unconscious of their necessity in the scheme.

Some hints as to the employment of figures to do certain things in a drawing may be gathered from the " Bank of Peru " sketch on Fig. 88, in which the figures were put in in ink deliberately from photographs without previous pencil drawing. The dark mass of the car on left shows the use of a vehicle to give a defined break to the lower line of a direct elevation and intensify its whiteness if in stone. The figure on the road, indicated by a minimum expenditure of line and without shadow inflexion, shows the use of a figure to break the lower line and give distance and scale without contrast, serving to bring the elevation "through" to the roadway. The rest of the figures are simply rapid translations of actual photographic poses, and the actuality survives in a certain liveliness that is almost invariably missing when the introduction of freely-drawn figures is attempted from memory. An effective trick is the strongly accentuated light on the building to the right of entrance given by the V-shaped composition of the group formed of contrasted light and dark figures.

In suggesting that figures should be drawn direct in ink

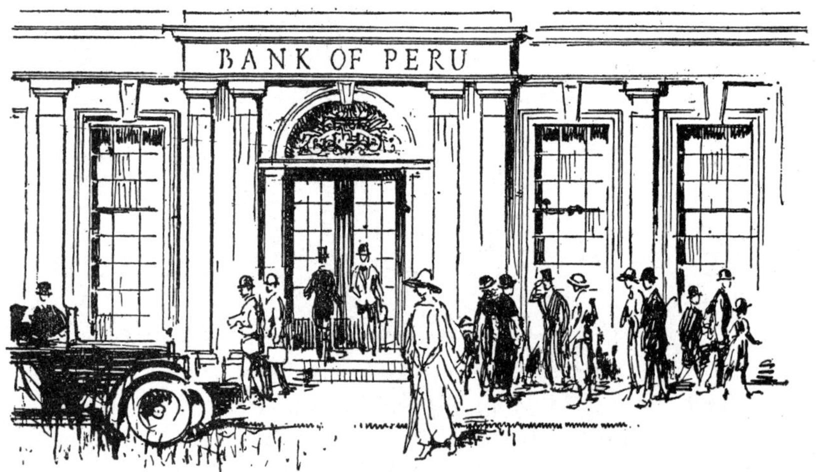

FIG. 88.

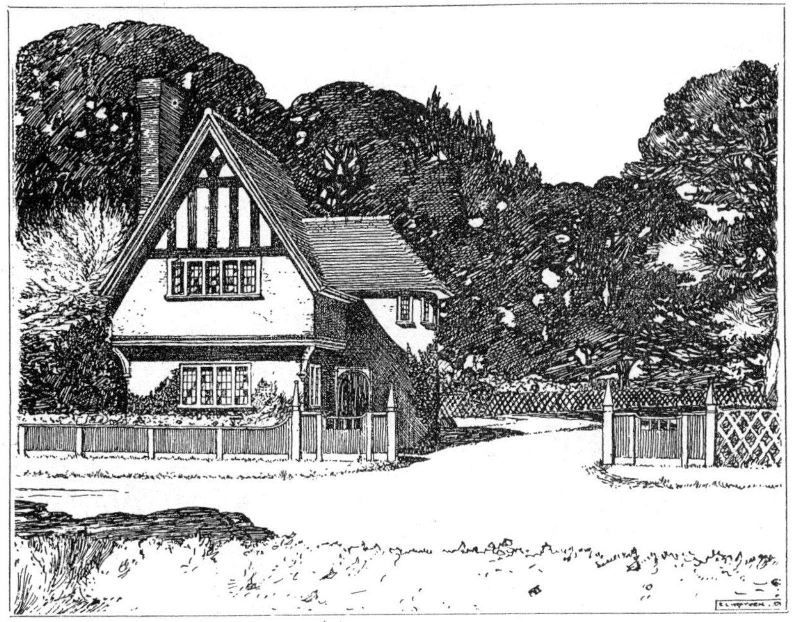

FIG. 89.—The Mount, Westerham, by E. L. WRATTEN.

to secure the freedom of actual drawing from life or photo, it is not meant that light and shade and composition should not be planned. This is best done by indicating weight of colour in soft dark pencil where the groups or single figures are needed, working on this afterwards and endeavouring to keep the same relative weight in ink. This is Brangwyn's method of obtaining the stereoscopic effect of receding groups of figures which is so characteristic and effective in his etchings.

Mr Wratten's drawing of "The Mount, Westerham" (Fig. 89), is a good example of colour in pen work combined with the touch of the professional architect. The handling of trees is an expert treatment of growth reduced to a flat unobtrusive mass which serves as a foil to the building.

The acquisition of professional draughtsmanship equal to the best modern standard of practice must be a labour of love. It can be approached in no other spirit if it is to succeed. The gradual addition of knowledge laboriously acquired is, according to Mr Robert Atkinson, who should know, "invaluable in installing the rudiments of taste, proportion, restraint, and many other qualities which would otherwise be neglected."

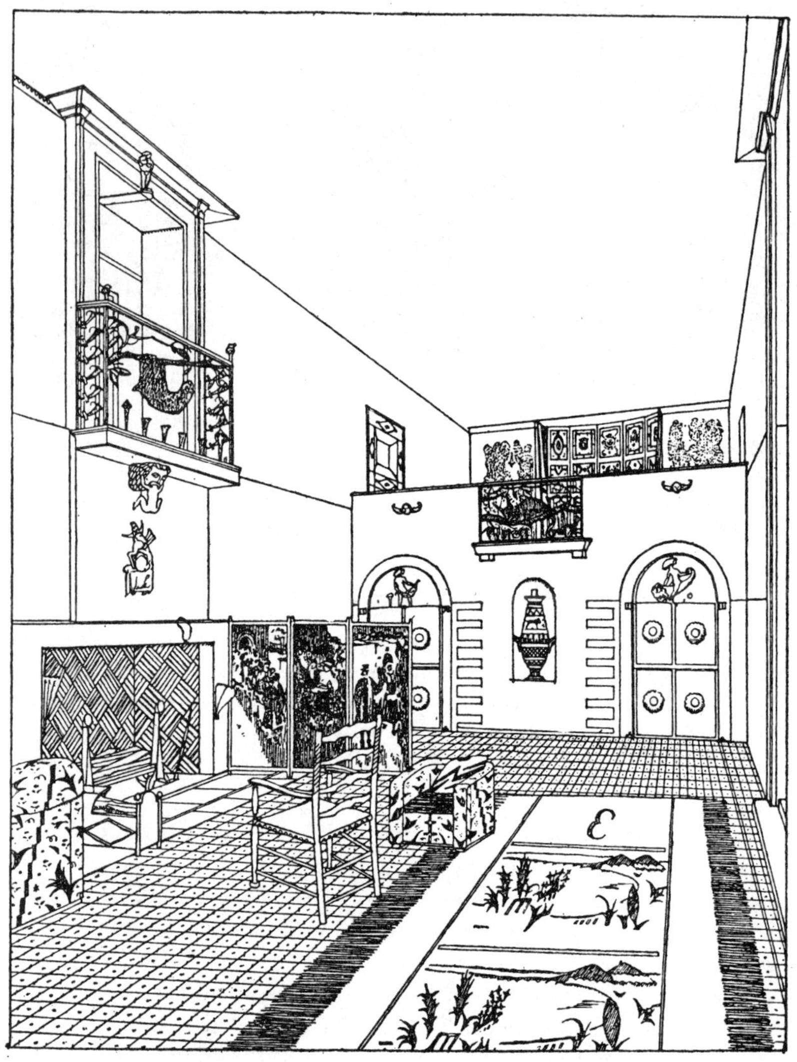

FIG. 90.—A Clever German Interior suggested in Pen Outline.

There is room only for the properly and thoroughly trained man who can think in terms of building and not *merely* draw buildings. "In draughtsmanship, for effect the structural problems are necessarily omitted; but it is obvious that the draughtsman must possess a very thorough knowledge of both historic ornament and constructive details." To quote Mr Atkinson again: "Designs may be called the expression on paper of voids and solids drawn in such a way as to convey

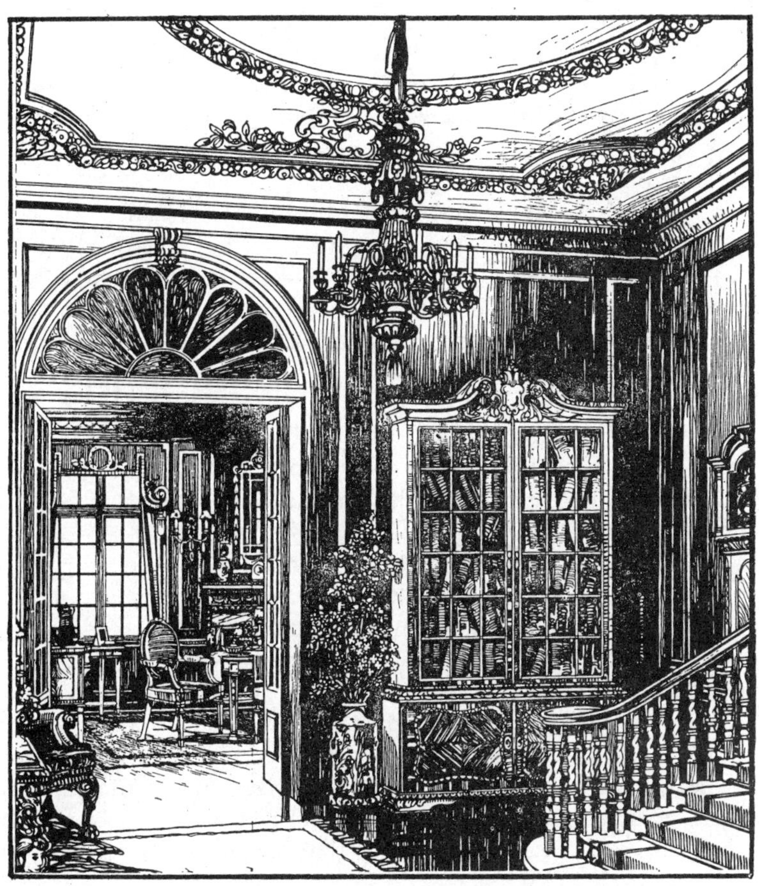

FIG. 91.—A Strong Treatment of a "Period" Interior.

an intelligible impression of the ultimate building. To achieve this result, rapid and accurate drawing of ornament and features is necessary. The *feeling* of the design can only be properly judged when the whole of the ornaments are placed in proper juxtaposition. Many such drawings may be necessary, and though each may be no more finished than the first, a gradual feeling will develop that the voids and solids are right and that the ornament is right.

"These drawings must be rapid and clear, and indication plays a great part in their preparation. When the *feeling* is right, more careful drawings are necessary. They are not wasted labour, but are made to satisfy the canons of taste, and should be masterpieces of rendered drawings, showing all lights and shadows. Even the most minute mouldings or ornaments may be too coarse or too light; their value can only be judged by careful projection of cast shadows in their relation to the general effect."

Mr Atkinson is quoted as authoritative evidence that the profession of architectural draughtsman is not to be lightly regarded: "A modern school of architectural draughtsmen is now arising who hope to revive the ancient glories of drawing, and are not satisfied with a perspective unless it is perfectly drawn, perfectly rendered, beautifully designed, and all sculpture or coloured decoration fittingly suggested."

To fill this programme adequately is obviously no mean task; but there are several men who are doing it, and only hard work is needed to join them in one of the definite ways of adding to the beauty and dignity of life.

A definite branch of modern architectural practice is the drawing of interiors, and the range of possibilities in this direction is wide: from the simple outline suggestions of Palmer Jones and the Viennese and German moderns (see Fig. 90), through the heavy architectural line shown in the advertisements for Warings herewith (Fig. 91), to the solid black and white of Fred Taylor's drawings for Heals. That the drawings of the future will be simpler is fairly certain, as the modern tendency is to leave something to the spectator's imagination, giving stimulus to thought rather than attention to detail.

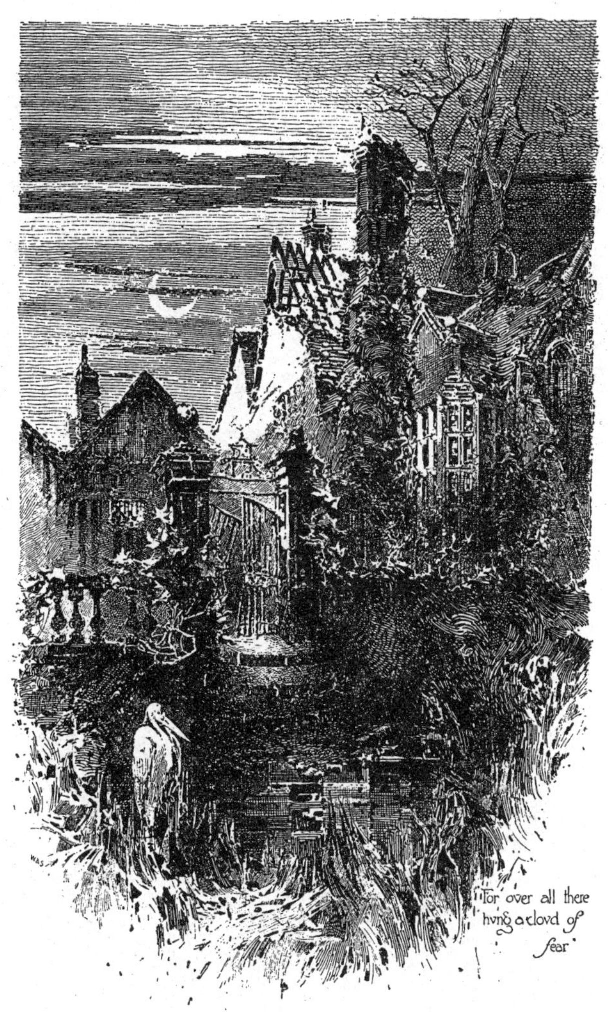

FIG. 91A.—An Example of the Complex Technique of RAILTON'S Later Work.

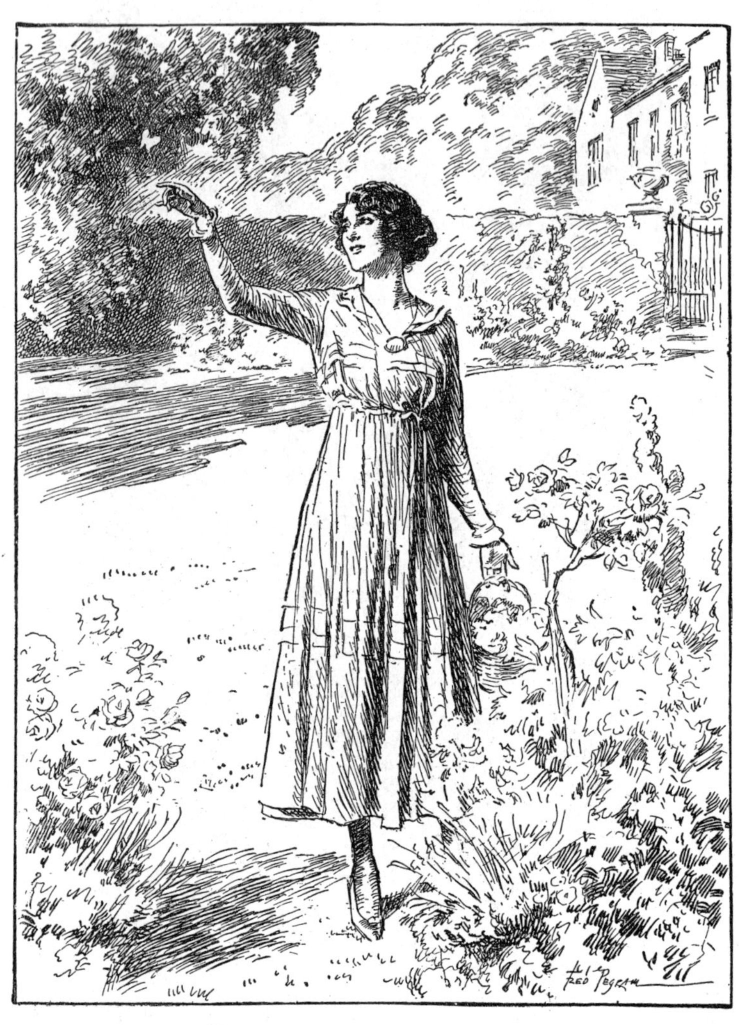

FIG. 92.—By FRED PEGRAM.

CHAPTER IX

MODERN PEN ILLUSTRATION

I. The Realistic School

BY realists must be understood those wise people who present nature as they believe she appears to other people. The fact that they see it the same way enables them to do this. They are eminently sane. Lacking the something that twists the normal mind into the abnormal state of genius, they are thoroughly equipped to deal with all the problems of actuality.

Absolute sanity is rare, and the small proportion of artists whose mentality prompts them in the safe and uneventful path of representational work prosper exceedingly.

Most artists graduate through periodical or magazine illustration, and it is difficult to recall more than one prominent name which has not been familiar in the editorial pages of the press. Bernard Partridge, F. H. Townsend, L. Raven Hill, Fred Pegram, Leo Cheney, H. M. Bateman, Frank Reynolds, E. J. Sullivan, and all the others have distinguished records in illustration, and all deal with life as it is generally understood, either in serious vein or in a spirit of kindly fun. A good illustrator with a universally understood style has only to get a few drawings into prominent papers to be a marked man in advertising circles, where everybody is keen to find new stars whose qualities have been revealed as suitable for the advertising constellation. Septimus E. Scott is the only prominent penman in advertising whose reputation did not come from illustration, and pen work is a minor activity of his, overshadowed by his work as a painter.

The popular magazines of a few years ago were illustrated mainly by pen drawings, and F. H. Townsend and Fred Pegram must have executed some thousands of drawings between them for publication as story illustrations. There is very little pen work in the magazines to-day; the editorial tastes have veered round to half-tone reproductions of wash drawings, which are not to be compared in artistic interest with good line work, but are nearer to the popular conception of life, which has been influenced by photography.

Pegram's work is the embodiment of neatness and clean finish; there are no loose ends (see Fig. 92). He is the ideal man for showing us athletic types of English men and women, beautiful children, and comfortable types of old people. His limitations are the inevitable result of his excellence in dealing with the refinements of life, and his labourers and country folk are unconvincing. They are not robust, the refinement obtrudes, and a patrician atmosphere pervades the simple cottage interior when Pegram draws it. His drawing seldom falters, but his vision is attracted by the comfortable side of life, glancing over the rougher places in search of it—an asset in advertising, where the rosy side of things cannot be too strongly emphasised.

Perfectly straightforward and sincere, Pegram's method shows no striving after style. It is pure drawing throughout, the subject first drawn in pencil and the ink applied to get the desired effect without fuss. The main characteristic of the actual technique is the heavy outline given to figures which are to stand out against a white or light background. Folds, shadows, and textures within this outline are kept subservient to it by lighter treatment. Textures are recognisable; a wool jersey, a tweed suit or skirt are wonderfully dealt with in strokes which are seldom long and never out of control. The secret of the appeal of such drawings to the business world lies in their complete presentation of its own ideas of things. The people in them are drawn with such stereoscopic accuracy, they are such solid realities, that the advertiser feels confident they will convey his message to the great majority.

The work of F. H. Townsend (see Fig. 99) achieves realism without the tightness of Pegram's technique. Townsend was interested in harmonious tone effects, and managed to convey incident with almost photographic accuracy in an unobtrusive technique of surprising freedom. He possessed a genius for hard work, and there was a story in the building up of most of his drawings. He worked entirely from models, and would go to infinite trouble to track them to earth for a particular subject. No one type persisted in his work, which dealt faithfully with all sorts and conditions of people. It is impossible to look at a Townsend without marvelling at the work involved in producing it, the studies from the model, the studies for accessories, for setting, for lighting, and the wonderfully free yet faithful translation into pen and ink of interiors and exteriors by night and by day. A London street at night or a cricket match in the blazing sunshine, a Mayfair drawing-room or a villa at Golder's Green would be conjured up with magical conviction in the prevailing atmosphere.

Bernard Partridge, another magician with a realistic pen, completes a great trio of pen draughtsmen whose work is peculiarly English. Partridge is now concerned with cartooning for *Punch*, but he has tackled almost every kind of drawing for that paper during the thirty odd years he has been associated with it. His best known book illustrations are the delightful realisations of Georgian modes and manners in "Proverbs in Porcelain." The technique in these is a little under the influence of Abbey's wonderful hair-line treatment in illustrating the "Old English Comedies," but it is a good blend with the more definite statement of Partridge's own interpretation, which resembles that of Abbey in its tranquillity and absence of sensational contrasts of light and dark.

Raven Hill is another of the *Punch* men with a genius for actuality, which he obtains with a free and hasty technique, reminiscent of Chas. Keene (see Fig. 93). He excels in presenting humorous and easily recognised types from all classes. It is probable that his quick grip of the possibilities of a joke makes him impatient of the actual drawing which is necessary to convey it to others. He is more interested in character than technique.

The mantle of F. H. Townsend, in the shape of the art editorship of *Punch*, has now fallen upon Frank Reynolds, a worthy successor in carrying on the tradition of good drawing and good fun. He is a believer in the efficiency of the curved line, and evidently sees life as a good round business. He does not often use professional models, relying upon himself, his family, or his friends for poses, which he is quite able to turn into the characters he wants by drawing upon a well-stocked storehouse of miscellaneous characteristics usefully located in his brain. His general method is the obviously expedient one of finding out what he wants and getting it economically in time and effort, if possible, but getting it anyhow. The directness and simplicity of Frank Reynolds's technique is deceptive; it all looks so easy, and perhaps more than that of

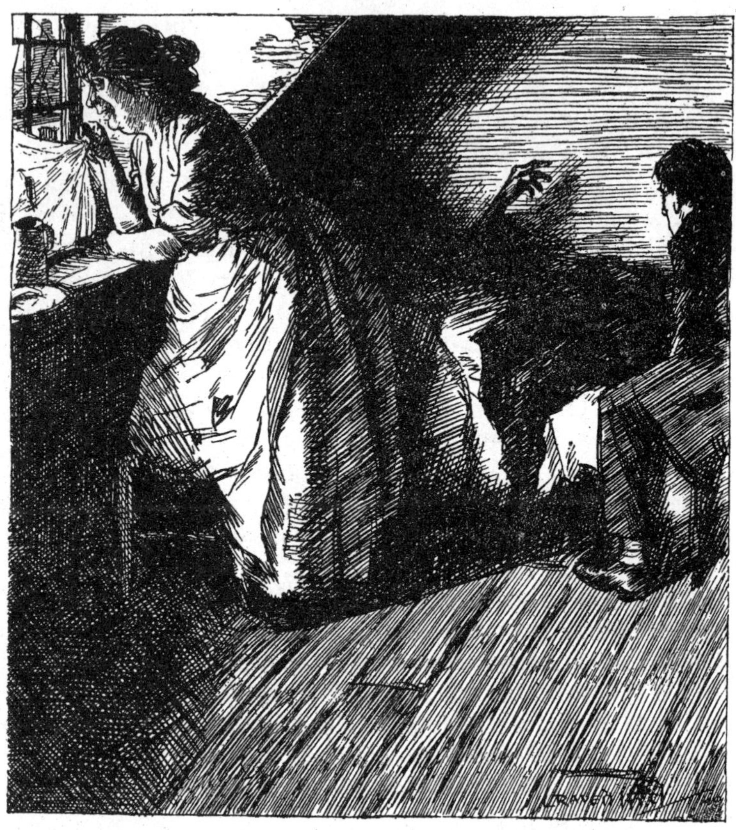

FIG. 93.—A Book Illustration by L. RAVEN HILL.

any other man justifies the definition given elsewhere in this book, that the chief element of style is the concealment of effort.

These names exhaust the list of pen draughtsmen in England who may be said successfully to hold the mirror up to nature, putting on record exactly what they see, without the intervention of temperamental arrangements of form, or the employment of distinctive line. But there is a crowd of good men

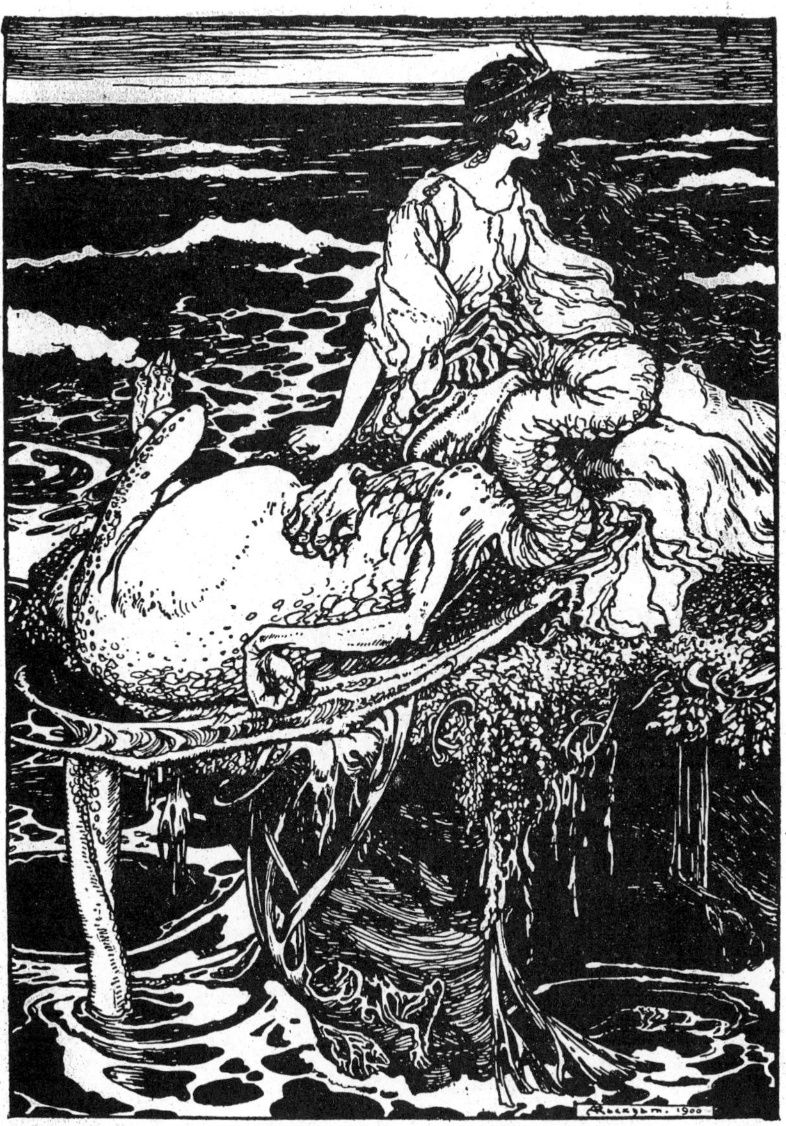

FIG. 94.—A Book Illustration by ARTHUR RACKHAM.

unwilling to knuckle down to the actual, who give us nature seen through more adventurous temperaments: E. J. Sullivan, a master of Rembrandtesque chiaroscuro and creator of the most intellectual pen line of to-day (see Figs. 1 and 17), which may be studied in his book, "Line." A. S. Hartrick, now mainly interested in lithography, but formerly a prolific illustrator with a flair for rural characters. Arthur Rackham, with

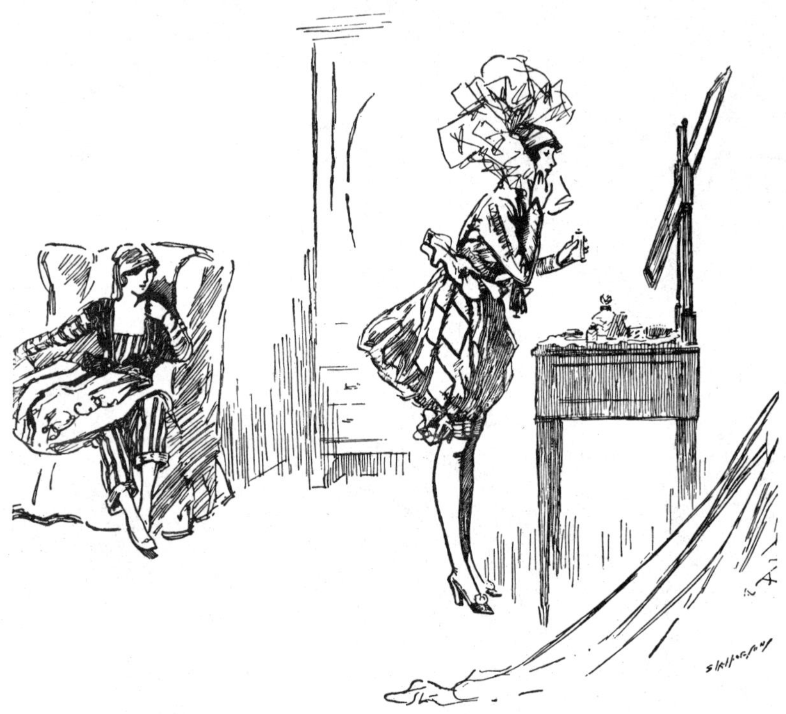

FIG. 95.—By the late CLAUDE SHEPPERSON, A.R.A.

a wonderful technique now mainly employed as a basis for colour illustrations to fairy lore (see Fig. 94). A. H. Shepherd, probably the greatest interpreter of "Society" foibles now Shepperson is no longer with us; an inspired draughtsman who can give us the smartest English girl or the rustiest farm hand with equal penetration in a style which is always distinguished.

Shepperson was an illustrator many years ago, specialising in "costume" subjects. But later he turned to the society note, for which his temperament was admirably fitted, and his subsequent drawings in *Punch* are classic examples of the ultimate in patrician atmosphere (see Fig. 95).

The Brocks, H. M. and C. E., are two of the most accomplished stylists in illustration to-day. H. M. draws with a decision and inevitability which is uncanny (see Fig. 135). All things, animate and inanimate, spring from his pen in a flexible technique which is the direct result of infinite study from nature. If it is more workmanlike than artistic, it still has the power to charm in its unfailing dexterity. He once illustrated

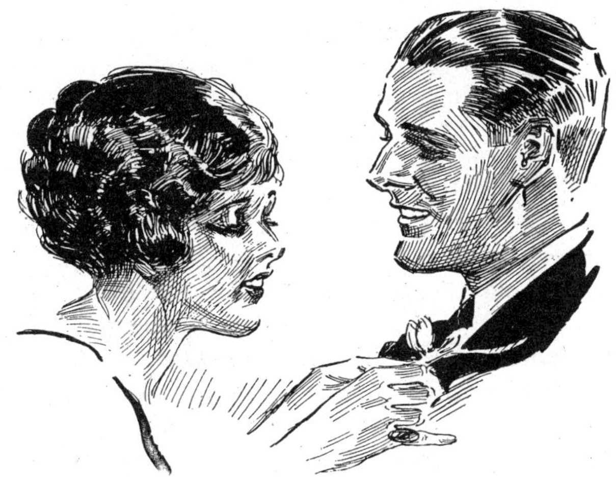

FIG. 96.—An Advertisement Drawing embodying the Ideal Young People of the Average Magazine Editor.

The importance of conformity to accepted types of good looks is a limitation wisely accepted by most illustrators.

a book on old furniture which revealed the connoisseur, and the accessories in his story and joke illustrations have a convincing quality even in the slightest suggestion, indicating texture and solidity as few other men can in deliberate work to that end.

Costume illustration, especially Georgian and early Victorian, has attracted both the Brocks, and each gives a different, but equally facile, rendering of the Georgian, which they re-create as a period, fortunately capturing the popular conception and " Beau Nash " atmosphere of the century.

Hugh Thompson and Abbey gave us the last word in

dealing with the manners and men of a slightly earlier period, and the Brocks may claim the Georgian and Victorian as peculiarly their own. Hugh Thomson's men and women were, perhaps, finer as interpretations of the spirit of a period (see Fig. 97), but, then, Thomson confined his attention strictly to that period, while the Brocks run the whole gamut of commercial illustration from children's books to advertising drawings, which makes their pre-eminence in costume illustration the more remarkable.

Pen drawing for the illustration of stories in the cheaper magazines is a big field for the artist's cultivation. But with strange unreason pen drawings are under a financial cloud in comparison with wash drawings, editors considering them less effective in conveying actuality and less impressive in the general make-up of the magazine.

In editorial estimation, therefore, pen drawing has degenerated so much that it is seldom found in our few remaining magazines with any pretensions to serious illustration, and many of the best penmen have deserted into advertising and etching. The big demand is now for comparatively cheap illustrations for the railway journey type of magazine and the more or less domestic journals, and some surprisingly good work is found in these which proves that rapidly produced work can be kept to a very fair standard in good hands.

A large percentage of the stories illustrated give opportunities only for drawing " nice boys," " strong " men, and the usually recognised type of beautiful girl in situations so recurrent as to be almost stereotyped ; yet the variety and interest discernible in the various treatments of these is a tribute to the power of the pen artists in conveying the infinite variety in types of people, similarly dressed and doing the same things. The tribute is the more deserved as the variety of type is achieved in the face of enforced conformity to certain accepted standards of beauty, strength, and niceness held by the wise editor as necessary for the prosperity of his magazine.

There is a smaller demand for more interesting work in the strenuous illustrations for adventure and detective stories, also a very limited market for nature drawings of the kind so admirably done by Warwick Reynolds, one of the strongest draughtsmen in illustration (see Fig. 132).

For the illustrator of adventure stories it is absolutely

essential to keep a good classified reference for details of incidental landscape, houses, furnishings, and implements, etc., of all periods and countries, to get local colour and prevent the editor from annoyance in letters pointing out that "white

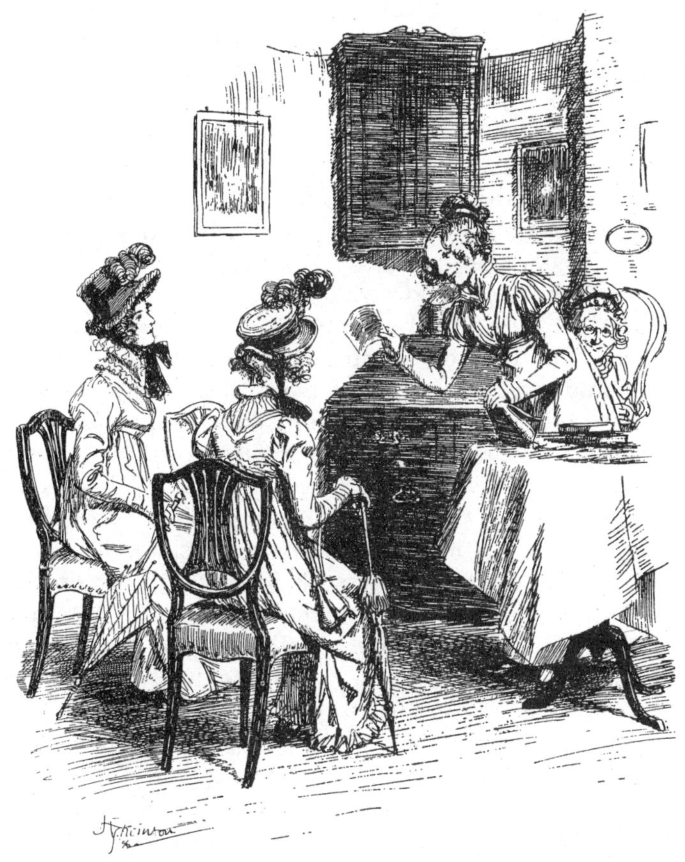

FIG. 97.—By HUGH THOMSON.

A good example of sympathetic "Period" illustration.

ducks are not worn in May at Spitzbergen," or similar alleged errors. Photographs of everyday life abroad are of the utmost value to the artist doing modern adventure stories or tales of life abroad, and such work to-day is generally convincing because it is based upon such authority or the artist's own travel notes. In illustrating tales concerned with times other than the present, details must necessarily be taken from work by other men who have searched them out, or else built up laboriously from reference books or museums, a very costly method indulged in by the great illustrators of more spacious days, but very difficult to manage in these commercial times.

The best type of illustration for adventure stories is that in which the interest is centred on good drawing and dramatic action, with convincing setting and lighting and an unobtrusive style or technique. Albert Morrow's pen drawings in *Cassell's Magazine* are good examples of this ; their present excellence is the result of many years' experience in work. Morrow evidently enjoys and treats in a spirit of adventure with the pen which gets both local colour and a decoratively rich patch on the magazine page.

Gordon Browne's drawings in Cassell's *World of Adventure* are also good examples of dash combined with accomplishment in making stirring incidents live on paper ; but his handling of the pen is more obtrusively clever than Morrow's, and to that extent less good for its purpose, the style tending to come in front of the interest of the incident.

Another stylist was the American illustrator, Howard Pyle, whose life story by Chas. D. Abbott, published by Harpers, is an inspiration to students as a record of sincere effort. His illustrations can be found in most American magazines prior to his journey to Italy, and ranges from the severe woodcut line adopted for his early fairy tales and used throughout his life for similar illustrations, to the strong incisive line used in the pirate stories and its delightful modification in such drawings as those for " The One Horse Shay " of Oliver Wendell Holmes (see Fig. 98).

Howard Pyle's work, apart from the deliberate use of Dürer's method in decorative illustration, was entirely the outcome of whole-hearted interest in striving to give the atmosphere of the works he illustrated. That " style " resulted, as it undoubtedly did, was beside the mark and incidental to a sincerity in work that involves infinite pains but brings great rewards.

He found some time from a life of incessant effort for teaching the younger generation, considering this a duty. The greatness of his conception of the undertaking is indicated in the following quotation from one of his letters on the subject : " I think first of all that they should be taught in the very beginning to believe that all they are learning of technique is only a dead husk in which must be enclosed the divine life of creative impulse. I think they should be stimulated to think things out of doors ; to talk of living things and to draw them, describing them maybe in words as well as in pictures."

There is a good deal in this idea of students writing down the scheme for an illustration before working on it as such.

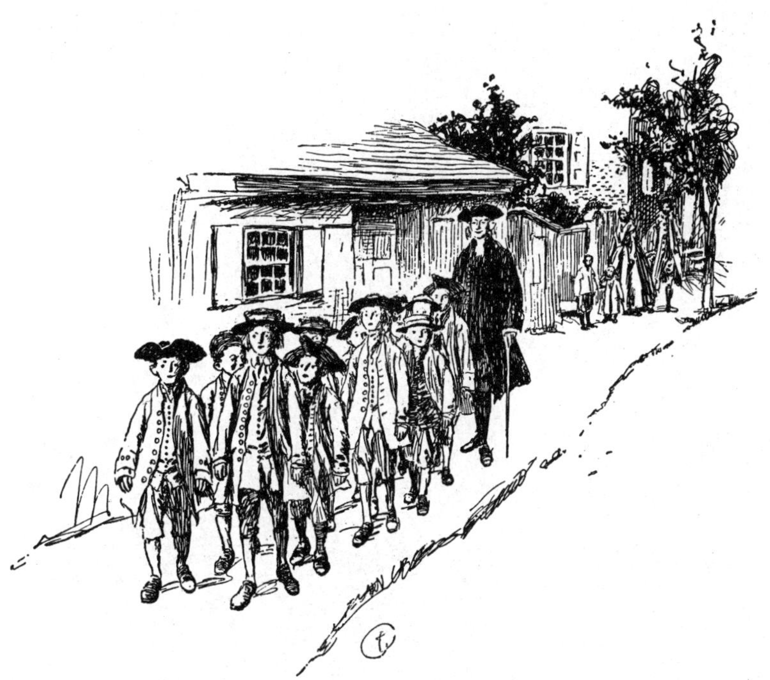

FIG. 98.—By HOWARD PYLE.

It helps the creative faculty to function in visualising a definite situation from the author's lines, and also reveals the line of approach, which can be tested by its pictorial result and used again if successful.

There is so much inspiring material by illustrators throughout the world that students should certainly be brought into touch with some of it. Rembrandt, Menzel, and Vierge are usually and rightly mentioned as outstanding examples of technical accomplishment. But if we analyse the majority of story illustrations now published, I think we shall find their

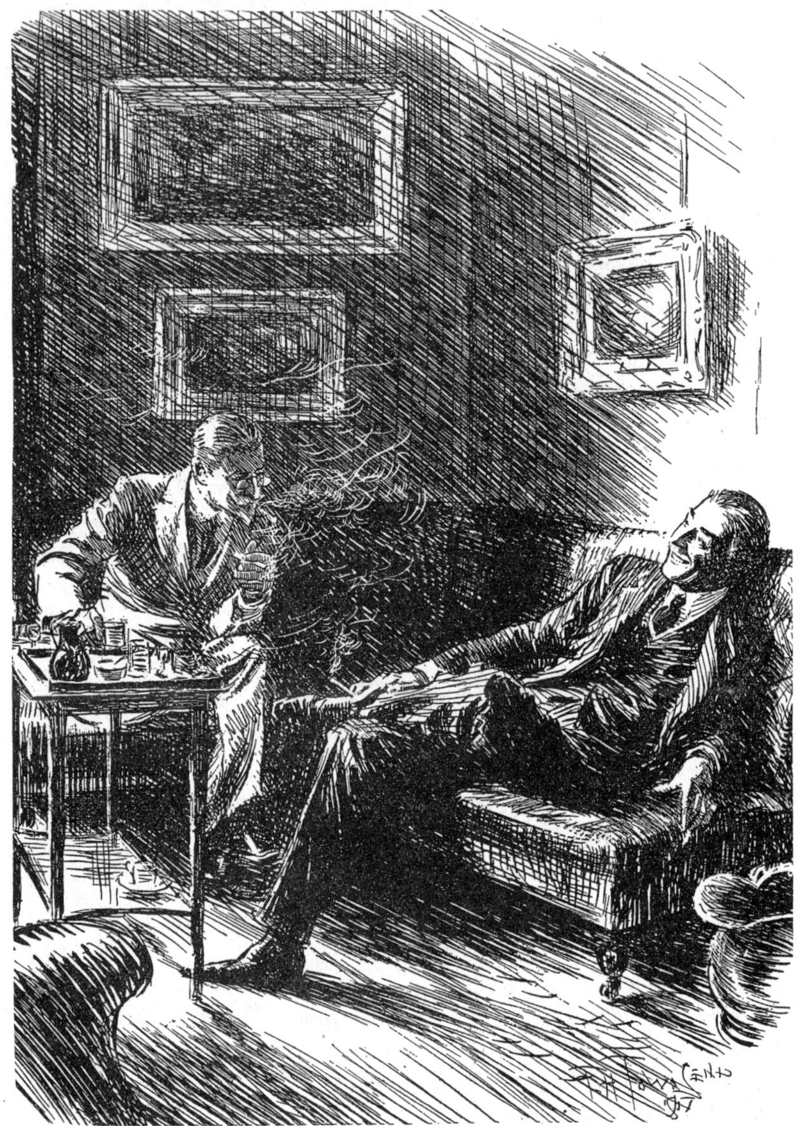

FIG. 99.—Masterly use of technique in a Drawing by F. H. TOWNSEND.

inspiration nearer to our own times in C. Dana Gibson and Montgomery Flagg of America, or F. H. Townsend, whose work as an illustrator is almost eclipsed by his later fame as a contributor of wonderful joke drawings to *Punch*.

Townsend's work represents pen drawing taken to its utmost limit of accurate representation. Its technique is complicated, for he used all kinds of devices in thickening lines or crossing them to get the tone he wanted. His drawing was spirited and convincing, acceptable alike to the artistic and lay public, and he was certainly our greatest master of facial expression. Sheer love of his art and passionate desire to give his best forced him to "get it right" at whatever cost to himself in trouble or expense. He not only used models for all his drawings, but went to infinite lengths in finding suitable ones for particular types if the names on his list yielded nothing just right. In fact, his pen drawings were prepared in much the same manner as an academician would set about a subject picture (see Fig. 99).

With Townsend's work as an objective, the hard-working student could not go very wrong, and pretty much the same may be said of the two great Americans, who differ from him only in the manner of their actual pen technique. All three stand for perfection in preparation, and to that extent at least they are admirable examples for students to follow. Townsend's technique is easily followed at a little distance, and many men whose work can be traced to a too sincere admiration for it do this without the necessary equipment in knowledge or preliminary care.

Gibson's technique is particularly unapproachable by the copyist, as it depends on swift interpretation of modelling and texture, with the pen substituted for the usual charcoal or pencil. His work, therefore, is useful to the student only as an example of perfection in a method which must be developed in a similar way on personal lines (see Fig. 27).

Montgomery Flagg's illustrations show what can be done in this way, for he was undoubtedly influenced by Gibson and proceeded in similar workmanlike fashion. The style evolved has less freedom from affectation, but is more printable, insomuch as it is more dependent on open line and has no diluted ink effects as in many of Gibson's drawings, which necessitate work by the process man (see Figs. 100 and 101).

Admitting the pronounced technique in Flagg's drawings as a defect, it is amply atoned for in the brilliance of the characterisation and drawing. The stages by which Flagg reached his present mastery are all interesting. Always a competent draughtsman, he commenced with an astonishingly "bright" technique in which the whole drawing appeared to glitter, and a curious mannerism in making heads too large. The glitter gradually toned down and heads became normally proportioned, but for some time his technique remained brittle

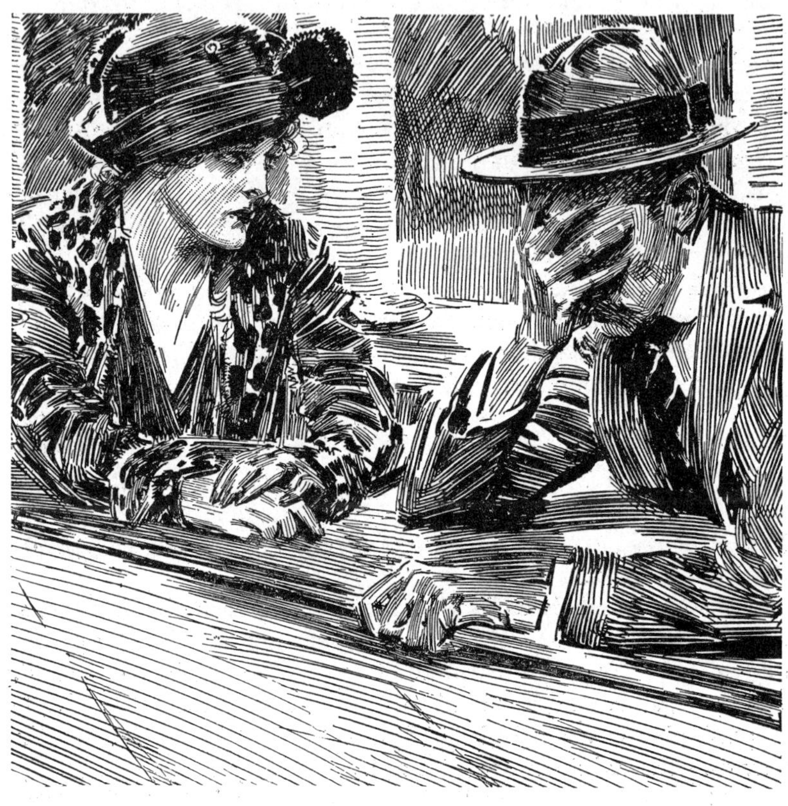

FIG. 100.—Colour in Line. A Wonderfully "Slick" Magazine Illustration by JAMES MONTGOMERY FLAGG.

until the inevitable result of direct study from the model prevailed in softening his line work to closer affinity with that of his early master, Gibson. Next, he worked for some time on his own types rendered practically in the Gibson technique, arrived at not by imitation but by logical progression on lines deliberately chosen. His present wonderfully expressive style is obviously derived from reconsideration of this penultimate stage, broadened in effect and simplified in line.

For illustrating the light literature which forms the major interest in magazines, Flagg's work is so universal in appeal that it may be taken as a standard, and an analysis of its qualities will show the essentials in perfect story illustration :—

1. It should add to the interest of the story.

Flagg's drawings always fulfil this condition because he has a keen literary sense and sufficient general knowledge to realise the author's intention as to types and situations.

Illustration must interpret the plot and stimulate the reader's

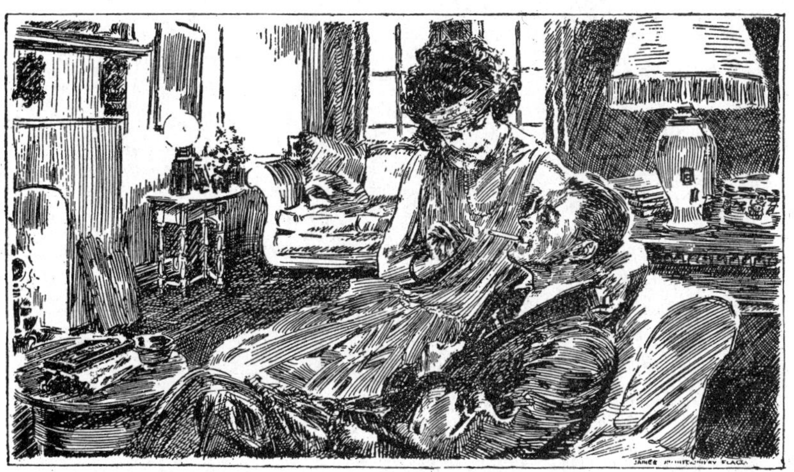

FIG. 101.—By JAMES MONTGOMERY FLAGG.

interest in its characters, or it is waste of time and money. If the impression made is disturbed by the artist's faults either in conception or execution, the story would be much better without his drawings.

2. It should create a definite atmosphere.

Reality or romance is conjured up immediately by Flagg's treatment of his figures and indication of their surroundings. If the action of the story centres round a French café, for instance, it gives the quaint foreign differences which linger in the memory. The smiles of madame, the polite waiters, the solicitous care of the proprietor for his guests, if not actually shown, are brought to mind in the subtle handling of types and environment.

3. It should attract the reader to the story.

A tale illustrated by Flagg stands a fair chance of being the first read in any magazine. Most readers glance at the illustrations first and, according to the degree of interest aroused, read or postpone reading the stories.

4. It should decorate the page.

This is not a matter of technique alone, although in Flagg's work this is all sufficient. Weight of colour and placing of figures has much to do with success. Editors are fond of irregular silhouette drawings, the type brought in to the irregularities. Under such circumstances the distribution of light and dark is important, as the type may take up the greys of a drawing and leave a spot of white or black isolated.

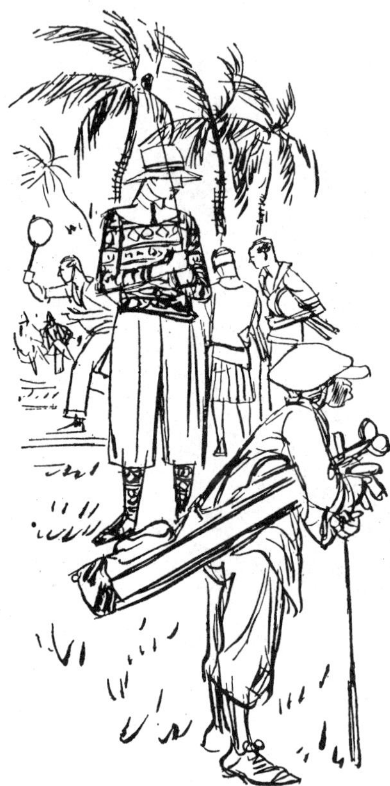

FIG. 102.—Summer Resort Illustration by WALLACE MORGAN.

5. It should print clean and bright.

Flagg's work at all stages is an object lesson in keeping materials at concert pitch. New pens, clean ink, dusted boards are necessities of perfection in printing line.

If no English illustrator since Townsend has the complete mastery of a Gibson or Flagg, we have, nevertheless, some good men, ranging from those on novelettes and boys' and girls' papers, to the better known ones on the shilling magazines. Students should certainly see what these are doing month by month in order to understand what is being used, and determine to do better.

The real test of having done at least as well is to get work published. Students often think that their work is better than much that appears in print, and they may be right; but it

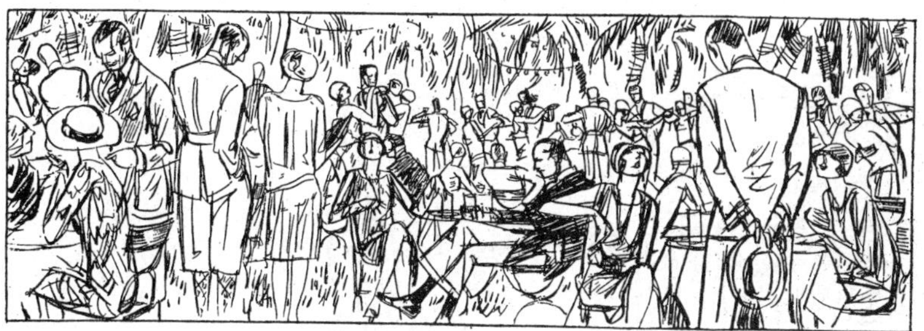

FIG. 103.—Summer Resort Illustration by WALLACE MORGAN.

may be better in fifty different ways without being right for an editor's purpose.

Monotony of subject in line illustration for the cheap magazines is due to immovable obstacles which the budding illustrator must take into consideration, however confident that the quality of his work constitutes an irresistible force. The obstacles are: similarity in the plots of the stories, similarity in the dress of the characters, and editors' fixed ideas of beautiful young women and strong young men. The editor generally knows what is most pleasing to his readers, and it is his business to get it. So, unless you can convince him that you know better, your work must fit in with his ideas if it is to see daylight in his paper. Once "published" and therefore admitted to the great band of men whose job it is to make authors intelligible at sight, artists usually find editors very

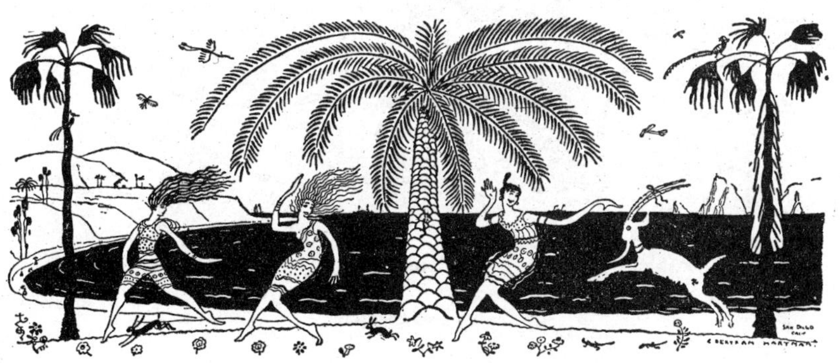

FIG. 104.—Illustration to Advertisement for San Diego by E. BERTRAM HARTMAN.

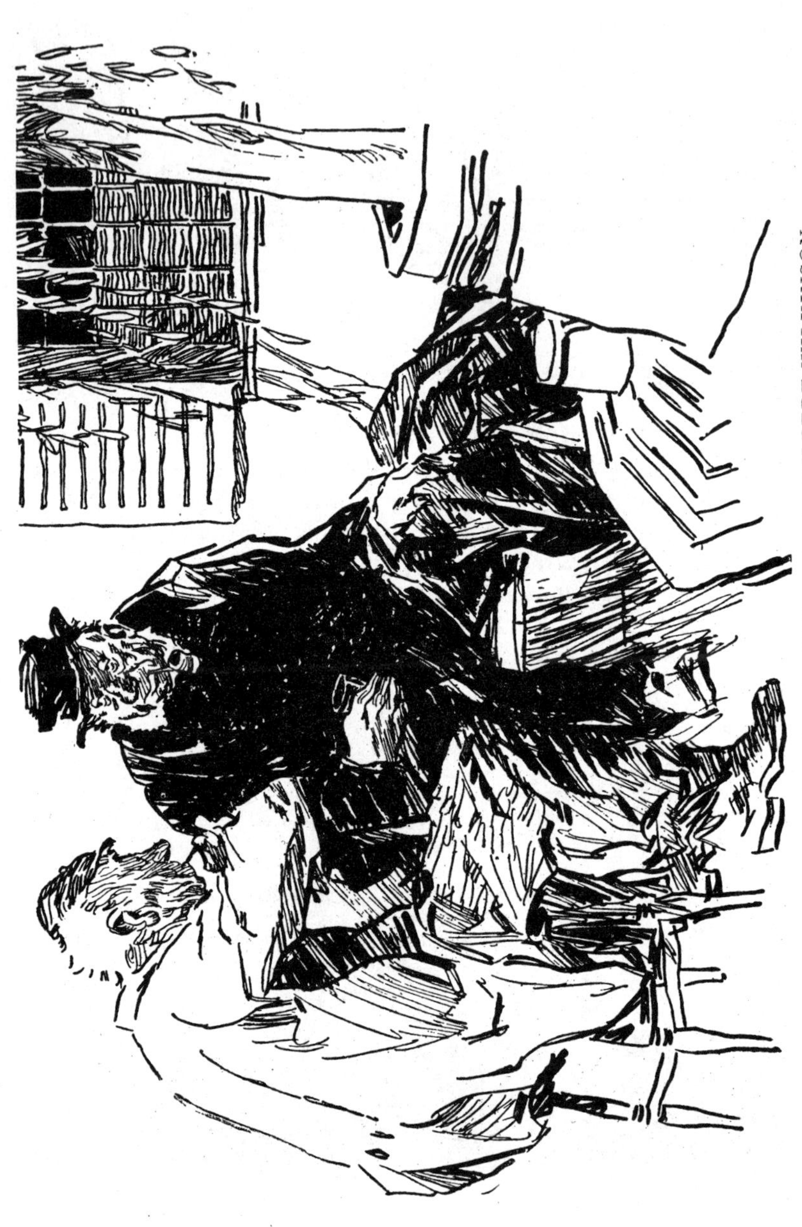

FIG. 105.—A "Character" Illustration by GILBERT WILKINSON.

amenable to ideas, helpful towards their expression within the limits of their readers' comprehension and sometimes beyond, if, in their infinite wisdom, they see that the slight mental effort involved will not decrease their circulation and may possibly increase it.

Types are half the battle, and good types depend on suitable models. Moral: find the right types in actuality and draw them until they become part of your mental equipment, enabling you to reproduce similar character and features in using other models for position and lighting, and in an emergency without models at all. Work done consistently without models usually proclaims the fact pretty plainly in lack of human interest; the worst fault in illustrating which must impress readers with its reality or fail in establishing the subtle bond of sympathy implied in human interest.

Few illustrators get this quality. The average drawing is practically a diagram of one, two, or more figures smartly drawn, but empty, as it must be unless the artist's genius can triumph over the conditions of dash and hurry necessitated by cheap prices.

Of those who can, the most individual is perhaps Gilbert Wilkinson, who is as interesting in serious mood as he is in humorous (Fig. 105), and can draw most alluring girls in just the right clothes. Graham Simmons, with a technique almost too clean and clever, shows good types of men, and dresses them in good clothes. Wallis Mills applies the Du Maurier tradition in technique to extremely modern people in society drawings of much vitality. Bertram Prance has a useful facility in execution, and represents the public point of view so exactly that he is eminently safe with any story. Thomas Henry is also a safe man, and improves daily. Arthur Ferrier, whose girls are much admired by those who know, trusts to these to carry very little effort in illustrating (see Fig. 127).

All these men know their job very thoroughly and are in demand. There are wide differences between their styles, their types, and their treatments of plots and situations. But they have a common bond in understanding what editors want; so study of their various methods is the surest road to similar knowledge and success.

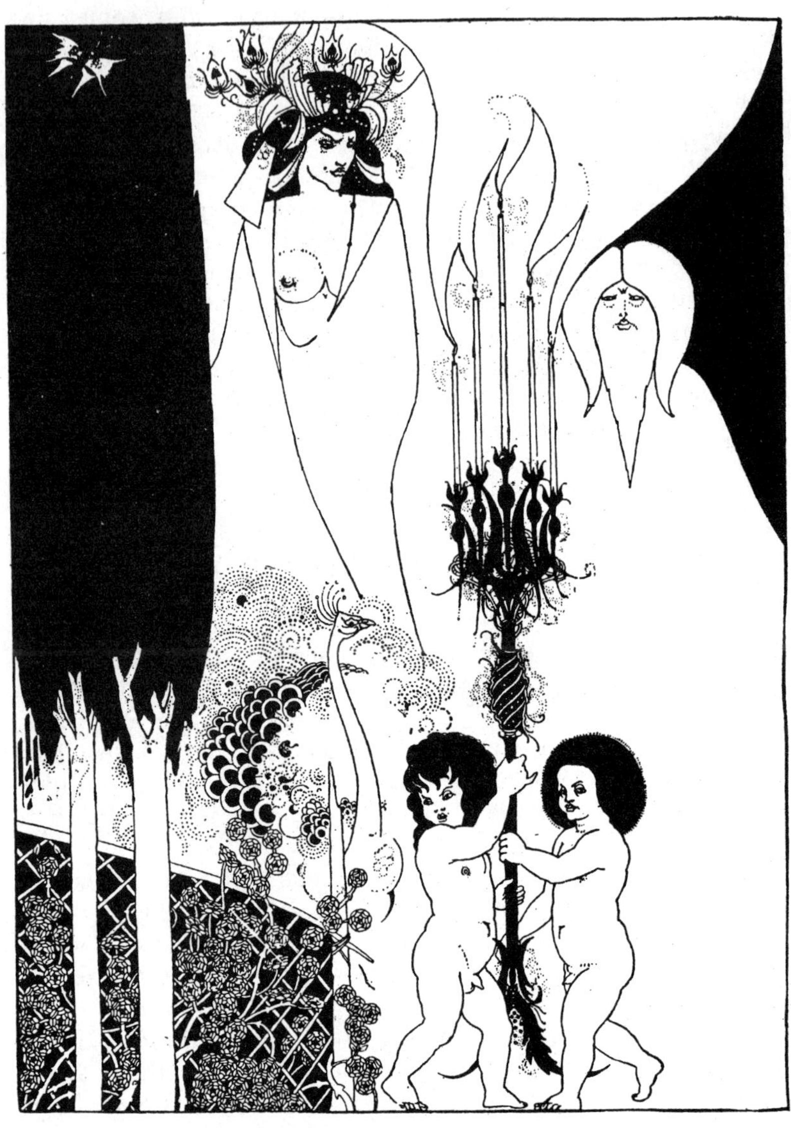

FIG. 106.—AUBREY BEARDSLEY. Drawing for "Salome."
The Eyes of Herod.

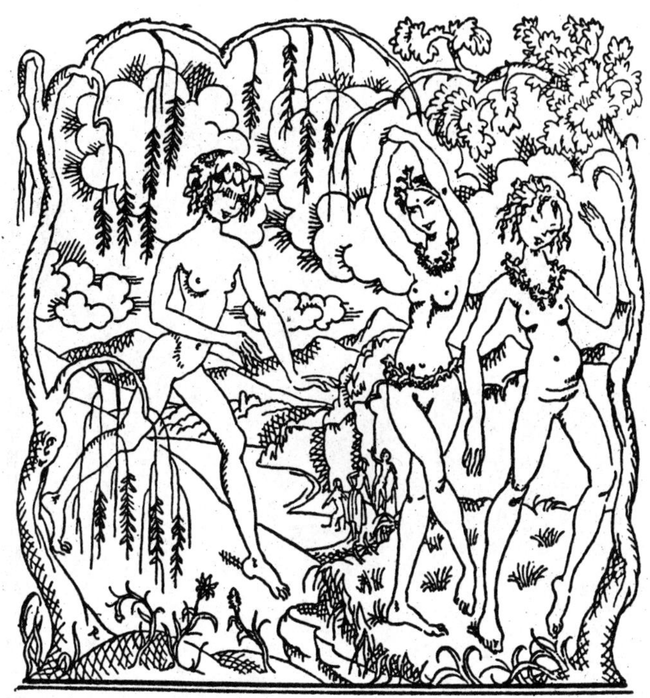

FIG. 107.—Book Illustration by ALBERT RUTHERSTON.

II. THE INDEPENDENTS AS INSPIRATION

Curiously enough, most individualists acquire their style from an overwhelming admiration, in the first place, for some outstanding artist whose work affects them at an impressionable age. Very few evolve it entirely from their own experience. It may be impossible to trace the derivation in the ultimate development, but it is generally to be discovered either with the aid of the artist concerned or from a knowledge of his early hero worship.

Beardsley, who burst upon the world in early numbers of *The Studio*, marks the beginning of a new era in the revival of the decorative method of illustrating books. Like most great geniuses he was misunderstood, laughed at, and talked or scoffed out of the brotherhood of the established artists of that day.

But Beardsley's fame grew rapidly, and was soon far

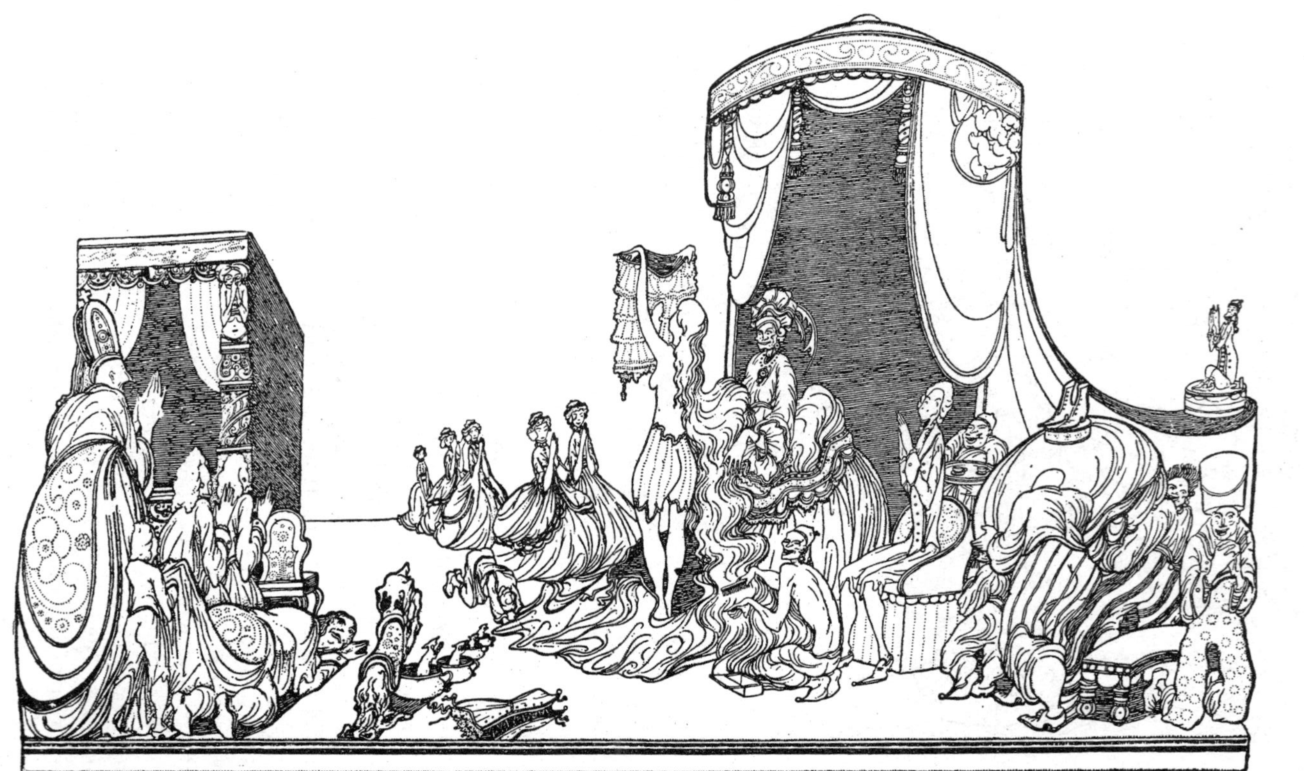

FIG. 108.—Book Illustration by ALAN ODLE.

An imaginative treatment showing the influence of the eighteenth-century caricaturists.

greater than that of his critics, many of whom became belated admirers. The literary men, showing more tolerance and vision in facing a new force, were immediately enthusiastic in recognition of his genius, and publishers responded with commissions. Beardsley was assured of congenial work, and produced a comparatively large quantity of drawings in the very few years before his early death.

The drawings were wayward, often *macabre*, but as examples of black and white placing or design they are superb, and have certainly inspired more students and converted more laymen to a new outlook on illustration than those of any other illustrator (see *frontispiece* and Fig. 106).

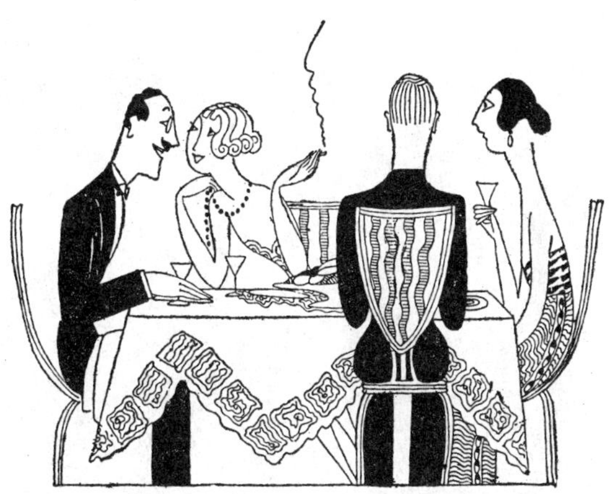

FIG. 109.—Society as seen by " FISH."

A number of present-day exponents of decorative illustration have obviously graduated under the Beardsley influence, and have profited by Beardsley's usefully selective eye in the use of Japanese " notan " or placing. Three examples of contemporary illustrators who owe much to their early allegiance to Beardsley will sufficiently demonstrate this. " Fish," whose diverting " Eve " drawings and society satires seem very far from Beardsley, was an ardent student of his work, and got nearer than anyone else to working in his actual convention. That she did not carry it on was possibly due to a commission to illustrate society doings for a magazine. She responded with new types and new handling served with much of the master's charm of line and disposition of pattern, added to her own witty pictorial comment on human frailty (see Figs. 109 and 121).

John Austen's early work in black and white was directly inspired by Beardsley, but he drew too well in the academic sense to get inside the essentially unreal convention, and

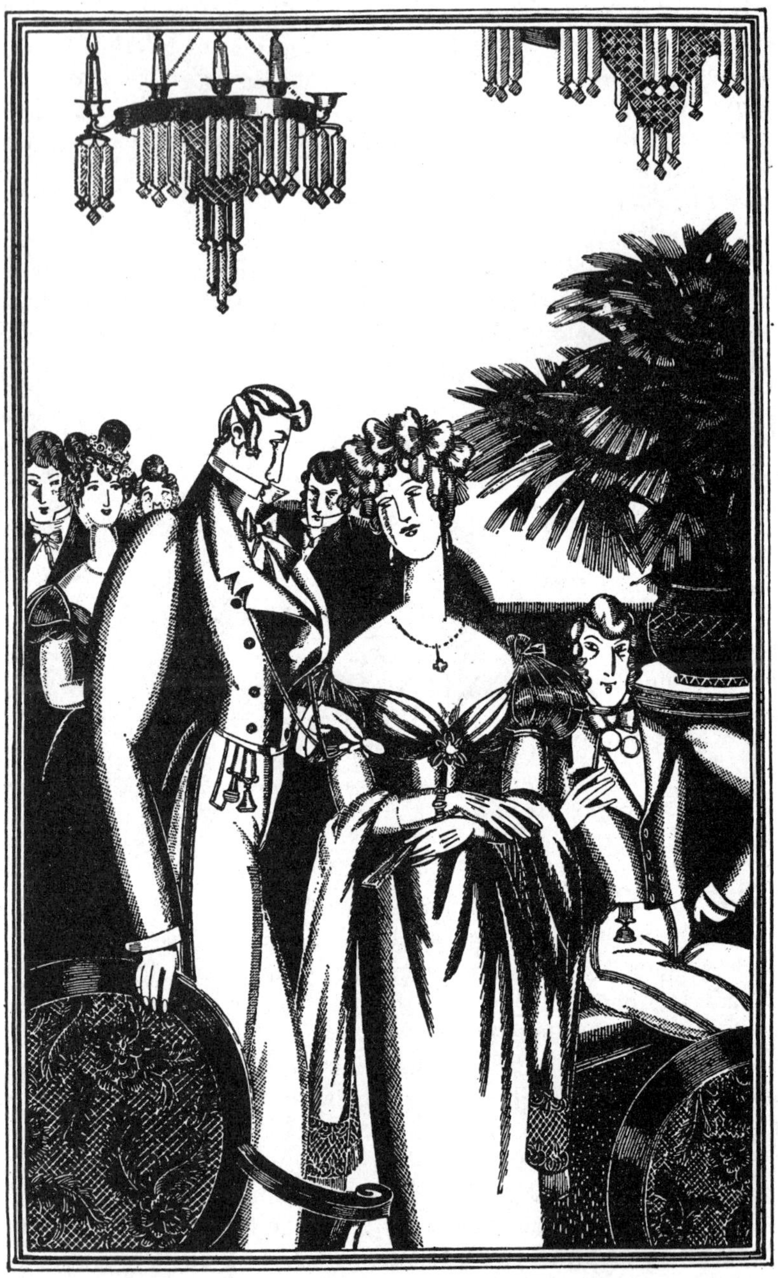

FIG. 110.—A Book Illustration by JOHN AUSTEN.

mistook the wood for the trees in concentrating on the richness of pattern which sometimes occurred in Beardsley. Seemingly heading for artistic suicide, Austen's genius triumphantly emerged with an entirely personal style embracing his capacity to draw the natural figure (see Fig. 110).

Alan Odle, one of the greatest of our imaginative illustrators, was a disciple, and even yet elects to work occasionally in a convention which reminds of the master, although his powers

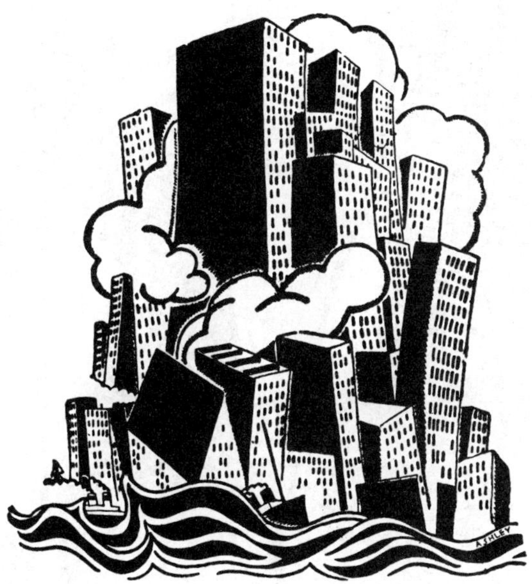

FIG. 111.—By ASHLEY HAVINDEN. The new note applied to advertising.

of draughtsmanship and satirical humour are generally employed on subjects peculiarly his own (see Fig. 108).

This list could be extended with names well known in many countries, including whole "schools" or "groups" in France, America, and Germany, showing the immense possibilities of the influence of a courageous and well-informed innovator.

The inevitable aftermath of Beardsley was a crop of imitators of his technique and imaginative style, all anxious to demonstrate their own originality in weird drawings, a phase which soon passed, consumed by its own intensity, leaving an entire generation impressed with Beardsley's name as the cause of

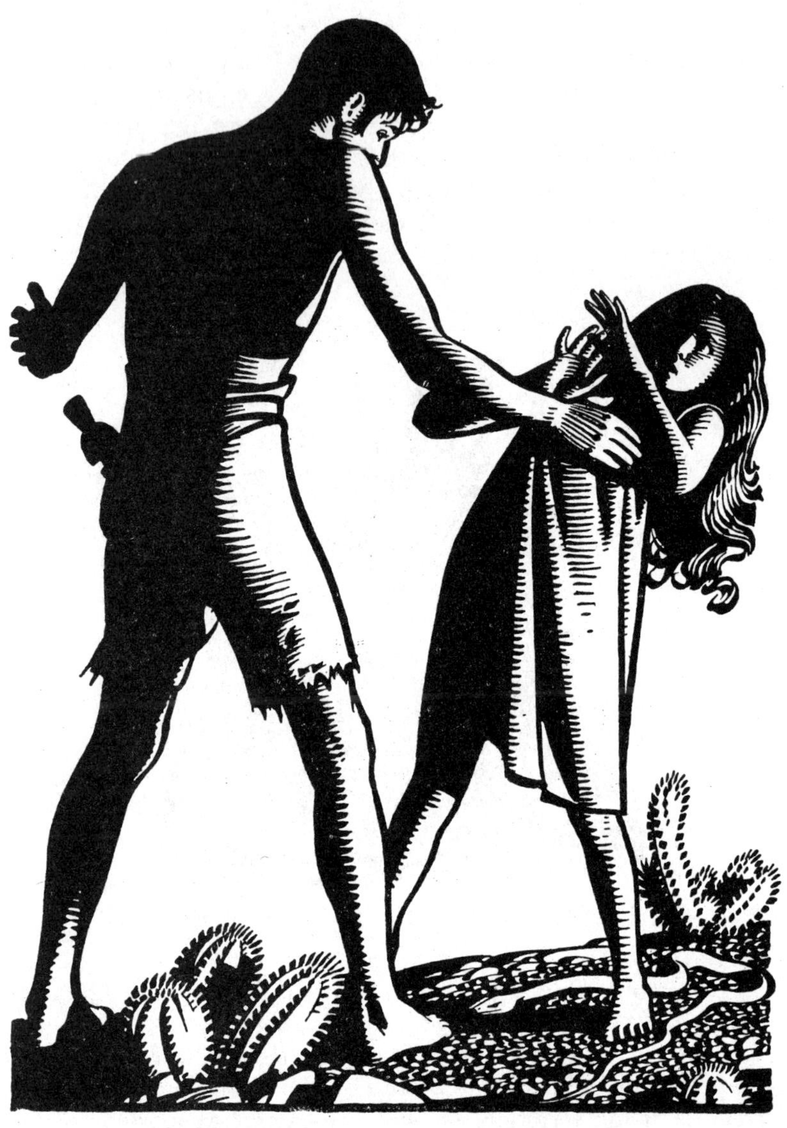

FIG. 112.—Pen Illustration by KEITH HENDERSON.
Showing deliberate use of wood-engraving technique.

all the trouble, and among these the cultured few aware of his portent in the whole future of black and white illustration. In the " Savoy " and " Yellow Book " is enshrined the history of Beardsley's immediate influence on his contemporaries, a practical demonstration of the usefulness of an outstanding personality.

The revolution in art caused in the first place by the early "post-impressionists" in France, and in England by the formation of the "London Group," had an almost instant effect on illustration and commercial drawing, and dealt a final blow to the supremacy of the naturalistic manner for such purposes. The accompanying illustrations (Figs. 108, 110, 112, 113, and 114) give some indication of the modern trend in which design, to the elimination of the fussy detail and accessories of the realistic school, comes into its own again, thus enlarging considerably the scope of the decorative and commercial artist. Figs. 111, 115, and 116 show how the new note may be struck successfully in advertising, and arrest the attention by its novelty.

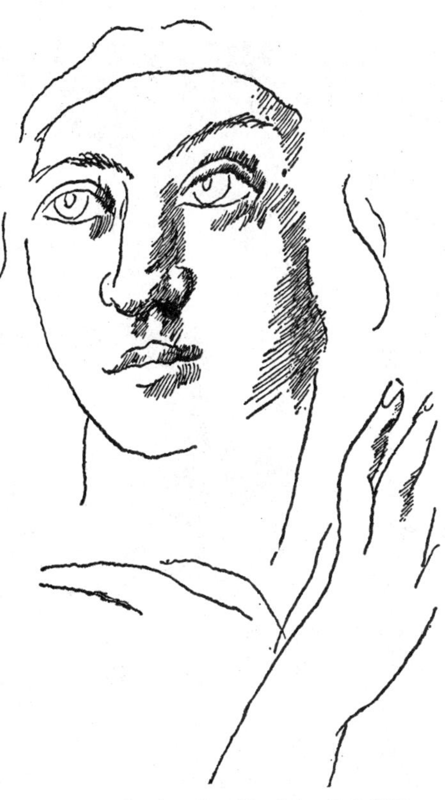

FIG. 113.—Study of a Head by ROGER DE LA FRESNAYE.

Soon after the "London Group" became a recognised factor, the war came, and with it the rebels' great opportunity. The public grew receptive, with changed conditions, of any novelty in art, and it needed only the services of astute wire-pullers to sway the "official" recognition of "war artists" mainly to the new school. The War Museum shows the results, certainly much more interesting than the type of thing we should have had from the academic school, and really valuable as a record of war mentality; a passing phase even with many of the artists represented, for Nevinson and Wadsworth, to mention only two of the best known, have returned to representational work, showing but slight traces of their former heroics.

But the art world owes much to the genius and courage of these men. Things can never get back to the self-satisfied

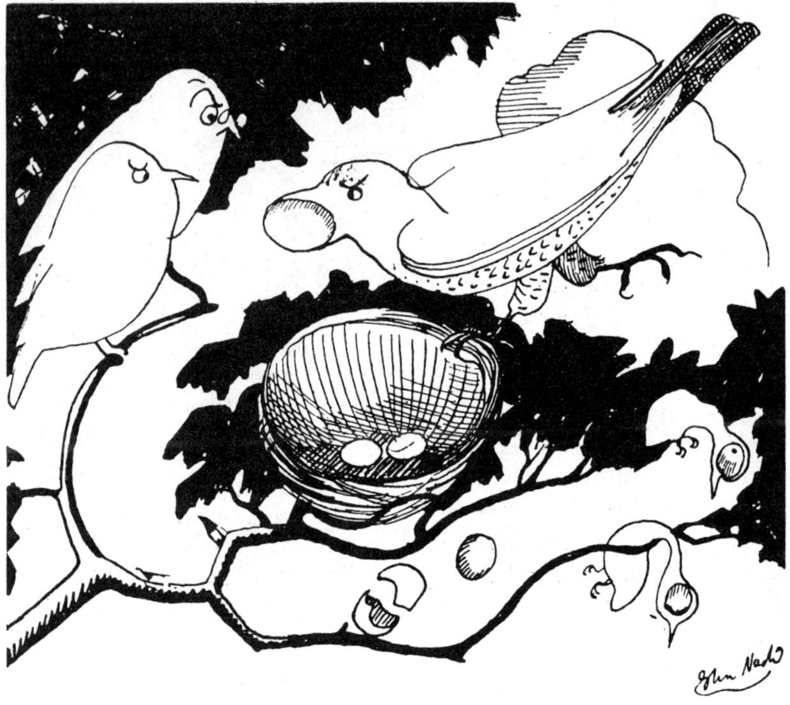

FIG. 114.—By JOHN NASH. One of a Series of Amusing Pen Decorations in the Modern Style, representing the Months.

stagnation which had set in when they determined to stir them up. There is interest and vitality in the schools to-day, and we see the young people experimenting with weird and wonderful techniques the while they unconsciously learn to draw much better than the average student of old.

In decorative illustration we draw for a more sophisticated public, educated to respond to the power of clever suggestion, consequently a school of decorative illustration has emerged peculiar to the modern " smart " magazines all over the world.

Its influence is slowly permeating English periodicals, conservative to the last, and the demand will probably increase, although it is hardly likely to equal that for good naturalistic work.

The student with something to say is generally most interested in how things have been put by others. By close attention to what has been done the possibilities of a medium are quickly grasped, and it is quite a workable idea to select the method of expression which most appeals to one, and strike out from this to evolve one's own method on the basis of personal impressions of things rendered in a similar convention. For instance, the drama may interest a student to the extent of wishing to make decorative drawings of stage situations, which is a big undertaking. It may help him greatly to set out in the manner of an admired master. Making notes from the actual stage, he gets to understand the process of turning these notes into a homogeneous drawing; in fact, he sees how it is done. His drawings at first will be frankly imitative, but the habit of looking at things with a set purpose, reducing colour and complicated form and line to manageable pattern, will facilitate the acquirement of a definite method in which he can progress to a style of his own.

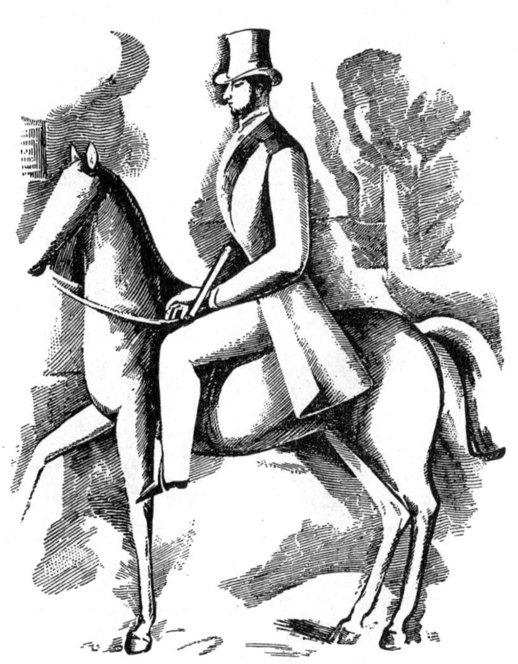

FIG. 115.—A French Advertisement, clever and arresting in its child-like technique.

There is an increasing field open at the present time for the illustrator with a markedly personal style, and as the accompanying illustrations (Figs. 108, 110, 112, 114) show, the art of illustration in pen and ink is just as alive now as at any of its great periods. Originality is in demand by the more critical section of the public, and this demand is well satisfied by such men as John Austen, Alan Odle, the Nashes, Keith Henderson, all of whom have made a name for themselves in their own distinctive way, and are producing work that will live beyond their own time. Students should analyse the handling of men whose work attracts them, and try to discover exactly why things have been done in certain ways. It is a fascinating and profitable way of acquiring knowledge. Some men, the few really great artists, will baffle all efforts at analysis. The naïveté of John Nash, for example, is entirely elusive in expression of a vision in almost superhuman accord with the facts of nature, which can but inspire one to approach the world reverently and humbly even as he does. But most pen draughtsmen give their methods, if not their magic, away in a thorough study of a dozen or two of their drawings, and a student may legitimately profit by the inspiration gained from ripe experience in one who rouses him to sufficient enthusiasm for hero-worship.

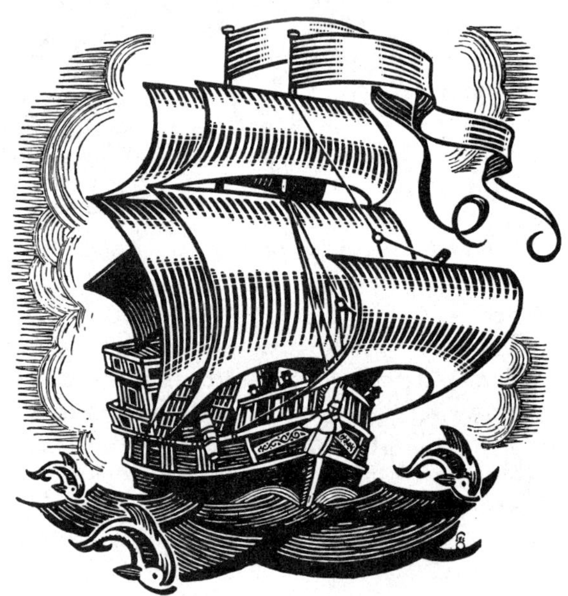

FIG. 116.—By F. G. COOPER.

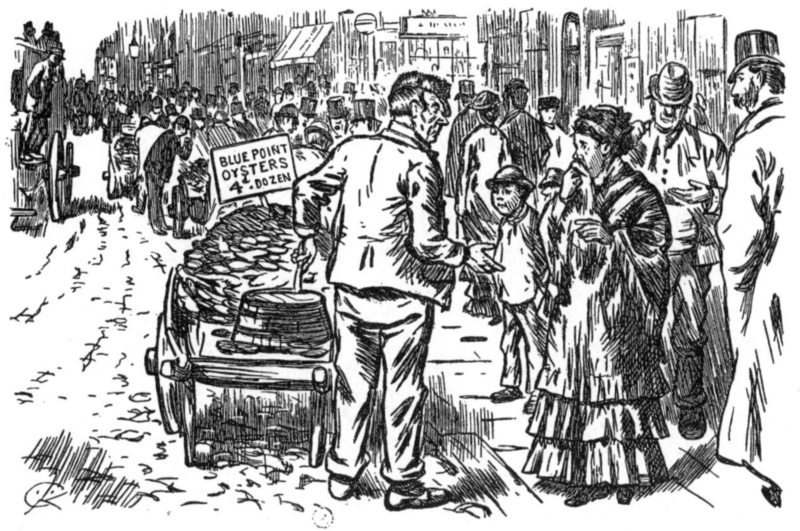

FIG. 117.—A Drawing by CHARLES KEENE, to whom many modern humorists in line pay sincerest flattery.

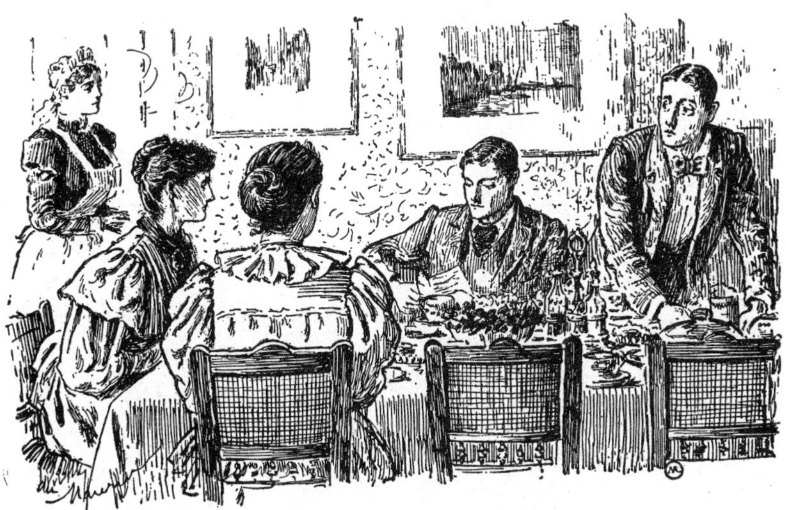

FIG. 118.—A Drawing by GEORGE DU MAURIER.
A characteristic drawing of the horribly dressed period the artist struggled with.

CHAPTER X

HUMOROUS ILLUSTRATION

DRAWINGS for the comic papers and humorous and satirical work for the general news and magazine prints are one of the brightest hopes for English pen drawing, although advertising may create a greater demand in the future.

English comic papers are much more conservative than those on the Continent, and it is rare as yet to find anything startling in technique. English editors probably understand the national temperament in insisting on "natural" drawings, but a slightly more adventurous outlook is called for, or the public, educated by advertising drawings, will be ahead of the fare provided and bored by the general repetition of *Punch* models. Even America—enemy of the modern note in publicity work—is more venturesome than we are in encouraging such attempts at gaiety in technique as C. Bertram Hartman's rendering of "Californian Coast Sport," obviously inspired by continental artists (see Figs. 102, 103).

It is the ambition of most pen draughtsmen to appear in *Punch*, and the English tradition of illustrating jokes rather than making funny drawings is founded on this desire for the hall-mark of the most famous comic journal.

Ninety per cent. of the joke drawings in *Punch* and its many clever rivals are illustrations more or less dependent on their text for intelligibility, and many would serve equally well for any joke in merely representing two or more ordinary people just talking, well drawn, and lending a certain interest to the text, but really superfluous and quite useless without words to explain them.

A typical *Punch* drawing, therefore, is funny only when we take the joke with it; but there are others, Frank Reynolds, the art editor, Bert Thomas, Fougasse, and Bateman, for instances, who are quite capable of provoking laughter by their actual handling of the human species, and can show us the funny aspect of our fellows as well as any continental or American artists.

A man is either a humorous artist, or he is not. Many illustrators fail to realise this, and are aided and abetted by editors in doing illustrations for jokes which can do quite well without their help. Veritable humorists see the funny side of things pictorially, and do their plain duty in intensifying it for those who look to them for laughter in a dull world.

It is not always the "funny man" of the art school who

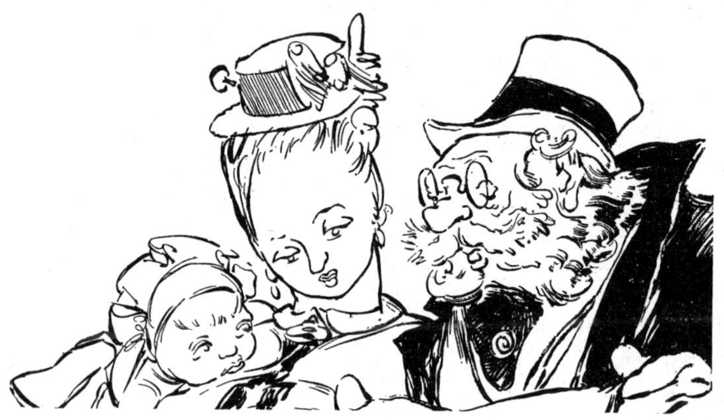

FIG. 119.—By the late WILL DYSON. Portion of a caricature showing the individual treatment that brought world fame to this artist.

blossoms into the best professional joke maker. I have seen the dawn of several reputations, and have an idea that it is very difficult to spot winners in this direction. An air of settled melancholy and hopeless pessimism in speech are no detriment, and a generous allocation of brain is usually indicated.

Art school sketch clubs are often the means of revealing the potential joke man, although the powers that be seldom encourage students to develop their sense of fun; in fact, drawing for comic papers is hardly mentionable in their august hearing, and a student who openly declared his intention of devoting his life to it would most likely meet opposition, or be thought not quite nice.

Not that this matters in the least, for the humorist in embryo cannot look for help to any art master except for the

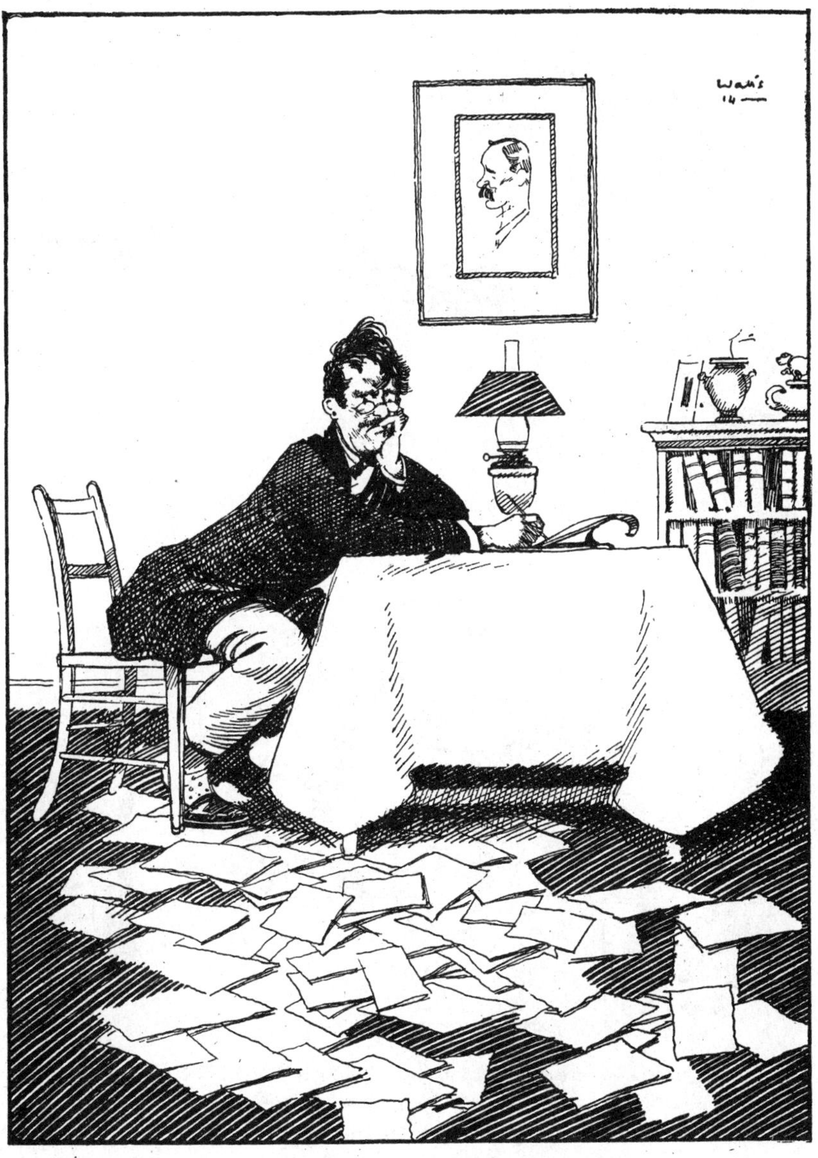

FIG. 120.—By ARTHUR WATTS. "The Caricaturist."
Arthur Watts has an intensely personal method and the power to show the funny aspect of everyday things.

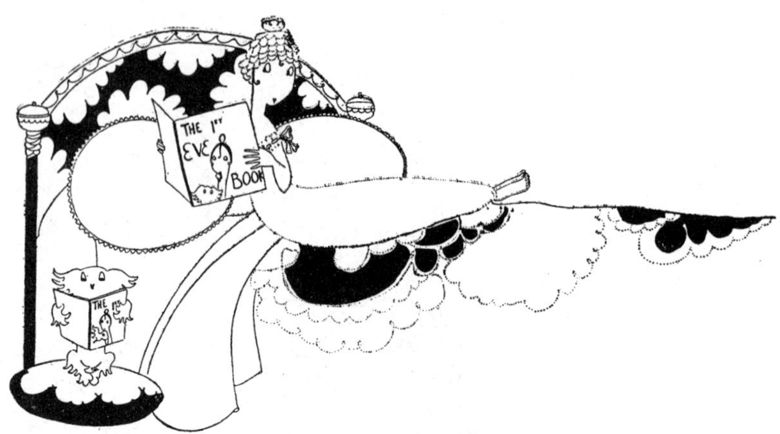

FIG. 121.—The Famous " FISH " Type of Girl. Showing the Beardsley influence, and adding interest to many magazine pages here and in America.

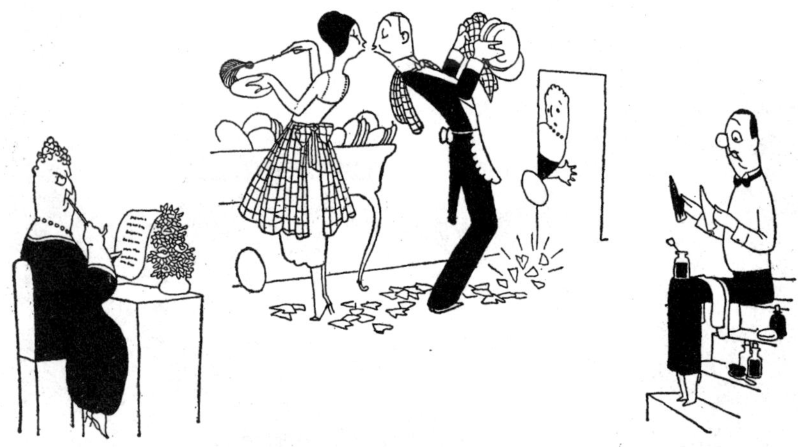

FIG. 122.—Three Illustrations by GLUYAS WILLIAMS, one of America's greatest pictorial humorists.

This type of illustration, long in demand for " Society " magazines, is invading the cheaper papers.

preliminary training in drawing and anatomy which he needs in common with all artists dealing with the human figure. The rest is entirely a matter of personal observation and temperament, and most comic men develop their gifts in this direction after trying to suppress them in some serious occupation.

The notion of a man whose obvious mission in life is to make the world brighter, suppressing his birthright to design dull wall-papers or paint second-rate pictures, is in itself a joke of some magnitude, for it is impossible to conceive a more useful career, or one bringing greater rewards from one's fellows than that of comic artist.

It is not easy to give advice to the would-be comic artist,

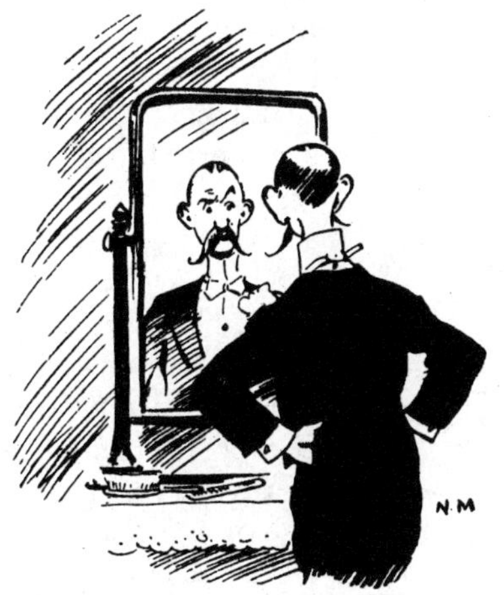

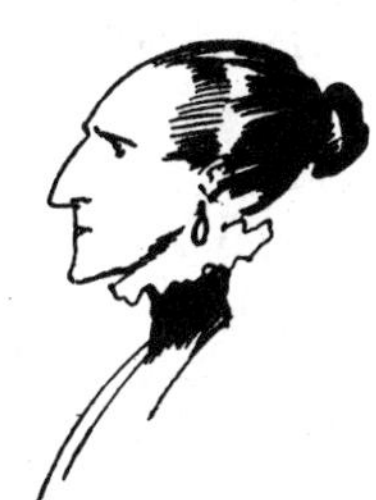

FIGS. 123 and 124.—Economy of Line in Pictorial Sarcasm by NORMAN MORROW.

beyond the usual admonition to draw well, and even that must be modified to draw *easily*, or at least appear to draw easily, for the greatest asset in funny drawing is that it appears spontaneous and simple, with all evidence of effort and preparation out of sight. We must feel that the artist was the first to enjoy the joke.

H. M. Bateman is an outstanding example of careful preparation, carefully hidden, for the apparent simplicity and "done straight away" appearance of his work is deceptive. His people are studies from life (Figs. 50 and 125), exaggerated sometimes in the actual process of sketching and sometimes afterwards from quite "straight" sketches which are priceless as actual portraits.

Gilbert Wilkinson, on the other hand, is blessed with a

perfect visual memory, and can take his "picture" complete as it afterwards appears without actual notes of any kind. This power to re-create a scene from memory is the greatest gift vouchsafed to a joke merchant, and Wilkinson is the only man I have met who can really afford to rely upon it in getting the widest contrasts in facial character and expression, bodily attitudes, and even clothes and furnishing accessories. His command of all necessary detail is so sure, that in technique he concentrates on conveying life and vigorous happiness in pen work that is obviously a romp all the time. He is constantly adding to his gallery of amusing puppets, but we see his favourites again and again; his old "Man About Town," his "Minx," and his lovably impudent "Gutter-Snipes" are our favourites too (see Fig. 105).

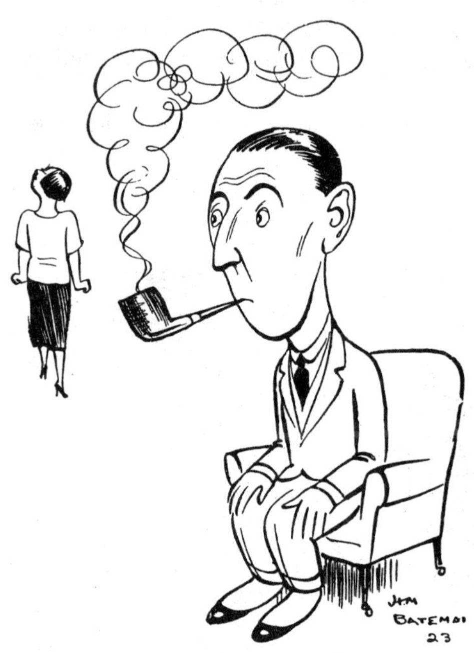

FIG. 125.—By H. M. BATEMAN.
The pen used solely to convey an idea and not allowed to stray from it.

Leo Cheney is a thoroughly efficient craftsman and genuine humorist with a habit of "thinking with the pen" which students might adopt with advantage (see Fig. 126). He enjoys the translation of ideas into pen and ink so much that he is constantly extending his range of types by memory sketching, filling reams of paper with extremely interesting notes of things recently observed. He has, perhaps more than any other pen draughtsman, the useful ability to show things in very complete detail without losing the spontaneity of the joke, being in this sense only a worthy follower of F. H. Townsend, who achieved this result in an entirely different way.

Townsend was an ardent admirer of Charles Keene, and one can trace his admiration in the technique of his drawings. Cheney is also an admirer of Keene, but his line is not influenced in any perceptible degree by Keene or any other " old master " ; in fact, one can trace its evolution as an entirely personal thing, from his early preoccupation with old English types, slightly

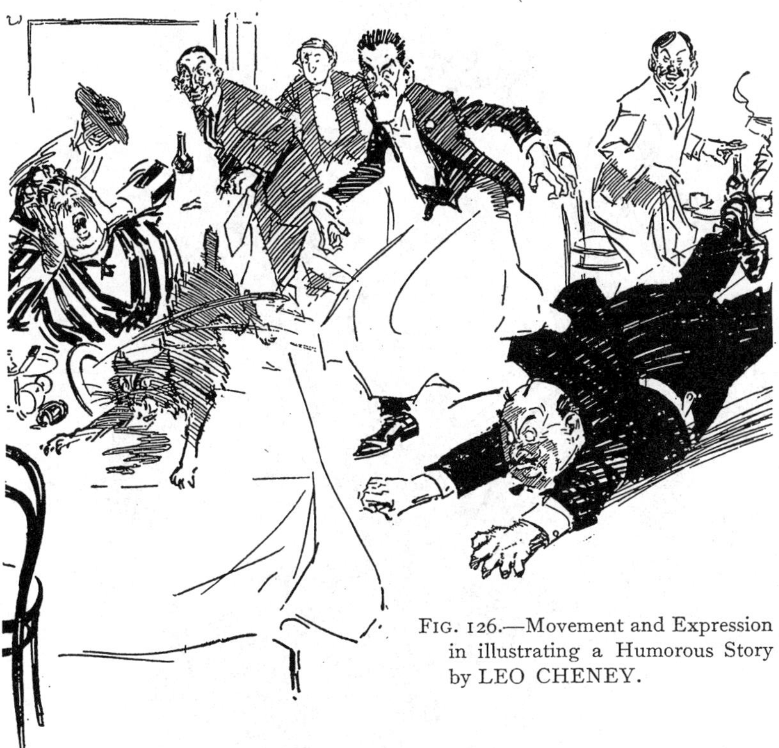

FIG. 126.—Movement and Expression in illustrating a Humorous Story by LEO CHENEY.

influenced by Cecil Alden (or Caldecott), to its present highly sophisticated efficiency.

Those who only know Keene's drawings in *Punch* (see Fig. 117) would hardly suspect the wonder and sensitiveness of his pen line.

Keene, in turn, was a disciple of Rembrandt, and so we trace the moderns back to the mighty master, acknowledged by all good pen draughtsmen as supreme in understanding of the mysteries of line and shadow. Graham Simmons, in whose beautiful work it is indeed difficult to find any trace of

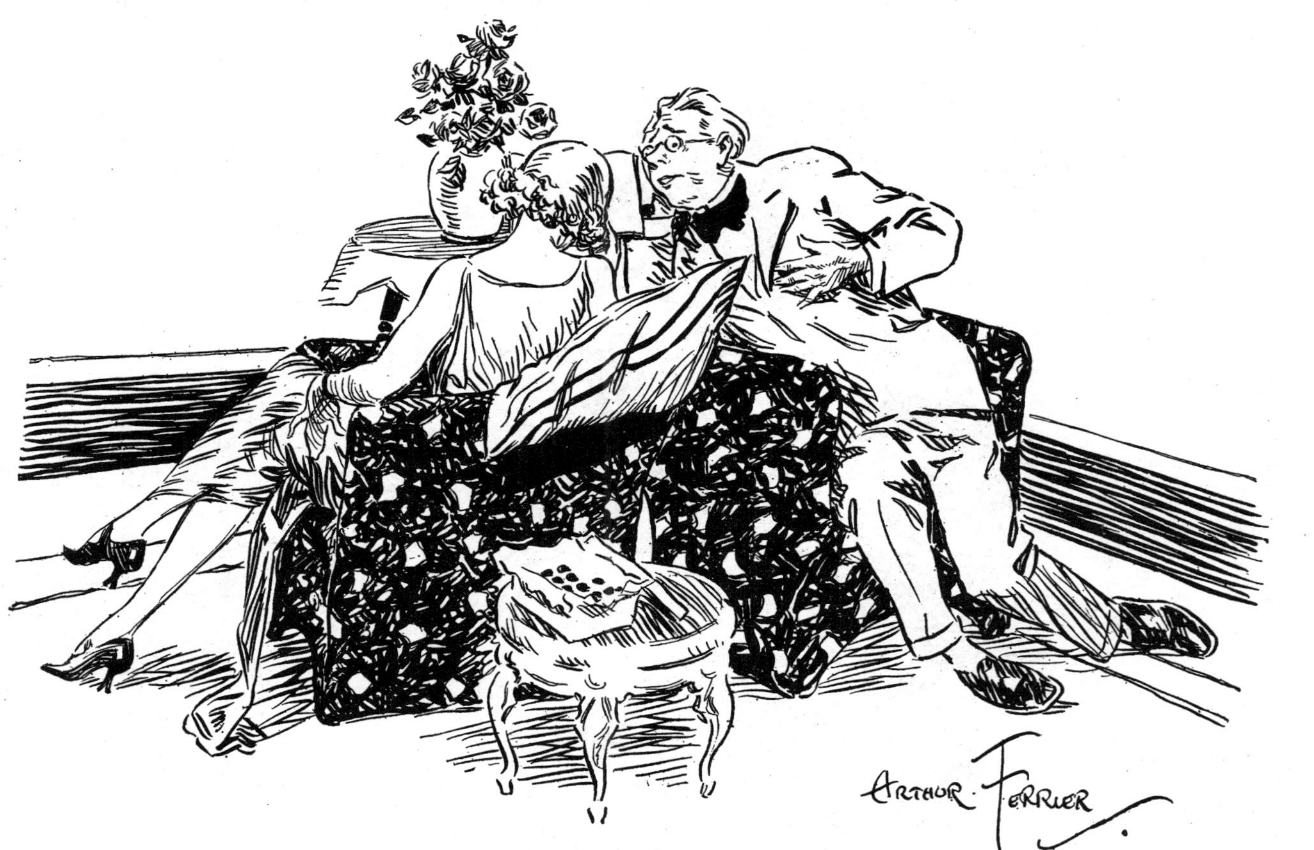

FIG. 127.—By ARTHUR FERRIER.

Good drawing and pleasant line, with no apparent effort; the editor's ideal.

Rembrandt's influence, advises the student of pen drawing to study both Rembrandt and Charles Keene, declaring that it is possible to find out from the etchings of the former all there is to learn.

Nearly all advice to students is given on the assumption that their ambitions are to run in some well-worn groove.

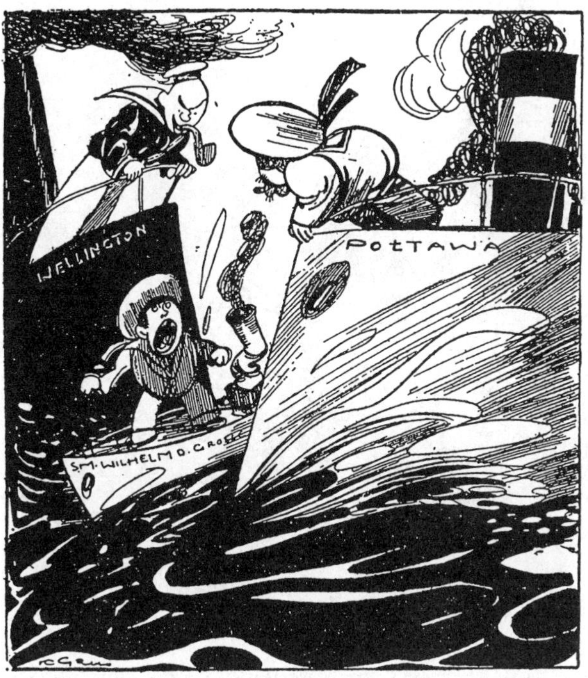

FIG. 128.—Vigorous Line in Caricature adopted by many Continental Caricaturists whose work on the whole is more vital and interesting than our own.

This is quite sensible, for there is no better advice to give, and its justification is that it works well in practice. The boy is always a hero worshipper and the student is merely the boy growing up, so give him a hero or two and he will follow them as he will not follow dry rules or dull experience.

Many students to-day, unfortunately, make heroes of their contemporaries, and we get "schools" of very young men whose sole equipment is a pronounced mannerism. But the amusing thing is that real drawing and real humour combined goes on, gaining new interest and greater perfection, borrowing perhaps a little from the amusing freaks in technique evolved by these young rebels, but otherwise taking very little heed of them.

The demand for humorous drawings is such that it calls for work from most men with a sense of humour, whatever form this takes. The exotic quaintness of Albert Rutherston (Fig. 107) and the Nashes (Fig. 114) finds expression in the illustration of

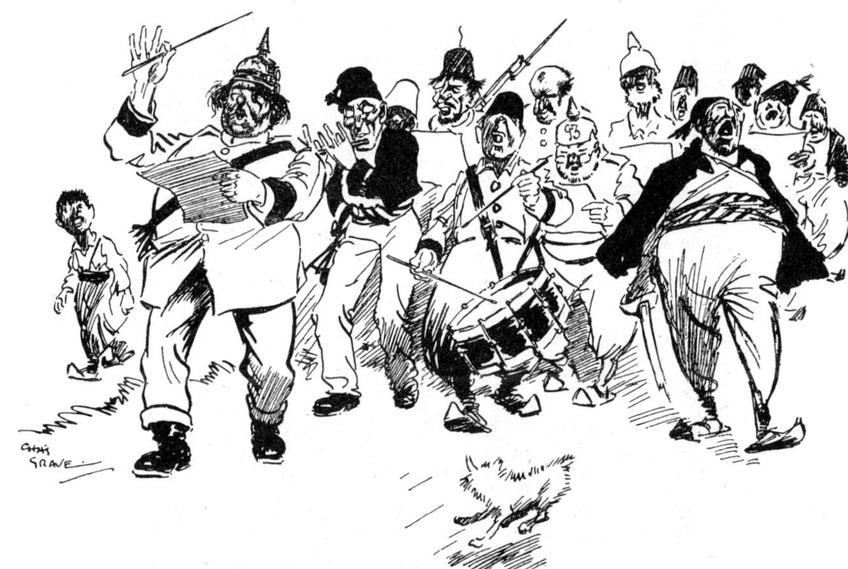

FIG. 129.—War Cartoon by CHARLES GRAVE, who rather specialises on the funny side of human woes, and is one of our best draughtsmen in line.

books in which the humour appeals mainly to those educated to subtleties, and at the other extreme we have the broad comicality of the children's comic papers employing an army of well-paid men unknown to fame until they break away into the better known papers, often published by the same firms and ever ready to welcome new men and assist them to fame.

Between these extremes there are crowds of papers using humorous work, and it not only pays artists to supply them, but pays men to deal in the placing of them with suitable papers. These "artists' agents" save the artist much worry and time, and enable him to get down to his own job and leave the commercial traveller part of the business alone.

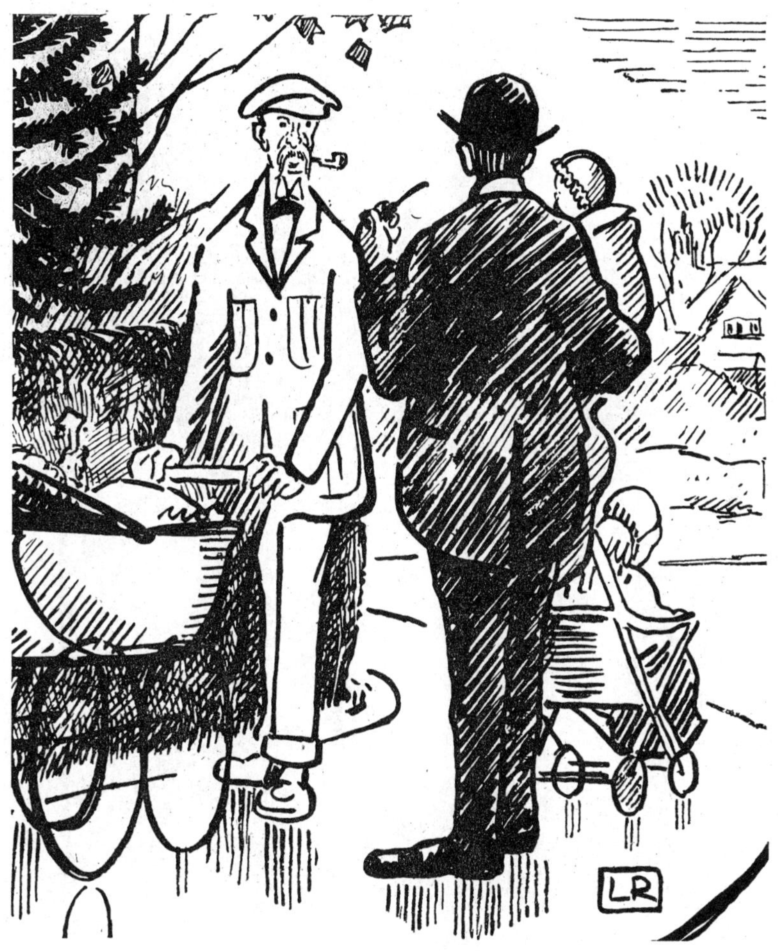

FIG. 130.—By LUDOVIC RODO.

An example of the concentration on " character " instead of detail and finish which " goes " better with French than English editors.

Naturally, these agents will only accept men whose work is in demand already or so obviously right for the market that they can see their way to the creation of a demand without risk of wasted efforts. The placing of immature work is no part of their business, as they find that it merely leads to trouble all round.

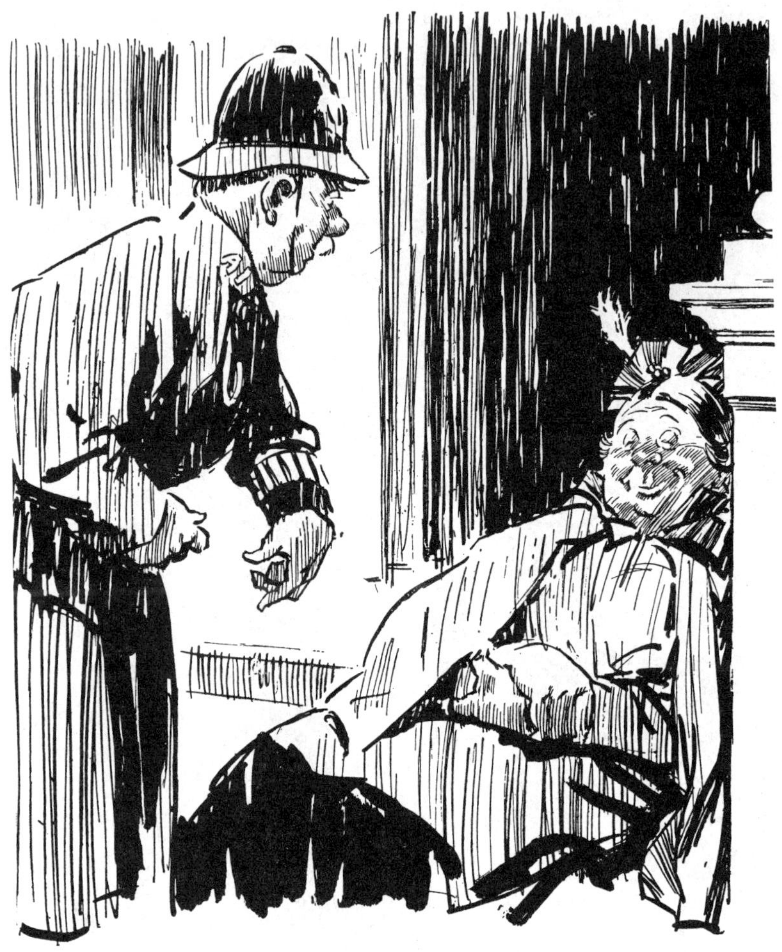

Fig. 131.—Part of a "Joke" Illustration by GEORGE WHITELAW, showing a crisp treatment which prints well owing to strong contrasts in colour and thickness of line.

A list of the principal agents is given below, but there are many others :—

Rogers & Co., 8 and 9 Bishop's Court, Chancery Lane, W.C.2.
Francis & Mills, 3 Arundel Street, Strand, W.C.2.

Sharmid, 6 Wells Street, Jermyn Street, S.W.1.
H. A. Young, 30 Fetter Lane, E.C.4.
Leigh Studios, 173-175 Fleet Street, E.C.4.
M. Elcock, 53 Fleet Street, E.C.4.
Mrs Cowper-Coles, 2 Aldridge Road Villas, S.W.11.
G. R. Cole, Oakbeams, Southgate, N.14.
Owen Aves, 20 Bedford Chambers, Covent Garden, W.C.2.
A. E. & R. J. Blanchard, 12 Red Lion Court, E.C.4.
Artads Ltd., 2 Crane Court, E.C.4.
Byron Studios, 8 Farringdon Avenue, E.C.4.
R. P. Gossop, 1 Henrietta Street, W.C.2.
H. E. Haffall, Stafford House, Norfolk Street, W.C.2.
S. Harford, 1 Henrietta Street, W.C.2.
H. E. Hassall, 40 Norfolk Street, W.C.2.
J. E. Gran, 173-175 Fleet Street, E.C.4.

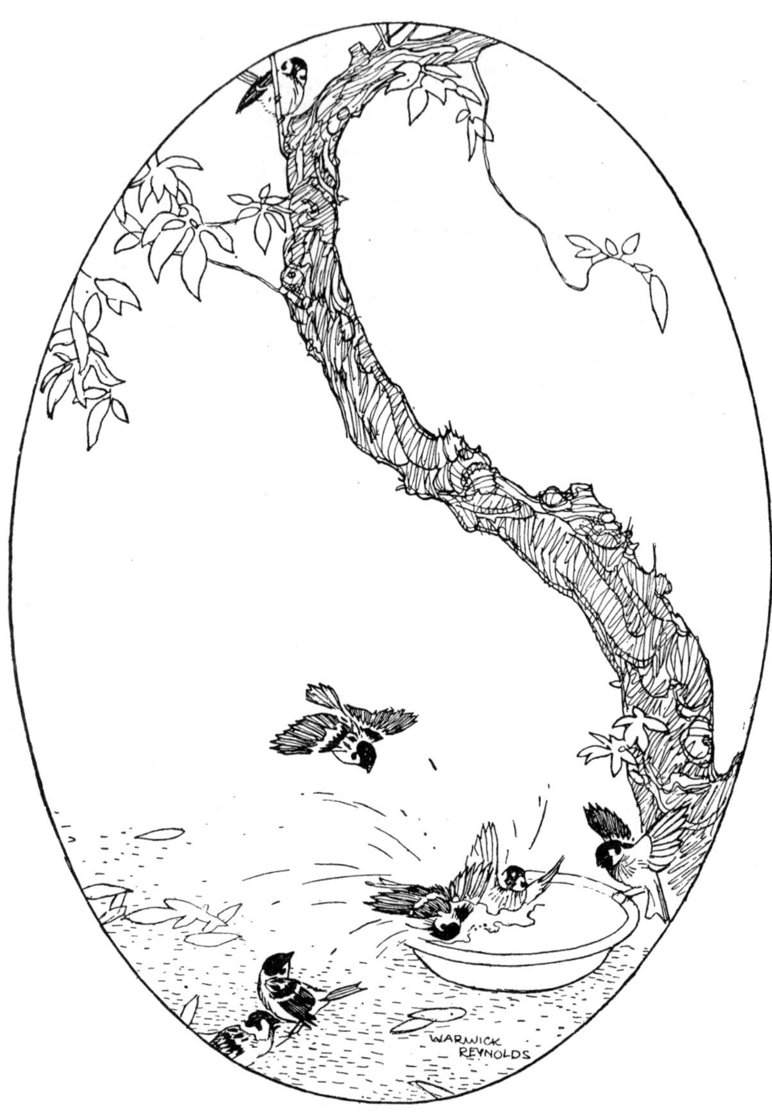

FIG. 132.—By the late WARWICK REYNOLDS.
A beautiful drawing with a subtle and intelligent idea to advertise soap.

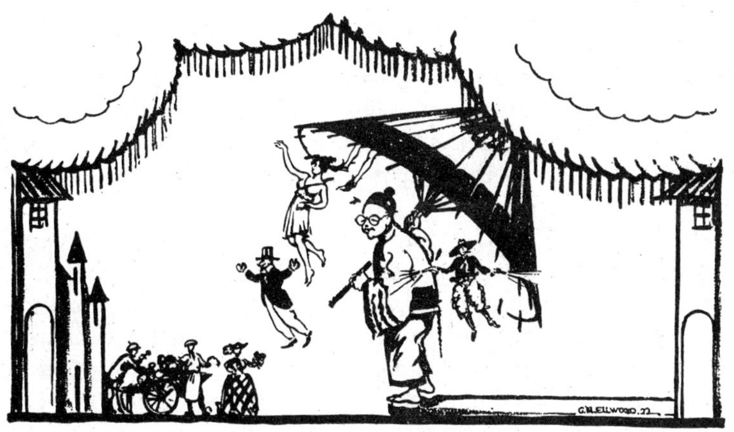

FIG. 133.—By G. M. ELLWOOD.
Theatrical advertisement in a combination of pen and brush line.

CHAPTER XI

PEN DRAWING FOR ADVERTISERS

IN the olden times of a few years ago it was impossible for a self-respecting artist to confess even a remote connection with the trade of advertising; the thing simply was not done. Advertising was east and art west in a very real sense. The persons who drew the "faces with and without whiskers," lions caught in nets, and tall ladies and gentlemen in tin clothes were not concerned with artistry. In those cheap days beyond recall, advertising was also cheap, although the proportion between the cost of drawings and cost of space in which to use them was probably about the same as it is to-day; then, perhaps, one to four guineas for the drawing and four to twenty for space. Now, ten to one hundred guineas for the drawing and forty to upwards of a thousand pounds for space.

It is obvious that space costing so much calls for good drawings and good copy writing to make it completely worth while. The direct effect of dearer space is to create a demand for better work from both artist and writer, for it is only the quaint survivals in trade who seek to save on the cost of space by putting cheap drawings into it. On the basis of present prices paid for drawings by firms who are really alive and determined to remain in the swim, it is easily understood why artists are no longer shy of being connected with advertising. It is quite on the cards that we may yet see a statue erected in the Aldwych Club to the first modernist to assist in advertising anything but himself.

Much ground has certainly been won in the last twenty years for the use of good design in advertising. The official schools of art now recognise a new outlet for serious work and encourage their students to exploit it. But their conception of the application of art to advertising is poster design, possibly because it conforms more to the spectacular tradition of the art schools in making a good show or inspection subject. Art masters are seldom in touch with the business end of advertising, and fail to realise its immensity. They vaguely realise it as a modern Tom Tiddler's ground, but can seldom show their pupils the easiest way in.

Comparison of the amount paid yearly for posters with that paid to artists for other kinds of drawings used in press and postal advertisements would perhaps have considerable influence on budding artists and induce them to devote their energies to doing good work in these minor fields of usefulness.

There is a constant demand for actuality in pen drawing to assist the sale of goods of all kinds. Pegram, Shepard, Leete, Cheney, Baumer, and Bert Thomas are but a few of the names prominent in graphic art which are constantly encountered in the advertising pages of the newspaper and magazine press. The work of some of these occurs more frequently in the advertisement than in the editorial pages, for the simple, human reason that the remuneration from advertisers is generally better than that obtainable from publishers.

The study of line drawing for newspaper and magazine illustration and advertising in connection with modern reproductive processes is fascinating, and the possibilities of technical discoveries are great. The potency of the pen in creating interest in goods and schemes by pictorial suggestion and representation offers constant opportunities to the competent artist. Franklin Booth in America, for instance, invented an entirely new pen technique which should inspire others to experiment, but has, unfortunately, inspired many to attempt the utterly impossible task of working in a method which is

Booth's alone, and which he alone can handle. Percy E. Syer, in England, experimented with an extremely interesting technique of vertical lines in a series of drawings for the Glasgow School of Accountancy, and another for a certain excellent beer. The effect is similar to wood-engraving, and attracts

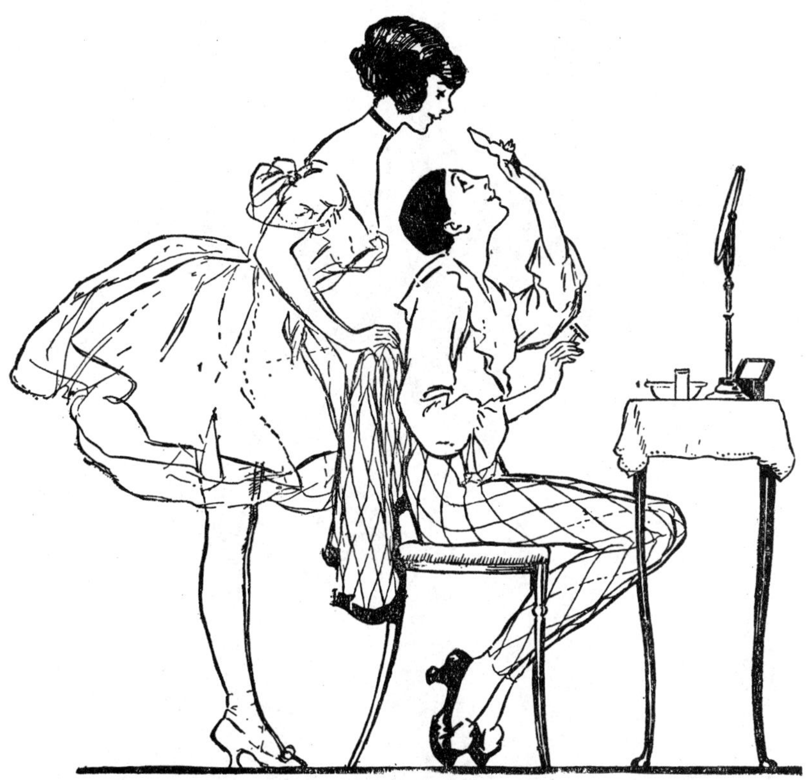

FIG. 134.—By LEWIS BAUMER.
Much is expressed by the employment of very few devices beyond the outlining of the principal features.

attention by a certain "body" which is the peculiar merit of its built-up pen lines.

The first necessity of advertising drawings is that they print well on rapid machines and indifferent surface papers. The ideal newspaper illustration for printing is one in clear and fairly stout outline, without close lines or cross-hatching to run together as the stereo wears; but it is not a great offence

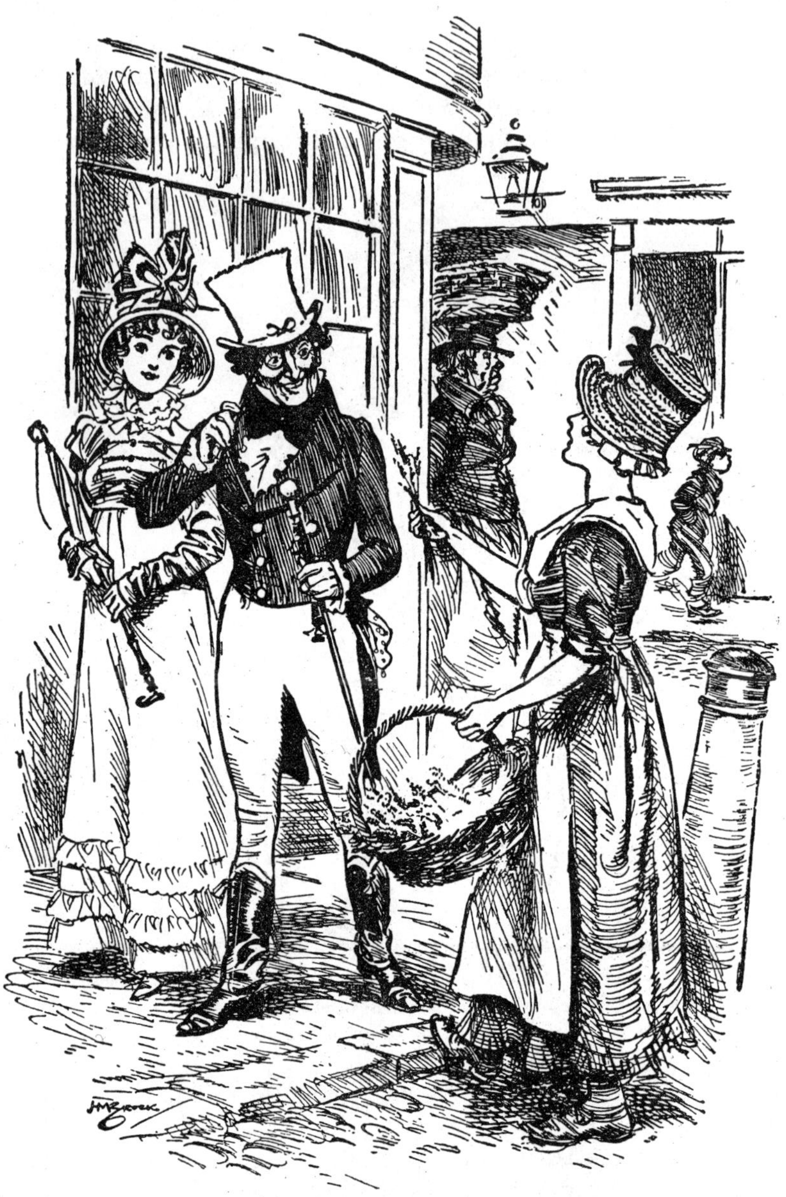

FIG. 135.—By H. M. BROCK. Introducing the famous Johnny Walker character invented by the late TOM BROWNE, R.I., and since treated in many ways by many famous artists.

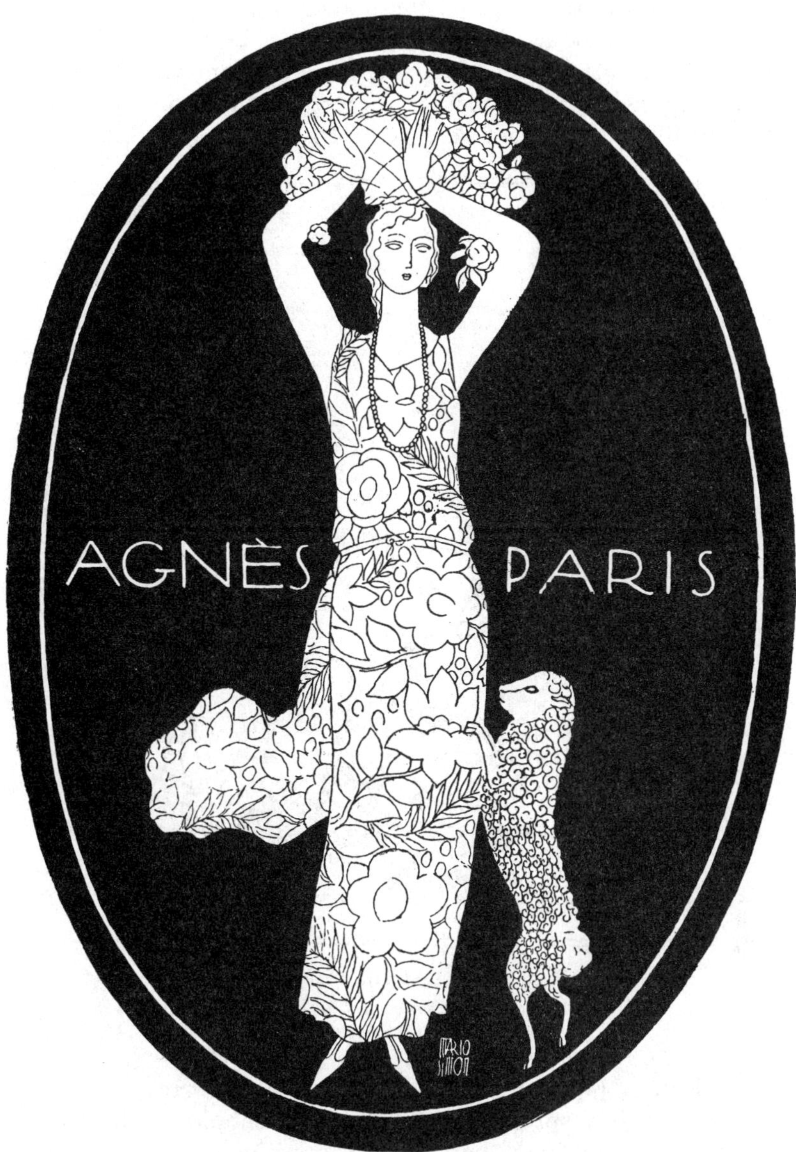

FIG. 136.—A French Drapery Advertisement by MARIO SIMON.
Well-designed silhouette with detail in thin pen outline is effective in advertising.

to wander away from the printer's ideal, for, frankly, anything that you can produce in pen and ink can be reproduced and printed in the modern newspaper press, and stands a fair chance of coming as drawn, which is merely another way of saying that it will be an exact replica of the drawing in black but

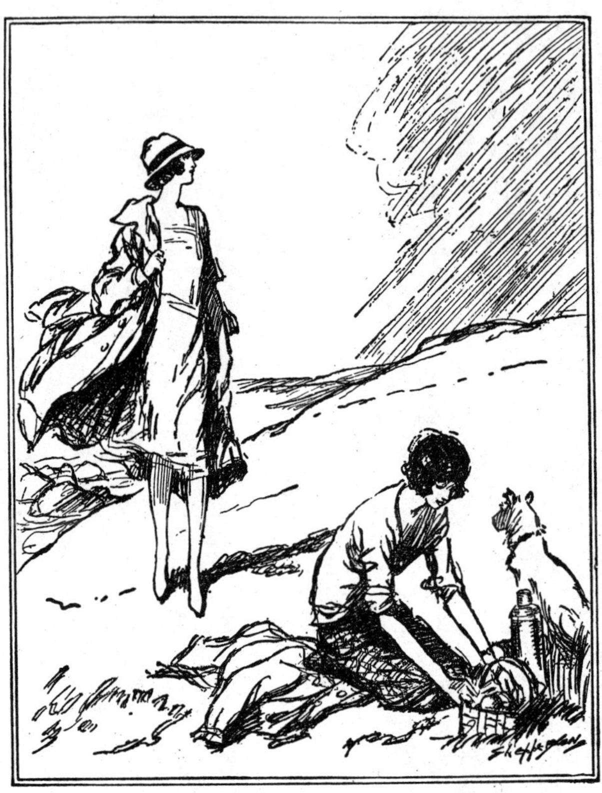

FIG. 137.—By the late CLAUDE SHEPPERSON, A.R.A.
The subtle pencil drawing is preserved in a technique in which it is merely emphasised and corrected in ink.

printed in a more or less uniform shade of grey, given by extremely thinly spread printing ink. It should be the aim of the artist to find a method which suits him, and at the same time averages the best results from these unalterable conditions, remembering always that it is his mission to produce good finished advertisements, not pretty drawings on immaculate Bristol board.

Let us consider the various forms of drawing used in advertising, first dividing them into broad and much embracing classes :—

1. "*Natural*" *Figure* with tone effects obtained by line treatment. The drawings most in demand and most likely to remain in demand in competition with all new stunts.

2. "*Semi-decorative*" *Figure.*—Figures solid black or white, but reality indicated by clever tricks of lighting in leaving high lights and suggesting shadows.

3. *Decorative Figure.*—Flat black and white with no attempt at light and shade.

4. *Decorative.*—Embracing a wide field of usefulness from mere borders to elaborate full pages involving lettering, figure, ornament, and the placing of type.

5. *Female Heads and Figures other than Fashion.*—There is a superstition that a drawing of a pretty woman will sell anything, and the vast number of men who cling to it are not well catered for by the schools, where pretty girls are more appreciated in reality than in drawings. For some occult reason the modern art student thinks it treason to his art to attempt such charming work.

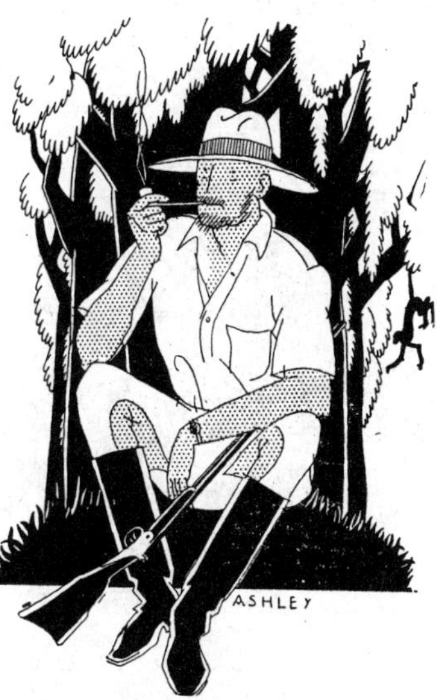

FIG. 138.—By ASHLEY HAVINDEN.
Clever semi-decorative suggestion of big game expeditions.

6. *Drawings of Goods and Buildings.*—A certain limited demand exists, but the English merchant is shy of seeing his beloved product or buildings treated with the transforming artistry they need to be interesting, and is inclined to let the artist loose on settings for the former only and very matter of fact renderings of the latter. These things they certainly do better in America.

The infinite variety of work comprised in these six categories will be apparent to all who read newspapers and magazines, which consist mainly of advertising matter nowadays. Nobody seems to mind very much, although the bulk of the matter used is atrocious in its utter disregard of artistry or even common sense.

But the general level of ugliness is being gradually lifted by the permeation of better stuff. The tendency is upward—and in this the artist who seriously intends to adopt the business may take comfort—the field is widening, and there is room both for men who adapt conventional methods to better things, and stronger men who can defy convention and by personality get their own way.

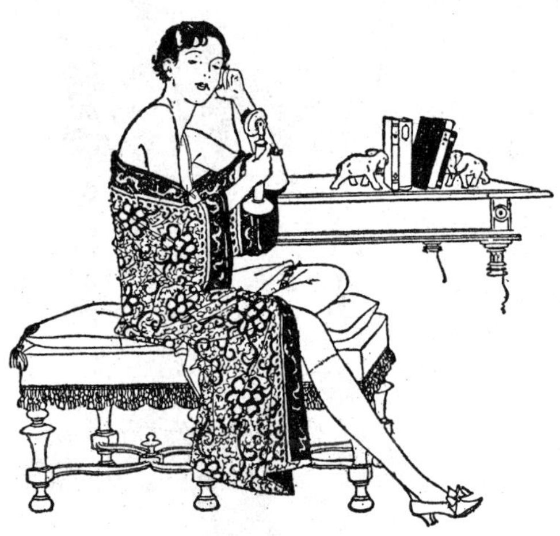

FIG. 139.—Formal Outline Treatment contrasted with Richly Drawn Pattern.

Pen line is the obviously right medium in designs for newspaper advertising, because it combines with printed matter much better than the big screen half-tone, which is the only alternative. There is affinity in the one and absolute hostility in the other between the illustration and its letterpress, and there is no reason to employ the offending half-tone as an approximate, but right effect can be obtained in pen line.

The infinite possibilities in line work executed with pen or brush are hardly touched in this country. We use it tentatively in comparison with the American advertisement artists' dash and vigour. Their drawings for pages in the *Saturday Evening Post*, for instance, are frequently made on a huge scale up to 3 ft. in height, and designs for borders I have seen made much larger than this.

On a board of this magnitude it is easy to see what you are doing, and it is also easy for others to see what you have done. In other words, it ensures good work and encourages experiment. Try it.

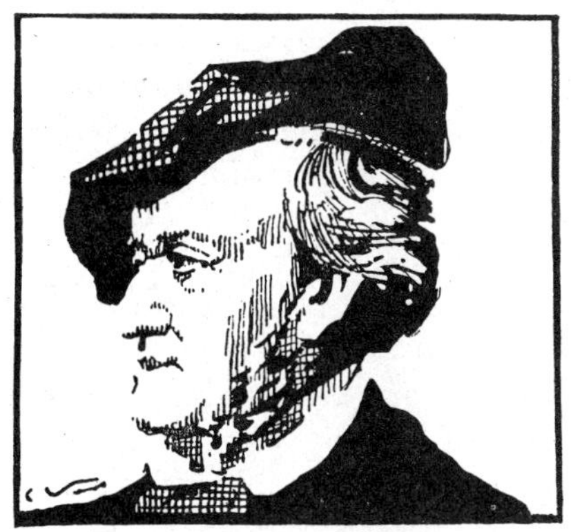

Fig. 140.—A German Advertisement, showing the effective use of Upright Lines in defining Features.

A little light on the procedure in making these huge drawings may be useful, as they are likely to awe the student as something miraculous. The usual way is to make the design on a much smaller scale, approximating to the size it is to be reproduced. This design is enlarged mechanically by photography before proceeding with the impressive finished drawing. By this method the qualities of the first sketch are preserved with added possibilities in good drawing and advertising "punch" from seeing it ready drawn for attack on the larger scale.

The best introduction to pen drawing for advertising is familiarity with American and continental papers over a few modern years. The quantity of pen work used in America alone is so vast that infinite variety of treatment for everything is discoverable, and it is well to see what others have done before striking out on the same adventures. France, Germany, Italy, Spain, Holland, and Sweden all address advertising from interestingly different angles, and their press work is provocative of new ideas. But the object in exploring the papers must be general information, not piracy, for the lift direct in modern advertising practice

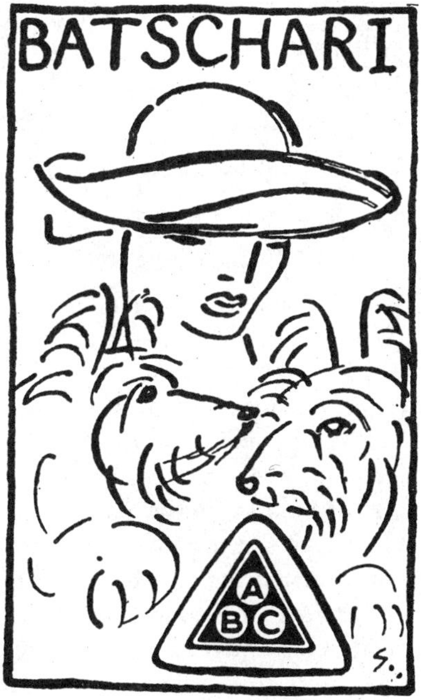

Fig. 141.—A German Advertisement. Rough pen note used with usual trade-mark.

is artistic suicide. Every one in the swim knows the outstanding men in other countries, and an imitator is not welcome unless he can adopt a style which depends as much on wit as design, and develop it on totally different lines ; a compliment paid to the original English artist " Fish " by the original American artist Gluyas Williams, or vice versa (Figs. 121 and 122).

America certainly leads in ornamental advertising ; her decorative artists are much better paid and can explore, therefore, with great thoroughness the authoritative sources of great work ; the Japanese for methods of placing and economy of line ; the East for exotic detail ; and the French engravers of the seventeenth and eighteenth centuries for dignity and opulent colour in massed differences of line. Study is maintained at white heat in conjunction with actual professional work, and accounts for the technical perfection and extraordinary beauty of the decorative pages found in the advertising side of most American magazines, their complete success due in great measure to the fine drawing compelled by the large size of the originals.

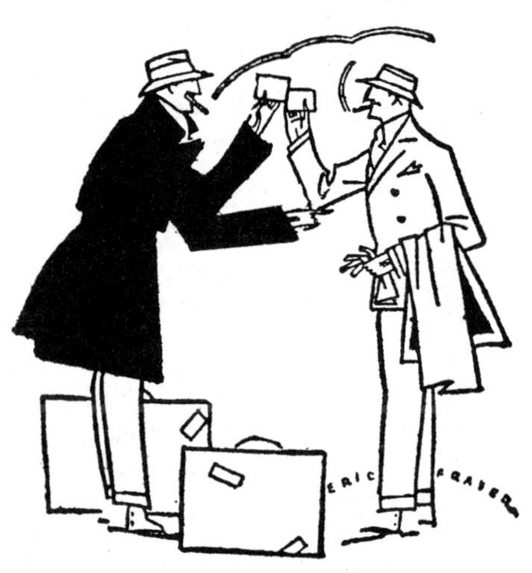

FIG. 142.—Conventional Treatment of the Modern Silhouette by ERIC FRASER.

The favourite type of pen drawing for smaller advertisements in America to-day is the figure vignette in pure outline, with light and shade suggested only by the merest thickening of line, or altogether omitted, the subject concerned with people either using the advertised goods or engaged in some occupation obviously bearing on their use. Such drawings are much in favour here as well ; but we do not give them the study and preliminary preparation necessary to compete with the Americans, in whose work there is so much more than appears to the uninitiated who admire its finished simplicity. This perfection is arrived at by a process of building up and elimination; building up by many drawings from actual people and objects arranged and rearranged to find the most arresting composition, with final elimination of everything but the barest lines necessary to express the meaning so simply that it is really difficult to miss.

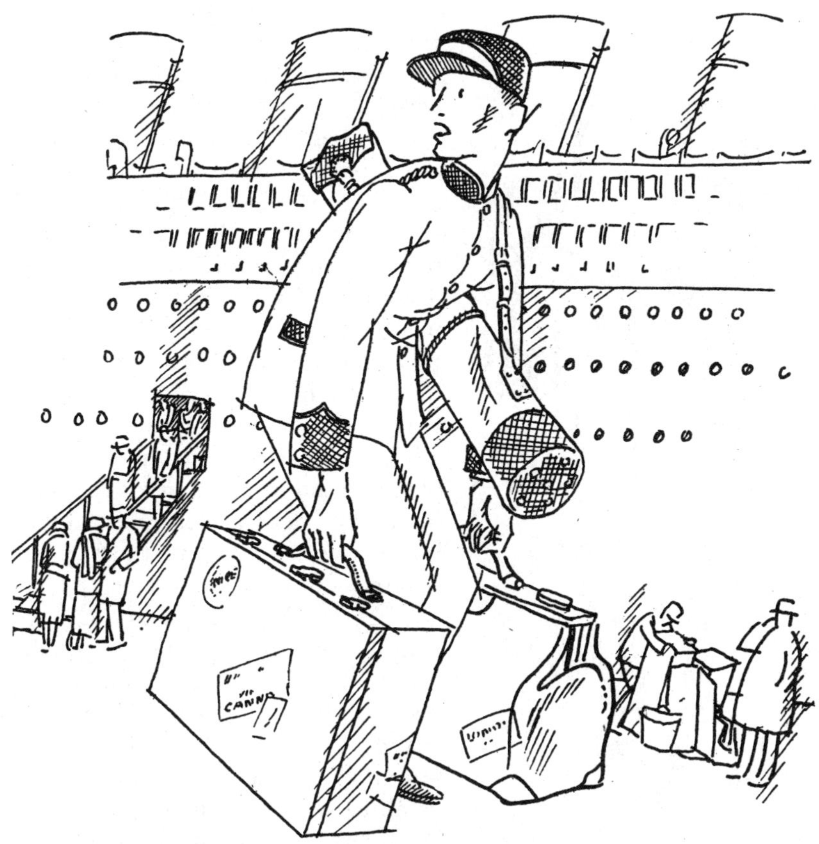

FIG. 143.—A Modern Pen Treatment by ASHLEY HAVINDEN, showing an effect of Studied Simplicity.

Study of the difference between the styles of various men working on drawings of this kind will show that the opportunity for individual treatment is increased rather than diminished by the severe restriction of line. Yet, curiously enough, if the preliminary study is omitted and the simplicity attempted with no other authority than the inner consciousness of the designer, a similarity between such attempts is immediately evident and accounts for the monotonous feebleness of such drawings. Get authority, therefore, with all thy getting, before starting out on the smallest drawing!

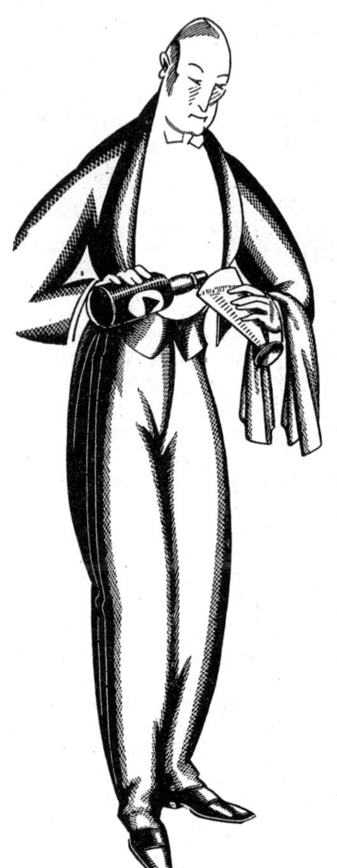

FIG. 144.—An Advertisement by JOHN AUSTEN.

The new note applied to advertising.

The number of business men who use decorative advertising in England is small in comparison with those who use naturalistic. So the best commercial policy for the coming draughtsman is to combine the qualities of both styles, making all his representations of people and things decorative in the sense that all fine drawings are decorative. The two heads for "Pepsodent" reproduced here illustrate this idea, for although naturalistic to the nth degree, they are, in colour, placing, and interesting modelling, intensely decorative, and give interest and vitality to the appeal printed with them.

The ability to draw happy people is not to be despised, especially if it can be managed without being fatuous. It is not easy to draw a smiling face in pen and ink, as the actual machinery establishing the smile calls for considerable tact in the management of lines. The smiling mouth is often divorced from the smiling eye, again the result of imperfect knowledge or preparation.

The debatable question of humour in advertising has influential support on the side that it *is* admissible. This is all to the good in a dull age, especially as we can certainly put up a strong set of artists on the humorous side.

A new kind of advertising is the sophisticated humour and

delicate irony employed in the Fortnum & Mason campaign, in which Stuart Menzies writes delicious recommendations of things to eat and drink, and Hendy, his artist accomplice, interprets them in pen pictures which bring the light and airy badinage well into the realm of practical salesmanship.

The notion of directing attention to goods by joking about

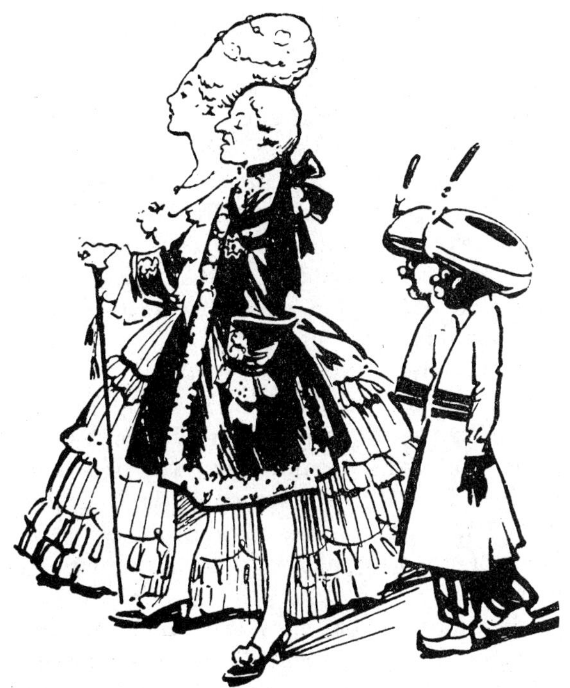

FIG. 145.—An Advertisement by G. M. ELLWOOD.

An example of the association of word and picture in demand by advertisers.

their origin, composition, and destination is so novel that it has taken the advertising world by storm; but it has certainly come to stay, and the artist who has a pretty wit and can spread the joy of life in helping to sell goods should certainly cultivate his gifts. Menzies' secret is that he enjoys writing advertisements; in fact, he enjoys everything, and for that very reason his temptations get home and sales result.

It was formerly an axiom of advertising that humour could be used only in selling to the half educated. Bateman, Fougasse, and Menzies have proved the contrary and launched a new era.

An excellent idea from every point of view, especially the artist's, is that of running long series of drawings like the "Cries of London" by Brock and Raven Hill, the "Travel" and "Ancient Crafts" by Cheney, and on simpler lines the "Quality," "Price," "Beauty," "Utility," etc., series for the General Electric Co. by myself, and the "Bondman" series by H. M. Bateman.

Reverting to naturalistic drawings and the decorative qualities that are desirable when they are used in advertisements, the late Claude Shepperson's work shows the perfect combination of the two. He was the greatest master of placing or composition in English pen drawing, and his advertising work so outstanding in contrasted light and dark that its mere distribution of colour gave it selling value or "punch." In this connection his drawings should be analysed and pondered over by students.

Baumer has some of the same qualities, but his strongest point is the delineation of aristocratic young persons of both sexes. No one can better suggest the perfect type of English girl. His drawing for Erasmic soap here reproduced shows his command of liquid decorative line, which, applied to convincing realism in drawing, lifts it well out of the rut, giving "punch" almost equal to Shepperson's, but obtained from quite different qualities.

Serious drawings of children are much in demand, and Septimus Scott and Lilian Hocknell are kept busy in supplying them, the former with strong line work of extreme facility and charm, evidently based on nature (see Fig. 26), the latter with thin, rather wiry pen line and a very complete understanding of children's little idiosyncrasies and the requirements of manufacturer and printer. Students attracted to the serious study of children for advertising could not follow a better mentor as to what is commercially "it' (see Fig. 158).

An amusing branch of advertisement work is the drawing of actual goods, usually very badly done, with occasional gleams of genius that show the possibilities. There will be a lot of this kind of thing in the future, and there is no reason why it should not develop on interesting lines. Photography, of course, leads the way in giving the actual, so there is a distinct boom in well-arranged pictures of cigarettes, scent, jewellery, cakes, etc., in suitable settings. Additional interest could be given by doing this better in pen and ink either as a translation of the photographic basis, or, better still, direct from "nature."

The Americans go in greatly for this kind of thing, and several of their best artists have shown that it has been a labour of love to make even patent foods and pairs of socks look their very best.

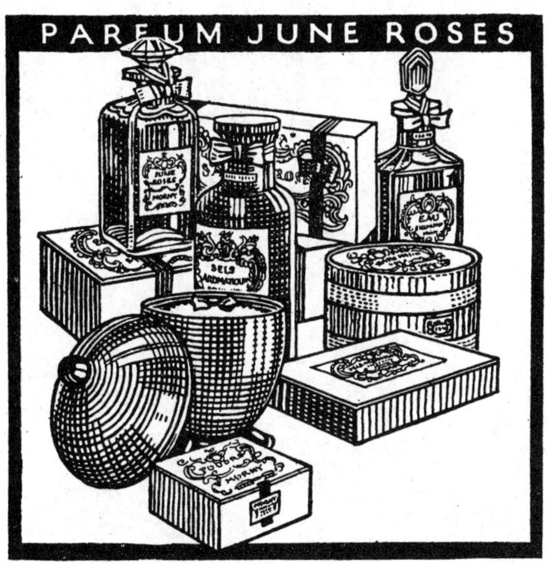

FIG. 146.—Pen Line suggested by Wood-Cutting, very definite and beautifully designed.

Drawings of goods depend for interest on technique, except in the minority of instances where goods or packings are beautiful or amusing in themselves. A dangerous tendency is abroad to regard extreme elaboration in line as a factor in success. It is not; elaborate work will never cover poverty of invention or failure in seizing the right point of view. In point of fact it is almost true to say that conscious elaboration beyond the minimum of effort to obtain truth is wrong, unless the interest is definitely shifted from the objects to the technique. When a branded packet, for instance, is shown in the foreground, objects not on sale but bearing on the product indicated in the background are purposely kept down in interest.

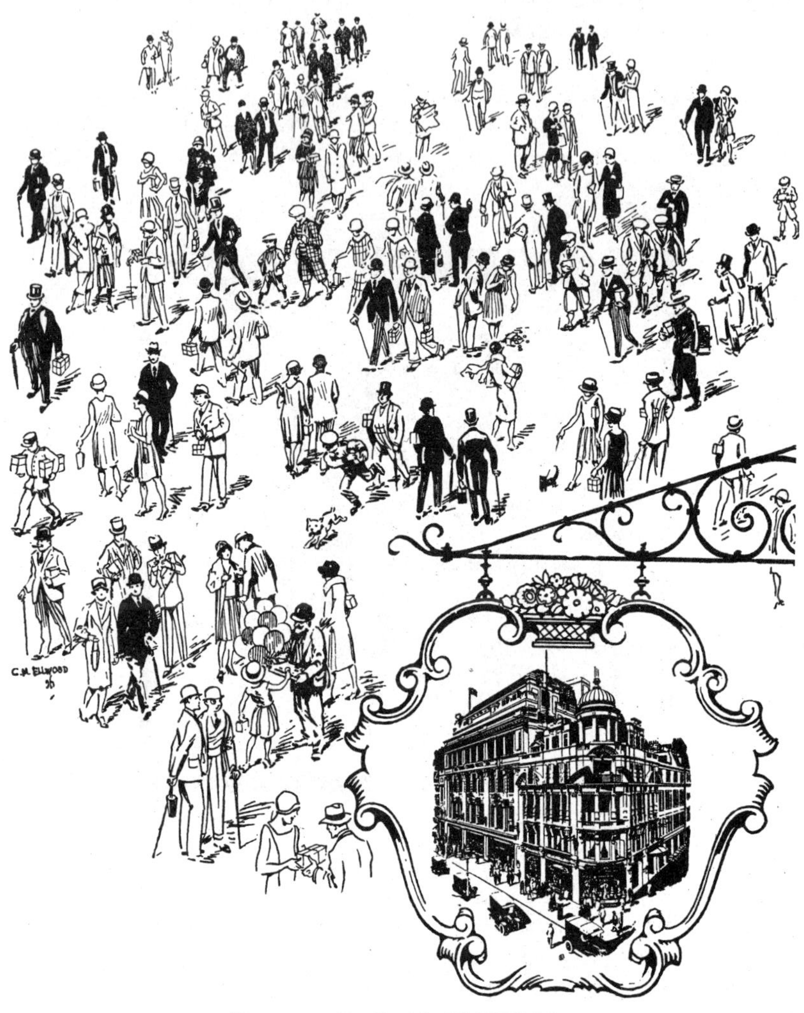

FIG. 147.—By G. M. ELLWOOD.

Illustration drawn for full newspaper page, showing to what extent an open treatment will reduce and print.

Elaborate work has a certain fascination, it is true, for both artist and public; the one feels that he is giving full measure and the others that they are getting it, and should be proportionately grateful. But the fact remains that they are not, and elaboration as such is proved wrong in loss of force. When there is something fundamentally right in the work to carry it, the sin is not deadly ; but it is waste, because the fundamental rightness would have more chance to function without it.

A flagrant example of over-elaboration is shown in the advertisement on Fig. 148, in which everything is emphasised and nothing is vital. There is considerable technical accom-

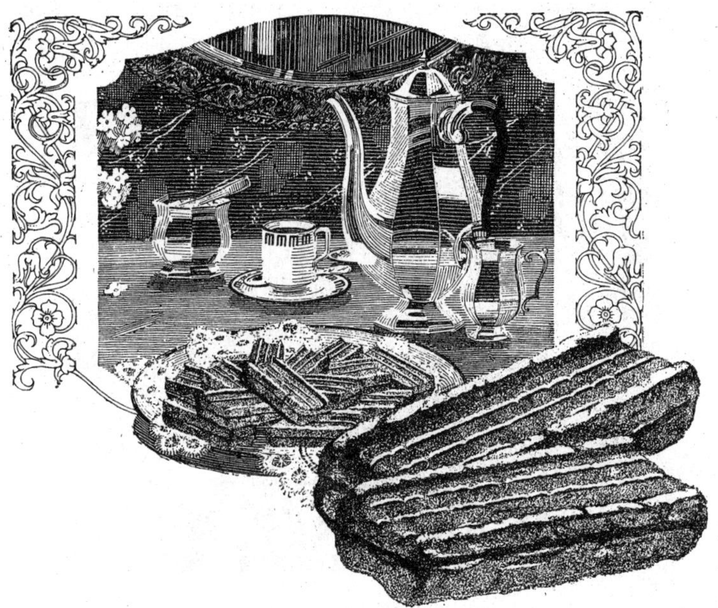

FIG. 148.

plishment in the complete performance, but the evident desire to show this cleverness to the utmost defeats its end. It is like the opening chorus of a musical comedy, where every one is singing so loudly that nothing comes over but noise. It may not be the fault of the artist, but the advertisement is killed by facts where beautiful subtleties would keep alive the main idea that one should desire a certain delectable biscuit more than any other.

There is no such thing as " correct " technique in advertising line work. The only test of method is a pleasing result, and all kinds of instructions and warnings in text-books on pen drawing go by the board in actual practice; for instance, the axiom of illustration that the background should never be stronger in line than the foreground objects does not function, as it is often expedient to throw lightly treated objects into prominence with very heavy pen strokes.

The possibility of indulging in interesting experiments is one of the compensations of the artist condemned to draw dull things. These experiments may be towards simplicity on the lines of the old wood-cutters of the early days of printing, or towards intriguing elaboration as practised by the modern

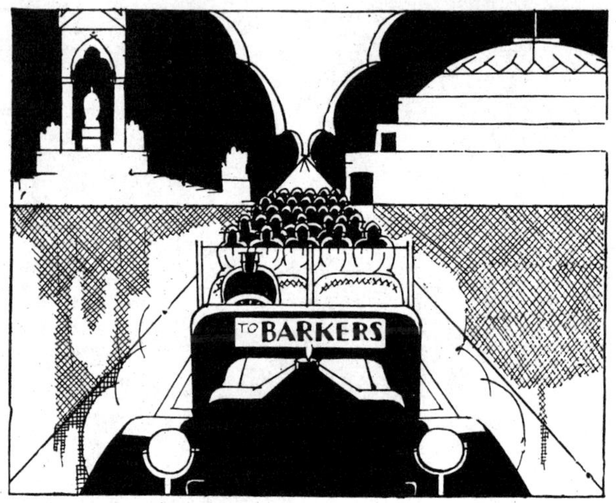

FIG. 149.—Original advertising idea by ERIC FRASER.

Americans. Their success will depend on the taste and trained perception of the executant in not exceeding the limit of fitness in either direction.

Drawings of buildings are a feature of advertising, as nearly every business man is anxious to show the aspect of his shop or works at some time. The old idea of exaggerated size is happily extinct, as it is hardly compatible with the modern slogan, "Truth in Advertising"; but the most truthful generally like their premises in favourable perspective. The present tendency is to have sketches rather than detailed drawings; to suggest the general aspect of the building and not make a catalogue of its exact number of bricks. Architectural drawings are also in demand for railways and tours generally, and there is a future for specialists in this direction.

It is hoped that the illustrations to this Chapter will give the student a fairly comprehensive insight into the various manners and techniques most in demand by advertisers at the present day. They represent a careful selection of what is, in the author's opinion, some of the best contemporary work produced in this field both in England and America, a serious study of which should amply repay the effort. Comparison with the advertisement pages of the average periodical of twenty years back will show the enormous strides already made towards a higher standard of good drawing and good ideas in this branch of pen drawing, and give some indication of the immense possibilities which lie ahead.

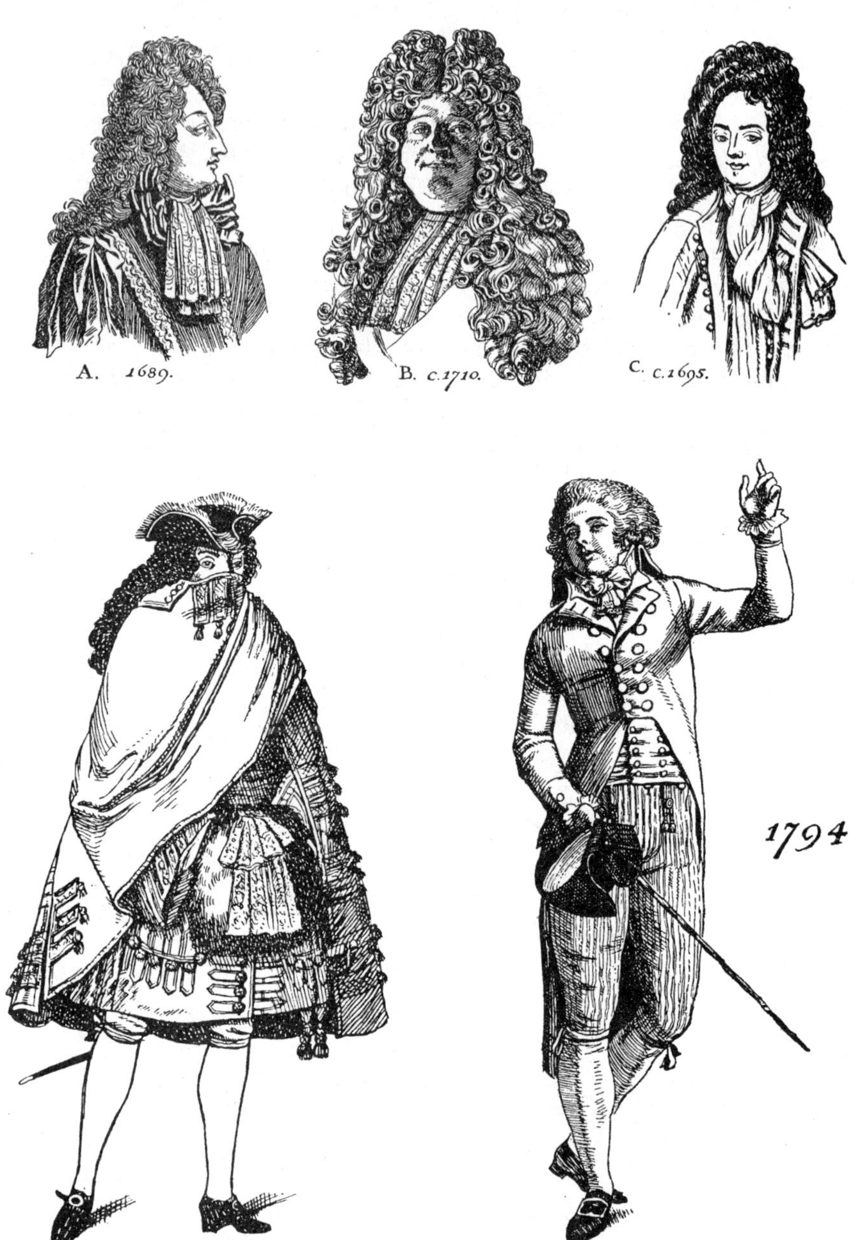

FIG. 150.—Drawings for Costume by RANDOLPH SCHWABE.
Accuracy combined with feeling for the period.

CHAPTER XII

FASHION DRAWING IN PEN AND INK

MORE individuality in the technique of fashion work is the immediate demand, and those fashion artists who will take the trouble to develop on these lines will find an increasing call on their services in the advertisement departments of the big West End houses. With these

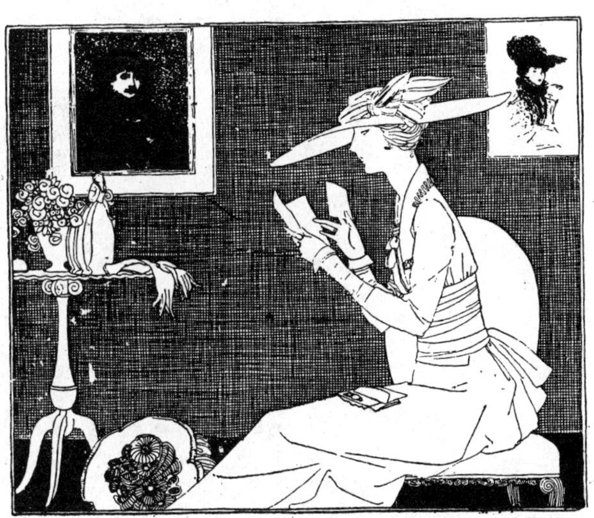

FIG. 151.—Decorative Fashion Drawing (American) by THE KEESES. An early example of a type of drawing now much in request.

advertisers the great endeavour is to get the character and speciality of their establishments reflected in all their press announcements, and a distinctive type of wearer and style of presentation is needed to supplement the exclusive name block, generally the only thing which effectively separates one announcement from another, apart from the dividing lines set

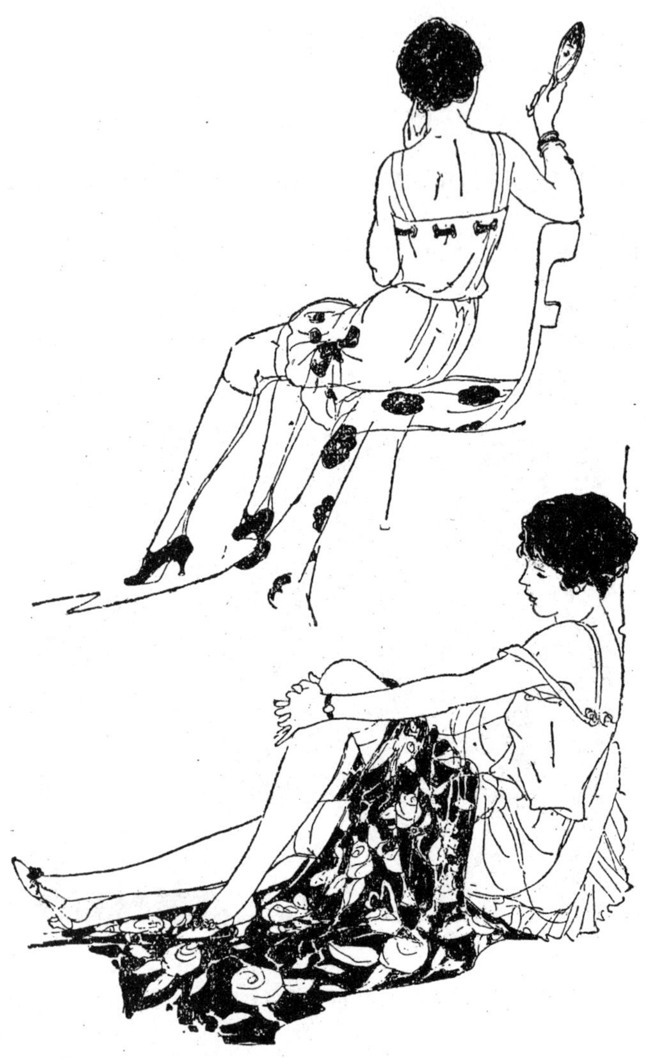

Fig. 152.—American Stocking Advertisements, showing the possibilities of Natural Treatment in Fashion work.

by the papers. A glance at current drapery advertising will demonstrate the commonplace similarity in technique which mainly holds the field, with a very few brilliant exceptions—Bessie Ayscough an outstanding one in feminine fashions, and George Roller in men's wear. Miss Ayscough's sketches are instantly recognisable and looked for by half the women in the kingdom, and George Roller's authority in sports wear is unquestioned by those who know. In spite of the great possibilities suggested by such drawings to the wideawake advertisers, the majority of drapery announcements, representing a weekly expenditure of thousands of pounds, give the impression of a distribution of stock blocks by wholesalers, so dead is the level of execution, owing mainly to the dearth of fashion artists with a strong sense of style.

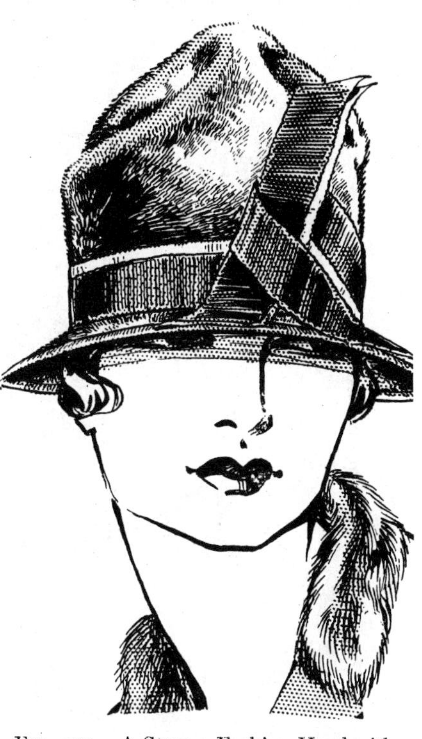

FIG. 153.—A Strong Fashion Head with Hat in sufficient detail to show Trimming and Texture.

Distinctive style usually goes with intuitive perception, and its exponents often tire of fashion's restrictions and desert it for book illustration or other more attractive, if less remunerative, occupations. The fact remains that fashion drawing can be both fascinating and remunerative to those who cultivate a recognisable flair for smartness and produce something that stands out from the colourless and insipid average.

All character and individuality seems to desert the fashion artist's pen in a supreme effort to show frocks in complete detail, and, after all, this detail is generally wasted, for it is quite a matter of opinion whether a fashion sketch should embody petty details of pattern, etc., or concentrate on the " line " which is so much more vital, allowing the artist a free hand in presenting an alluring impression of the general effect, and leaving detail to the descriptive matter.

"Personally, I consider it quite a mistake to pay too great attention to detail, and would rather see a smart sketch err on the side of 'abandon' and 'go,'" says Mr Laurence Calhaem

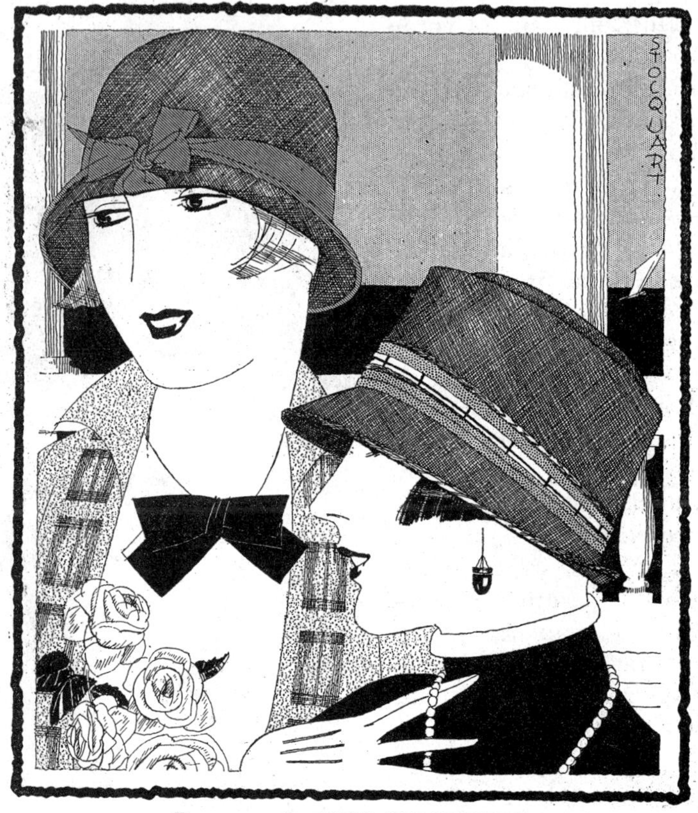

FIG. 154.—By MISS STOCQUART.
Fashions in Hats, combining the modern note with selling detail.

of Jays, who speaks for the exclusive house. But in work intended for wholesalers' catalogues, detail is essential, and there is no reason why it should not be added to drawings already full of spirit and right in "line" by artists incapable of these qualities but interested in working out delicate patterns.

Mr Calhaem's advice to the novice is to cultivate an individual style and also a certain adventurous abandon in his drawing, even though it may not at first find favour commercially, for he will be developing on right lines, as all big advertisers tend to insist on exclusive methods in the illustration of their press advertising.

Artists generally have a very inadequate conception of the scope in fashion work, and are inclined to scoff and avoid it. They see the inartistic catalogue illustrations and lament the superiority of French and American drawing without con-

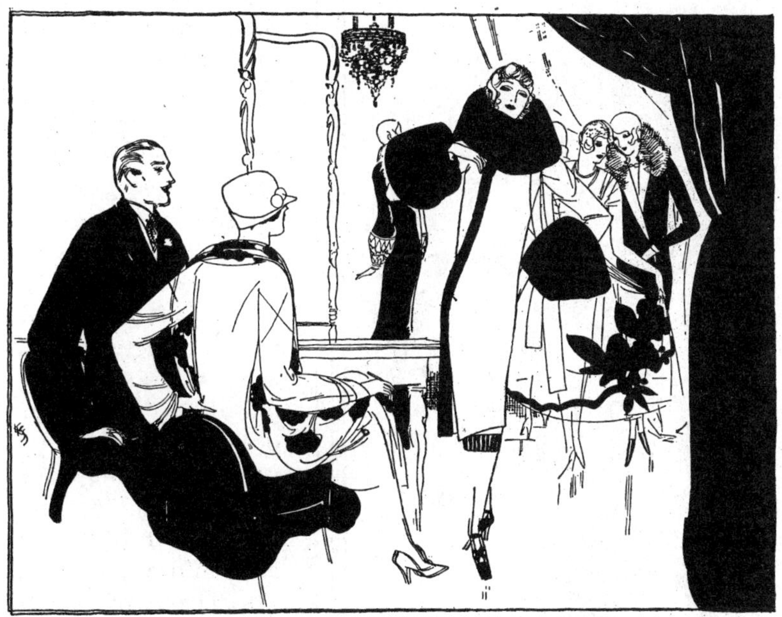

FIG. 155.—Effective use of Solids with Economy of Line in a Fashion Drawing by KATHERINE STURGES.

sidering the immense possibilities in offering better style to the awakening perceptions of English costumiers and tailors, many of whom go to France and America for such work for lack of variety at home.

It is difficult to find a better practical training in illustration or any figure work than a thorough course of sketching from the splendid poses which are second nature to the West End mannequin. The big houses will give facilities for this to an artist who can show drawings promising effectiveness in their advertising, and the draughtsman with confidence in his powers can use fashion drawing in this way as a stepping-stone to illustration, and will very likely find it fascinating and remunerative enough to abandon the ultimate aim, or combine it with the serious business of fashion as a *main* occupation.

It is useful to know the work of the great Frenchman, Drian, one of the pioneers of quite natural fashion drawing. Drian makes no concessions to the conventions of trade; his figures are always beautifully drawn from nature, their costumes treated as drapery which may or may not stress the essential features of the dress, but invariably makes a picture which every woman wants to look like. He seldom does fashion drawings nowadays, being more interested in etchings of beautiful women and children; but occasional pages of costume sketches and drawings of smart women for advertisers, like Lery's perfumes, show that he is still foremost in the modes.

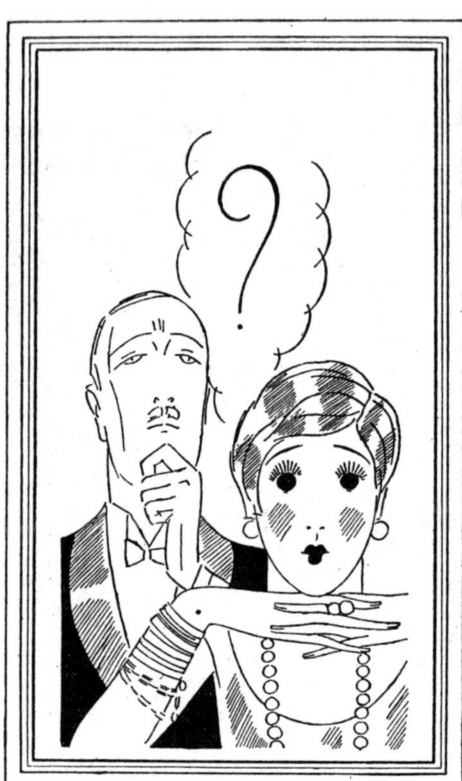

FIG. 156.—By E. G. BENITO.
Decorative use of Essential Lines typical of the modern tendency in illustration.

From Drian to the next best is a far cry, even in Paris, and we have in England few fashion artists comparable with the French second line of defence. There is room, therefore, for many good men or women who can get the French note of extreme smartness. One of our younger illustrators, "Forster," could, and he would, run Drian more closely than his French rivals, but I think Forster is quite satisfied with the flood of illustration work which surges round him, and is hardly likely to desert it in order to undertake the improvement of English fashion drawing (see Fig. 157).

Many enter the rather crowded ranks of purely commercial fashion drawing and acquire a certain facility in turning out "drawings that are wanted," according to the formulæ laid down by fashion schools. They are generally assured of

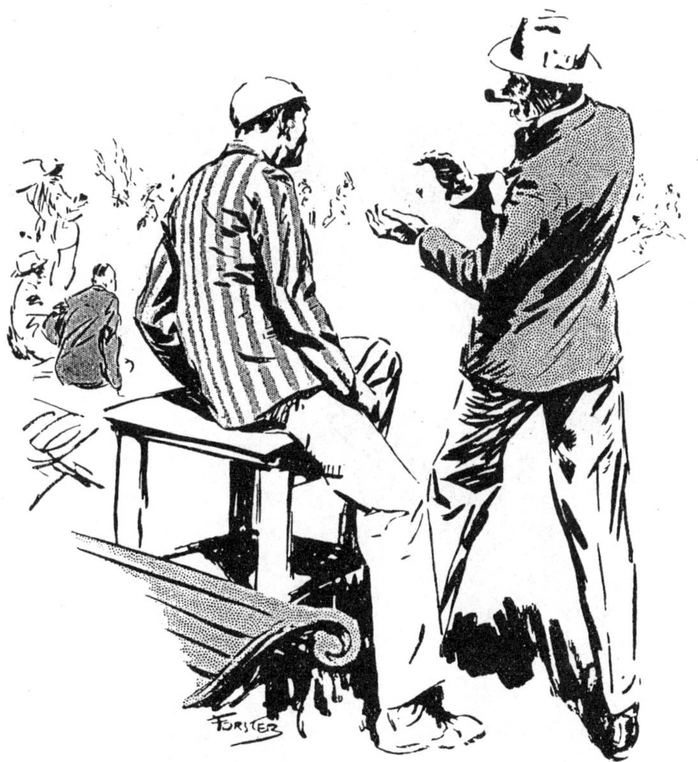

FIG. 157.—Men's Fashion Drawing by FORSTER.

work of a kind, and if they can stand the monotonous repetition of six stock poses, with face and hands to pattern, they can be pretty certain of employment by people who act as farmers for this kind of thing. It has no remote connection with art or drawing, being a purely mechanical business of manipulated tracing paper and careful retracing of lines, only saved from being mechanically executed by the facts that fashions change with great rapidity and human fingers are cheaper than the elaborate machinery it would involve.

It is an occupation very much the same as typing, but a little more interesting, perhaps, and useful to crowds of girls who are content with a dead-end occupation. Those whose artistic ambitions are active will do well to leave it alone and strike out boldly for a line of their own—the only hope of making fashion work tolerable and remunerative to an artist.

In addition to work for costumiers and wholesale houses, there is a considerable amount to be done for fashion papers,

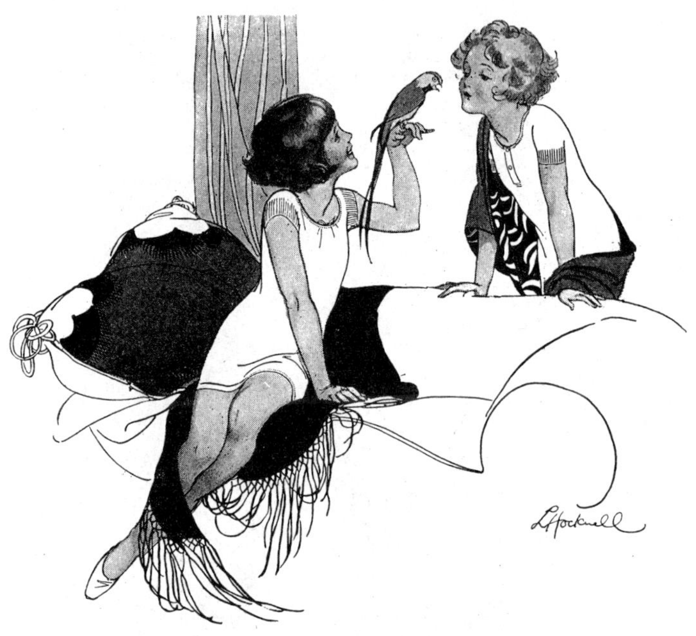

FIG. 158.—L. HOCKNELL has turned Children's Fashions in Underwear into Pleasant Pictures, achieving fame in the process.

and although most of it is reproduced in half-tone, a good number of the drawings are really pen drawings with light washes added. This method, which has much to recommend it in combining the advantages of both styles of drawing, is excellently employed by Miss E. Shepherd in her business-like work for " Good Housekeeping."

The reputation of a paper is often made by its star fashion artists. Miss Ayscough certainly recommends the *Daily Mail* to women. Miss Oliver gave renewed life to *The Ladies'*

Field, and Miss Lilian Young kept up interest in *The Gentlewoman*, then the foremost ladies' paper, for three or four decades, until she retired about ten years ago.

A post as fashion artist on an important paper is rather an enviable one, giving the entrée to a good deal of social life and the interesting world of expensive stuffs, laces, and trimmings covered by the term "West End Houses."

The latest development in fashion drawing is work needed for houses running press campaigns to sell "branded" goods

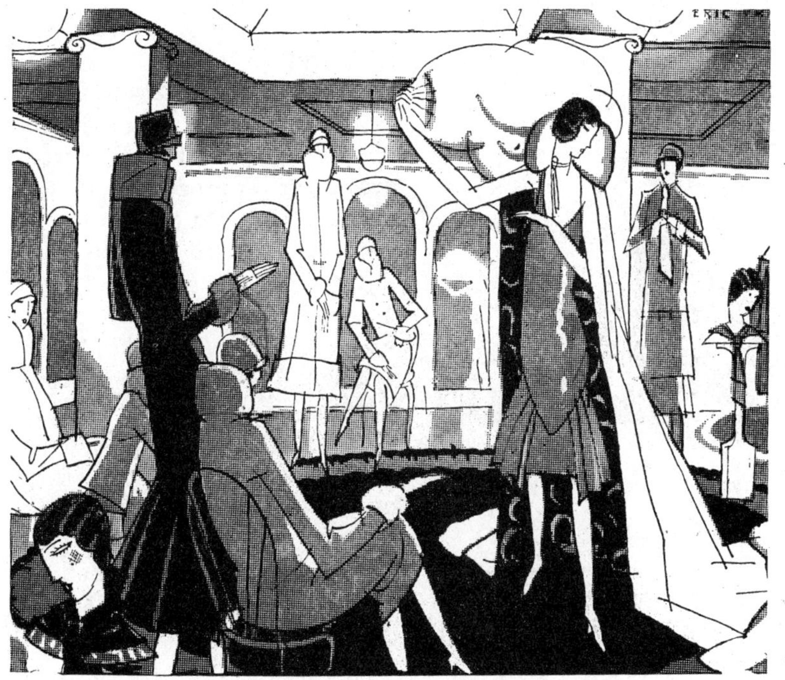

FIG. 159.—By ERIC FRASER.

Showing the abandonment of all fashion conventions, and giving its message at a glance.

such as "Aquascutum," "Dexter," "Zambrene," "Celanese," "Viyella," and hosts of others, all needing and willing to pay for really outstanding drawings to demonstrate their good qualities. This creates an inexhaustible demand for tip-top work, and an artist has but to demonstrate his ability in this direction to find a good deal of competition for his services—

often his exclusive services to one firm, like "Roller" for Burburys and "Caffyn" for Jays.

Nearly all big firms handling advertised brands of goods are ever open to suggestions for series fashion drawings in some novel and attractive technique either in line or wash. It never follows that their advertising managers are hostile to new ideas because they ask for conventional styles. Many will spend quite a long time in explaining *exactly* what they want, and warning a new artist on his first commission that he *must* conform to some supposed ritual, only afterwards to express their satisfaction with something entirely opposed in every possible way to instructions which they find it convenient to forget.

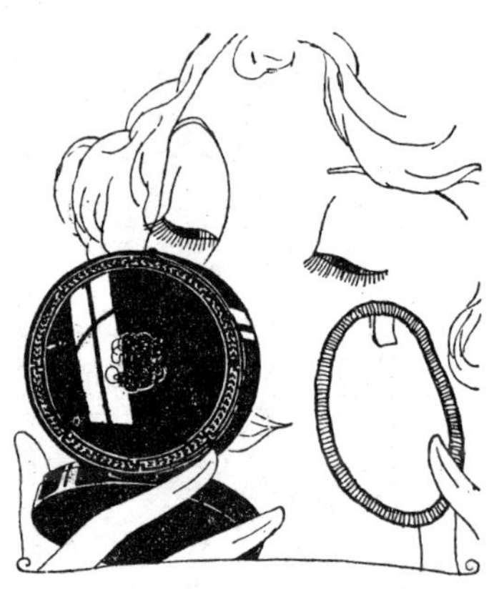

Fig. 160.—Deftness of Line in a Decoration by ELIZABETH LANSDELL.

Those who remember the old conventions of fashion work are most appreciative of the changes wrought by the acceptance of natural shape and movements in place of diagrams of seams and buttons on lengthened "figures" like wooden nine-pins. The pioneers deserve the thanks of the entire artistic fraternity in ridding the world of one form of useless ugliness, and at the same time opening a tremendous field of remunerative work not too difficult of access for the moderately clever, yet holding opportunities for outstanding genius to function in actual business-getting work of enormous importance to the national welfare.

This concludes the list of possible and profitable avenues to success for the pen artist at the present day. They are, as will have been observed, many and varied enough to offer a niche for almost any personality in this medium. As has been emphasised in the foregoing pages, and can never be emphasised too strongly, the expression of a genuine and definite personality is one of the most important aims to be achieved in the quest for the elusive quality of "style." The beginner must learn to derive his inspiration from his own self, and not to rely for it in what he finds in the work of some favourite master. But hand in hand with this must go the perseverance to carry on in the face of the numerous disappointments that at the start always fall to his lot, and the patience to persist when work seems only a dull and difficult grind. Inspiration is the direct result of a long and arduous battle with technique, and if these pages provide for their readers any material aid in this battle, their author will feel satisfied that something at least has been accomplished.

INDEX TO TEXT AND ILLUSTRATIONS

Figures in black type indicate page numbers of illustrations

A

B

C

D

E

F

G

H

I

J

K

L

M

N

O

P

R

S

T

V

W

Y

A CATALOG OF SELECTED

DOVER BOOKS

IN ALL FIELDS OF INTEREST

A CATALOG OF SELECTED DOVER BOOKS IN ALL FIELDS OF INTEREST

CONCERNING THE SPIRITUAL IN ART, Wassily Kandinsky. Pioneering work by father of abstract art. Thoughts on color theory, nature of art. Analysis of earlier masters. 12 illustrations. 80pp. of text. 5⅜ x 8½. 23411-8

ANIMALS: 1,419 Copyright-Free Illustrations of Mammals, Birds, Fish, Insects, etc., Jim Harter (ed.). Clear wood engravings present, in extremely lifelike poses, over 1,000 species of animals. One of the most extensive pictorial sourcebooks of its kind. Captions. Index. 284pp. 9 x 12. 23766-4

CELTIC ART: The Methods of Construction, George Bain. Simple geometric techniques for making Celtic interlacements, spirals, Kells-type initials, animals, humans, etc. Over 500 illustrations. 160pp. 9 x 12. (Available in U.S. only.) 22923-8

AN ATLAS OF ANATOMY FOR ARTISTS, Fritz Schider. Most thorough reference work on art anatomy in the world. Hundreds of illustrations, including selections from works by Vesalius, Leonardo, Goya, Ingres, Michelangelo, others. 593 illustrations. 192pp. 7⅛ x 10¼. 20241-0

CELTIC HAND STROKE-BY-STROKE (Irish Half-Uncial from "The Book of Kells"): An Arthur Baker Calligraphy Manual, Arthur Baker. Complete guide to creating each letter of the alphabet in distinctive Celtic manner. Covers hand position, strokes, pens, inks, paper, more. Illustrated. 48pp. 8¼ x 11. 24336-2

EASY ORIGAMI, John Montroll. Charming collection of 32 projects (hat, cup, pelican, piano, swan, many more) specially designed for the novice origami hobbyist. Clearly illustrated easy-to-follow instructions insure that even beginning papercrafters will achieve successful results. 48pp. 8¼ x 11. 27298-2

THE COMPLETE BOOK OF BIRDHOUSE CONSTRUCTION FOR WOODWORKERS, Scott D. Campbell. Detailed instructions, illustrations, tables. Also data on bird habitat and instinct patterns. Bibliography. 3 tables. 63 illustrations in 15 figures. 48pp. 5¼ x 8½. 24407-5

BLOOMINGDALE'S ILLUSTRATED 1886 CATALOG: Fashions, Dry Goods and Housewares, Bloomingdale Brothers. Famed merchants' extremely rare catalog depicting about 1,700 products: clothing, housewares, firearms, dry goods, jewelry, more. Invaluable for dating, identifying vintage items. Also, copyright-free graphics for artists, designers. Co-published with Henry Ford Museum & Greenfield Village. 160pp. 8¼ x 11. 25780-0

HISTORIC COSTUME IN PICTURES, Braun & Schneider. Over 1,450 costumed figures in clearly detailed engravings–from dawn of civilization to end of 19th century. Captions. Many folk costumes. 256pp. 8⅜ x 11¾. 23150-X

STICKLEY CRAFTSMAN FURNITURE CATALOGS, Gustav Stickley and L. & J. G. Stickley. Beautiful, functional furniture in two authentic catalogs from 1910. 594 illustrations, including 277 photos, show settles, rockers, armchairs, reclining chairs, bookcases, desks, tables. 183pp. 6½ x 9¼. 23838-5

AMERICAN LOCOMOTIVES IN HISTORIC PHOTOGRAPHS: 1858 to 1949, Ron Ziel (ed.). A rare collection of 126 meticulously detailed official photographs, called "builder portraits," of American locomotives that majestically chronicle the rise of steam locomotive power in America. Introduction. Detailed captions. xi+ 129pp. 9 x 12. 27393-8

AMERICA'S LIGHTHOUSES: An Illustrated History, Francis Ross Holland, Jr. Delightfully written, profusely illustrated fact-filled survey of over 200 American lighthouses since 1716. History, anecdotes, technological advances, more. 240pp. 8 x 10¾. 25576-X

TOWARDS A NEW ARCHITECTURE, Le Corbusier. Pioneering manifesto by founder of "International School." Technical and aesthetic theories, views of industry, economics, relation of form to function, "mass-production split" and much more. Profusely illustrated. 320pp. 6⅛ x 9¼. (Available in U.S. only.) 25023-7

HOW THE OTHER HALF LIVES, Jacob Riis. Famous journalistic record, exposing poverty and degradation of New York slums around 1900, by major social reformer. 100 striking and influential photographs. 233pp. 10 x 7⅞. 22012-5

FRUIT KEY AND TWIG KEY TO TREES AND SHRUBS, William M. Harlow. One of the handiest and most widely used identification aids. Fruit key covers 120 deciduous and evergreen species; twig key 160 deciduous species. Easily used. Over 300 photographs. 126pp. 5⅜ x 8½. 20511-8

COMMON BIRD SONGS, Dr. Donald J. Borror. Songs of 60 most common U.S. birds: robins, sparrows, cardinals, bluejays, finches, more–arranged in order of increasing complexity. Up to 9 variations of songs of each species.
Cassette and manual 99911-4

ORCHIDS AS HOUSE PLANTS, Rebecca Tyson Northen. Grow cattleyas and many other kinds of orchids–in a window, in a case, or under artificial light. 63 illustrations. 148pp. 5⅜ x 8½. 23261-1

MONSTER MAZES, Dave Phillips. Masterful mazes at four levels of difficulty. Avoid deadly perils and evil creatures to find magical treasures. Solutions for all 32 exciting illustrated puzzles. 48pp. 8¼ x 11. 26005-4

MOZART'S DON GIOVANNI (DOVER OPERA LIBRETTO SERIES), Wolfgang Amadeus Mozart. Introduced and translated by Ellen H. Bleiler. Standard Italian libretto, with complete English translation. Convenient and thoroughly portable–an ideal companion for reading along with a recording or the performance itself. Introduction. List of characters. Plot summary. 121pp. 5¼ x 8½. 24944-1

TECHNICAL MANUAL AND DICTIONARY OF CLASSICAL BALLET, Gail Grant. Defines, explains, comments on steps, movements, poses and concepts. 15-page pictorial section. Basic book for student, viewer. 127pp. 5⅜ x 8½. 21843-0

THE CLARINET AND CLARINET PLAYING, David Pino. Lively, comprehensive work features suggestions about technique, musicianship, and musical interpretation, as well as guidelines for teaching, making your own reeds, and preparing for public performance. Includes an intriguing look at clarinet history. "A godsend," *The Clarinet,* Journal of the International Clarinet Society. Appendixes. 7 illus. 320pp. 5⅜ x 8½. 40270-3

HOLLYWOOD GLAMOR PORTRAITS, John Kobal (ed.). 145 photos from 1926-49. Harlow, Gable, Bogart, Bacall; 94 stars in all. Full background on photographers, technical aspects. 160pp. 8⅜ x 11¼. 23352-9

THE ANNOTATED CASEY AT THE BAT: A Collection of Ballads about the Mighty Casey/Third, Revised Edition, Martin Gardner (ed.). Amusing sequels and parodies of one of America's best-loved poems: Casey's Revenge, Why Casey Whiffed, Casey's Sister at the Bat, others. 256pp. 5⅜ x 8½. 28598-7

THE RAVEN AND OTHER FAVORITE POEMS, Edgar Allan Poe. Over 40 of the author's most memorable poems: "The Bells," "Ulalume," "Israfel," "To Helen," "The Conqueror Worm," "Eldorado," "Annabel Lee," many more. Alphabetic lists of titles and first lines. 64pp. 5$\frac{3}{16}$ x 8¼. 26685-0

PERSONAL MEMOIRS OF U. S. GRANT, Ulysses Simpson Grant. Intelligent, deeply moving firsthand account of Civil War campaigns, considered by many the finest military memoirs ever written. Includes letters, historic photographs, maps and more. 528pp. 6⅛ x 9¼. 28587-1

ANCIENT EGYPTIAN MATERIALS AND INDUSTRIES, A. Lucas and J. Harris. Fascinating, comprehensive, thoroughly documented text describes this ancient civilization's vast resources and the processes that incorporated them in daily life, including the use of animal products, building materials, cosmetics, perfumes and incense, fibers, glazed ware, glass and its manufacture, materials used in the mummification process, and much more. 544pp. 6⅛ x 9¼. (Available in U.S. only.) 40446-3

RUSSIAN STORIES/RUSSKIE RASSKAZY: A Dual-Language Book, edited by Gleb Struve. Twelve tales by such masters as Chekhov, Tolstoy, Dostoevsky, Pushkin, others. Excellent word-for-word English translations on facing pages, plus teaching and study aids, Russian/English vocabulary, biographical/critical introductions, more. 416pp. 5⅜ x 8½. 26244-8

PHILADELPHIA THEN AND NOW: 60 Sites Photographed in the Past and Present, Kenneth Finkel and Susan Oyama. Rare photographs of City Hall, Logan Square, Independence Hall, Betsy Ross House, other landmarks juxtaposed with contemporary views. Captures changing face of historic city. Introduction. Captions. 128pp. 8¼ x 11. 25790-8

AIA ARCHITECTURAL GUIDE TO NASSAU AND SUFFOLK COUNTIES, LONG ISLAND, The American Institute of Architects, Long Island Chapter, and the Society for the Preservation of Long Island Antiquities. Comprehensive, well-researched and generously illustrated volume brings to life over three centuries of Long Island's great architectural heritage. More than 240 photographs with authoritative, extensively detailed captions. 176pp. 8¼ x 11. 26946-9

NORTH AMERICAN INDIAN LIFE: Customs and Traditions of 23 Tribes, Elsie Clews Parsons (ed.). 27 fictionalized essays by noted anthropologists examine religion, customs, government, additional facets of life among the Winnebago, Crow, Zuni, Eskimo, other tribes. 480pp. 6⅛ x 9¼. 27377-6

FRANK LLOYD WRIGHT'S DANA HOUSE, Donald Hoffmann. Pictorial essay of residential masterpiece with over 160 interior and exterior photos, plans, elevations, sketches and studies. 128pp. 9¼ x 10¾. 29120-0

THE MALE AND FEMALE FIGURE IN MOTION: 60 Classic Photographic Sequences, Eadweard Muybridge. 60 true-action photographs of men and women walking, running, climbing, bending, turning, etc., reproduced from rare 19th-century masterpiece. vi + 121pp. 9 x 12. 24745-7

1001 QUESTIONS ANSWERED ABOUT THE SEASHORE, N. J. Berrill and Jacquelyn Berrill. Queries answered about dolphins, sea snails, sponges, starfish, fishes, shore birds, many others. Covers appearance, breeding, growth, feeding, much more. 305pp. 5¼ x 8¼. 23366-9

ATTRACTING BIRDS TO YOUR YARD, William J. Weber. Easy-to-follow guide offers advice on how to attract the greatest diversity of birds: birdhouses, feeders, water and waterers, much more. 96pp. 5³⁄₁₆ x 8¼. 28927-3

MEDICINAL AND OTHER USES OF NORTH AMERICAN PLANTS: A Historical Survey with Special Reference to the Eastern Indian Tribes, Charlotte Erichsen-Brown. Chronological historical citations document 500 years of usage of plants, trees, shrubs native to eastern Canada, northeastern U.S. Also complete identifying information. 343 illustrations. 544pp. 6½ x 9¼. 25951-X

STORYBOOK MAZES, Dave Phillips. 23 stories and mazes on two-page spreads: Wizard of Oz, Treasure Island, Robin Hood, etc. Solutions. 64pp. 8¼ x 11. 23628-5

AMERICAN NEGRO SONGS: 230 Folk Songs and Spirituals, Religious and Secular, John W. Work. This authoritative study traces the African influences of songs sung and played by black Americans at work, in church, and as entertainment. The author discusses the lyric significance of such songs as "Swing Low, Sweet Chariot," "John Henry," and others and offers the words and music for 230 songs. Bibliography. Index of Song Titles. 272pp. 6½ x 9¼. 40271-1

MOVIE-STAR PORTRAITS OF THE FORTIES, John Kobal (ed.). 163 glamor, studio photos of 106 stars of the 1940s: Rita Hayworth, Ava Gardner, Marlon Brando, Clark Gable, many more. 176pp. 8⅜ x 11¼. 23546-7

BENCHLEY LOST AND FOUND, Robert Benchley. Finest humor from early 30s, about pet peeves, child psychologists, post office and others. Mostly unavailable elsewhere. 73 illustrations by Peter Arno and others. 183pp. 5⅜ x 8½. 22410-4

YEKL and THE IMPORTED BRIDEGROOM AND OTHER STORIES OF YIDDISH NEW YORK, Abraham Cahan. Film Hester Street based on *Yekl* (1896). Novel, other stories among first about Jewish immigrants on N.Y.'s East Side. 240pp. 5⅜ x 8½. 22427-9

SELECTED POEMS, Walt Whitman. Generous sampling from *Leaves of Grass*. Twenty-four poems include "I Hear America Singing," "Song of the Open Road," "I Sing the Body Electric," "When Lilacs Last in the Dooryard Bloom'd," "O Captain! My Captain!"–all reprinted from an authoritative edition. Lists of titles and first lines. 128pp. 5³⁄₁₆ x 8¼. 26878-0

THE BEST TALES OF HOFFMANN, E. T. A. Hoffmann. 10 of Hoffmann's most important stories: "Nutcracker and the King of Mice," "The Golden Flowerpot," etc. 458pp. 5⅜ x 8½. 21793-0

FROM FETISH TO GOD IN ANCIENT EGYPT, E. A. Wallis Budge. Rich detailed survey of Egyptian conception of "God" and gods, magic, cult of animals, Osiris, more. Also, superb English translations of hymns and legends. 240 illustrations. 545pp. 5⅜ x 8½. 25803-3

FRENCH STORIES/CONTES FRANÇAIS: A Dual-Language Book, Wallace Fowlie. Ten stories by French masters, Voltaire to Camus: "Micromegas" by Voltaire; "The Atheist's Mass" by Balzac; "Minuet" by de Maupassant; "The Guest" by Camus, six more. Excellent English translations on facing pages. Also French-English vocabulary list, exercises, more. 352pp. 5⅜ x 8½. 26443-2

CHICAGO AT THE TURN OF THE CENTURY IN PHOTOGRAPHS: 122 Historic Views from the Collections of the Chicago Historical Society, Larry A. Viskochil. Rare large-format prints offer detailed views of City Hall, State Street, the Loop, Hull House, Union Station, many other landmarks, circa 1904-1913. Introduction. Captions. Maps. 144pp. 9⅜ x 12¼. 24656-6

OLD BROOKLYN IN EARLY PHOTOGRAPHS, 1865-1929, William Lee Younger. Luna Park, Gravesend race track, construction of Grand Army Plaza, moving of Hotel Brighton, etc. 157 previously unpublished photographs. 165pp. 8⅞ x 11¾. 23587-4

THE MYTHS OF THE NORTH AMERICAN INDIANS, Lewis Spence. Rich anthology of the myths and legends of the Algonquins, Iroquois, Pawnees and Sioux, prefaced by an extensive historical and ethnological commentary. 36 illustrations. 480pp. 5⅜ x 8½. 25967-6

AN ENCYCLOPEDIA OF BATTLES: Accounts of Over 1,560 Battles from 1479 B.C. to the Present, David Eggenberger. Essential details of every major battle in recorded history from the first battle of Megiddo in 1479 B.C. to Grenada in 1984. List of Battle Maps. New Appendix covering the years 1967-1984. Index. 99 illustrations. 544pp. 6½ x 9¼. 24913-1

SAILING ALONE AROUND THE WORLD, Captain Joshua Slocum. First man to sail around the world, alone, in small boat. One of great feats of seamanship told in delightful manner. 67 illustrations. 294pp. 5⅜ x 8½. 20326-3

ANARCHISM AND OTHER ESSAYS, Emma Goldman. Powerful, penetrating, prophetic essays on direct action, role of minorities, prison reform, puritan hypocrisy, violence, etc. 271pp. 5⅜ x 8½. 22484-8

MYTHS OF THE HINDUS AND BUDDHISTS, Ananda K. Coomaraswamy and Sister Nivedita. Great stories of the epics; deeds of Krishna, Shiva, taken from puranas, Vedas, folk tales; etc. 32 illustrations. 400pp. 5⅜ x 8½. 21759-0

THE TRAUMA OF BIRTH, Otto Rank. Rank's controversial thesis that anxiety neurosis is caused by profound psychological trauma which occurs at birth. 256pp. 5⅜ x 8½. 27974-X

A THEOLOGICO-POLITICAL TREATISE, Benedict Spinoza. Also contains unfinished Political Treatise. Great classic on religious liberty, theory of government on common consent. R. Elwes translation. Total of 421pp. 5⅜ x 8½. 20249-6

MY BONDAGE AND MY FREEDOM, Frederick Douglass. Born a slave, Douglass became outspoken force in antislavery movement. The best of Douglass' autobiographies. Graphic description of slave life. 464pp. 5⅜ x 8½. 22457-0

FOLLOWING THE EQUATOR: A Journey Around the World, Mark Twain. Fascinating humorous account of 1897 voyage to Hawaii, Australia, India, New Zealand, etc. Ironic, bemused reports on peoples, customs, climate, flora and fauna, politics, much more. 197 illustrations. 720pp. 5⅜ x 8½. 26113-1

THE PEOPLE CALLED SHAKERS, Edward D. Andrews. Definitive study of Shakers: origins, beliefs, practices, dances, social organization, furniture and crafts, etc. 33 illustrations. 351pp. 5⅜ x 8½. 21081-2

THE MYTHS OF GREECE AND ROME, H. A. Guerber. A classic of mythology, generously illustrated, long prized for its simple, graphic, accurate retelling of the principal myths of Greece and Rome, and for its commentary on their origins and significance. With 64 illustrations by Michelangelo, Raphael, Titian, Rubens, Canova, Bernini and others. 480pp. 5⅜ x 8½. 27584-1

PSYCHOLOGY OF MUSIC, Carl E. Seashore. Classic work discusses music as a medium from psychological viewpoint. Clear treatment of physical acoustics, auditory apparatus, sound perception, development of musical skills, nature of musical feeling, host of other topics. 88 figures. 408pp. 5⅜ x 8½. 21851-1

THE PHILOSOPHY OF HISTORY, Georg W. Hegel. Great classic of Western thought develops concept that history is not chance but rational process, the evolution of freedom. 457pp. 5⅜ x 8½. 20112-0

THE BOOK OF TEA, Kakuzo Okakura. Minor classic of the Orient: entertaining, charming explanation, interpretation of traditional Japanese culture in terms of tea ceremony. 94pp. 5⅜ x 8½. 20070-1

LIFE IN ANCIENT EGYPT, Adolf Erman. Fullest, most thorough, detailed older account with much not in more recent books, domestic life, religion, magic, medicine, commerce, much more. Many illustrations reproduce tomb paintings, carvings, hieroglyphs, etc. 597pp. 5⅜ x 8½. 22632-8

SUNDIALS, Their Theory and Construction, Albert Waugh. Far and away the best, most thorough coverage of ideas, mathematics concerned, types, construction, adjusting anywhere. Simple, nontechnical treatment allows even children to build several of these dials. Over 100 illustrations. 230pp. 5⅜ x 8½. 22947-5

THEORETICAL HYDRODYNAMICS, L. M. Milne-Thomson. Classic exposition of the mathematical theory of fluid motion, applicable to both hydrodynamics and aerodynamics. Over 600 exercises. 768pp. 6⅛ x 9¼. 68970-0

SONGS OF EXPERIENCE: Facsimile Reproduction with 26 Plates in Full Color, William Blake. 26 full-color plates from a rare 1826 edition. Includes "The Tyger," "London," "Holy Thursday," and other poems. Printed text of poems. 48pp. 5¼ x 7. 24636-1

OLD-TIME VIGNETTES IN FULL COLOR, Carol Belanger Grafton (ed.). Over 390 charming, often sentimental illustrations, selected from archives of Victorian graphics–pretty women posing, children playing, food, flowers, kittens and puppies, smiling cherubs, birds and butterflies, much more. All copyright-free. 48pp. 9¼ x 12¼. 27269-9

LITTLE BOOK OF EARLY AMERICAN CRAFTS AND TRADES, Peter Stockham (ed.). 1807 children's book explains crafts and trades: baker, hatter, cooper, potter, and many others. 23 copperplate illustrations. 140pp. 4⅝ x 6. 23336-7

VICTORIAN FASHIONS AND COSTUMES FROM HARPER'S BAZAR, 1867–1898, Stella Blum (ed.). Day costumes, evening wear, sports clothes, shoes, hats, other accessories in over 1,000 detailed engravings. 320pp. 9⅜ x 12¼. 22990-4

GUSTAV STICKLEY, THE CRAFTSMAN, Mary Ann Smith. Superb study surveys broad scope of Stickley's achievement, especially in architecture. Design philosophy, rise and fall of the Craftsman empire, descriptions and floor plans for many Craftsman houses, more. 86 black-and-white halftones. 31 line illustrations. Introduction 208pp. 6½ x 9¼. 27210-9

THE LONG ISLAND RAIL ROAD IN EARLY PHOTOGRAPHS, Ron Ziel. Over 220 rare photos, informative text document origin (1844) and development of rail service on Long Island. Vintage views of early trains, locomotives, stations, passengers, crews, much more. Captions. 8⅞ x 11¾. 26301-0

VOYAGE OF THE LIBERDADE, Joshua Slocum. Great 19th-century mariner's thrilling, first-hand account of the wreck of his ship off South America, the 35-foot boat he built from the wreckage, and its remarkable voyage home. 128pp. 5⅜ x 8½. 40022-0

TEN BOOKS ON ARCHITECTURE, Vitruvius. The most important book ever written on architecture. Early Roman aesthetics, technology, classical orders, site selection, all other aspects. Morgan translation. 331pp. 5⅜ x 8½. 20645-9

THE HUMAN FIGURE IN MOTION, Eadweard Muybridge. More than 4,500 stopped-action photos, in action series, showing undraped men, women, children jumping, lying down, throwing, sitting, wrestling, carrying, etc. 390pp. 7⅞ x 10⅝. 20204-6 Clothbd.

TREES OF THE EASTERN AND CENTRAL UNITED STATES AND CANADA, William M. Harlow. Best one-volume guide to 140 trees. Full descriptions, woodlore, range, etc. Over 600 illustrations. Handy size. 288pp. 4½ x 6⅜. 20395-6

SONGS OF WESTERN BIRDS, Dr. Donald J. Borror. Complete song and call repertoire of 60 western species, including flycatchers, juncoes, cactus wrens, many more–includes fully illustrated booklet. Cassette and manual 99913-0

GROWING AND USING HERBS AND SPICES, Milo Miloradovich. Versatile handbook provides all the information needed for cultivation and use of all the herbs and spices available in North America. 4 illustrations. Index. Glossary. 236pp. 5⅜ x 8½. 25058-X

BIG BOOK OF MAZES AND LABYRINTHS, Walter Shepherd. 50 mazes and labyrinths in all–classical, solid, ripple, and more–in one great volume. Perfect inexpensive puzzler for clever youngsters. Full solutions. 112pp. 8⅛ x 11. 22951-3

PIANO TUNING, J. Cree Fischer. Clearest, best book for beginner, amateur. Simple repairs, raising dropped notes, tuning by easy method of flattened fifths. No previous skills needed. 4 illustrations. 201pp. 5⅜ x 8½. 23267-0

HINTS TO SINGERS, Lillian Nordica. Selecting the right teacher, developing confidence, overcoming stage fright, and many other important skills receive thoughtful discussion in this indispensible guide, written by a world-famous diva of four decades' experience. 96pp. 5⅜ x 8½. 40094-8

THE COMPLETE NONSENSE OF EDWARD LEAR, Edward Lear. All nonsense limericks, zany alphabets, Owl and Pussycat, songs, nonsense botany, etc., illustrated by Lear. Total of 320pp. 5⅜ x 8½. (Available in U.S. only.) 20167-8

VICTORIAN PARLOUR POETRY: An Annotated Anthology, Michael R. Turner. 117 gems by Longfellow, Tennyson, Browning, many lesser-known poets. "The Village Blacksmith," "Curfew Must Not Ring Tonight," "Only a Baby Small," dozens more, often difficult to find elsewhere. Index of poets, titles, first lines. xxiii + 325pp. 5⅜ x 8¼. 27044-0

DUBLINERS, James Joyce. Fifteen stories offer vivid, tightly focused observations of the lives of Dublin's poorer classes. At least one, "The Dead," is considered a masterpiece. Reprinted complete and unabridged from standard edition. 160pp. 5³⁄₁₆ x 8¼. 26870-5

GREAT WEIRD TALES: 14 Stories by Lovecraft, Blackwood, Machen and Others, S. T. Joshi (ed.). 14 spellbinding tales, including "The Sin Eater," by Fiona McLeod, "The Eye Above the Mantel," by Frank Belknap Long, as well as renowned works by R. H. Barlow, Lord Dunsany, Arthur Machen, W. C. Morrow and eight other masters of the genre. 256pp. 5⅜ x 8½. (Available in U.S. only.) 40436-6

THE BOOK OF THE SACRED MAGIC OF ABRAMELIN THE MAGE, translated by S. MacGregor Mathers. Medieval manuscript of ceremonial magic. Basic document in Aleister Crowley, Golden Dawn groups. 268pp. 5⅜ x 8½. 23211-5

NEW RUSSIAN-ENGLISH AND ENGLISH-RUSSIAN DICTIONARY, M. A. O'Brien. This is a remarkably handy Russian dictionary, containing a surprising amount of information, including over 70,000 entries. 366pp. 4½ x 6⅛. 20208-9

HISTORIC HOMES OF THE AMERICAN PRESIDENTS, Second, Revised Edition, Irvin Haas. A traveler's guide to American Presidential homes, most open to the public, depicting and describing homes occupied by every American President from George Washington to George Bush. With visiting hours, admission charges, travel routes. 175 photographs. Index. 160pp. 8¼ x 11. 26751-2

NEW YORK IN THE FORTIES, Andreas Feininger. 162 brilliant photographs by the well-known photographer, formerly with *Life* magazine. Commuters, shoppers, Times Square at night, much else from city at its peak. Captions by John von Hartz. 181pp. 9¼ x 10¾. 23585-8

INDIAN SIGN LANGUAGE, William Tomkins. Over 525 signs developed by Sioux and other tribes. Written instructions and diagrams. Also 290 pictographs. 111pp. 6⅛ x 9¼. 22029-X

ANATOMY: A Complete Guide for Artists, Joseph Sheppard. A master of figure drawing shows artists how to render human anatomy convincingly. Over 460 illustrations. 224pp. 8⅜ x 11¼. 27279-6

MEDIEVAL CALLIGRAPHY: Its History and Technique, Marc Drogin. Spirited history, comprehensive instruction manual covers 13 styles (ca. 4th century through 15th). Excellent photographs; directions for duplicating medieval techniques with modern tools. 224pp. 8⅜ x 11¼. 26142-5

DRIED FLOWERS: How to Prepare Them, Sarah Whitlock and Martha Rankin. Complete instructions on how to use silica gel, meal and borax, perlite aggregate, sand and borax, glycerine and water to create attractive permanent flower arrangements. 12 illustrations. 32pp. 5⅜ x 8½. 21802-3

EASY-TO-MAKE BIRD FEEDERS FOR WOODWORKERS, Scott D. Campbell. Detailed, simple-to-use guide for designing, constructing, caring for and using feeders. Text, illustrations for 12 classic and contemporary designs. 96pp. 5⅜ x 8½. 25847-5

SCOTTISH WONDER TALES FROM MYTH AND LEGEND, Donald A. Mackenzie. 16 lively tales tell of giants rumbling down mountainsides, of a magic wand that turns stone pillars into warriors, of gods and goddesses, evil hags, powerful forces and more. 240pp. 5⅜ x 8½. 29677-6

THE HISTORY OF UNDERCLOTHES, C. Willett Cunnington and Phyllis Cunnington. Fascinating, well-documented survey covering six centuries of English undergarments, enhanced with over 100 illustrations: 12th-century laced-up bodice, footed long drawers (1795), 19th-century bustles, 19th-century corsets for men, Victorian "bust improvers," much more. 272pp. 5⅝ x 8¼. 27124-2

ARTS AND CRAFTS FURNITURE: The Complete Brooks Catalog of 1912, Brooks Manufacturing Co. Photos and detailed descriptions of more than 150 now very collectible furniture designs from the Arts and Crafts movement depict davenports, settees, buffets, desks, tables, chairs, bedsteads, dressers and more, all built of solid, quarter-sawed oak. Invaluable for students and enthusiasts of antiques, Americana and the decorative arts. 80pp. 6½ x 9¼. 27471-3

WILBUR AND ORVILLE: A Biography of the Wright Brothers, Fred Howard. Definitive, crisply written study tells the full story of the brothers' lives and work. A vividly written biography, unparalleled in scope and color, that also captures the spirit of an extraordinary era. 560pp. 6⅛ x 9¼. 40297-5

THE ARTS OF THE SAILOR: Knotting, Splicing and Ropework, Hervey Garrett Smith. Indispensable shipboard reference covers tools, basic knots and useful hitches; handsewing and canvas work, more. Over 100 illustrations. Delightful reading for sea lovers. 256pp. 5⅜ x 8½. 26440-8

FRANK LLOYD WRIGHT'S FALLINGWATER: The House and Its History, Second, Revised Edition, Donald Hoffmann. A total revision–both in text and illustrations–of the standard document on Fallingwater, the boldest, most personal architectural statement of Wright's mature years, updated with valuable new material from the recently opened Frank Lloyd Wright Archives. "Fascinating"–*The New York Times.* 116 illustrations. 128pp. 9¼ x 10¾. 27430-6

PHOTOGRAPHIC SKETCHBOOK OF THE CIVIL WAR, Alexander Gardner. 100 photos taken on field during the Civil War. Famous shots of Manassas Harper's Ferry, Lincoln, Richmond, slave pens, etc. 244pp. 10⅝ x 8¼. 22731-6

FIVE ACRES AND INDEPENDENCE, Maurice G. Kains. Great back-to-the-land classic explains basics of self-sufficient farming. The one book to get. 95 illustrations. 397pp. 5⅜ x 8½. 20974-1

SONGS OF EASTERN BIRDS, Dr. Donald J. Borror. Songs and calls of 60 species most common to eastern U.S.: warblers, woodpeckers, flycatchers, thrushes, larks, many more in high-quality recording. Cassette and manual 99912-2

A MODERN HERBAL, Margaret Grieve. Much the fullest, most exact, most useful compilation of herbal material. Gigantic alphabetical encyclopedia, from aconite to zedoary, gives botanical information, medical properties, folklore, economic uses, much else. Indispensable to serious reader. 161 illustrations. 888pp. 6½ x 9¼. 2-vol. set. (Available in U.S. only.) Vol. I: 22798-7
Vol. II: 22799-5

HIDDEN TREASURE MAZE BOOK, Dave Phillips. Solve 34 challenging mazes accompanied by heroic tales of adventure. Evil dragons, people-eating plants, bloodthirsty giants, many more dangerous adversaries lurk at every twist and turn. 34 mazes, stories, solutions. 48pp. 8¼ x 11. 24566-7

LETTERS OF W. A. MOZART, Wolfgang A. Mozart. Remarkable letters show bawdy wit, humor, imagination, musical insights, contemporary musical world; includes some letters from Leopold Mozart. 276pp. 5⅜ x 8½. 22859-2

BASIC PRINCIPLES OF CLASSICAL BALLET, Agrippina Vaganova. Great Russian theoretician, teacher explains methods for teaching classical ballet. 118 illustrations. 175pp. 5⅜ x 8½. 22036-2

THE JUMPING FROG, Mark Twain. Revenge edition. The original story of The Celebrated Jumping Frog of Calaveras County, a hapless French translation, and Twain's hilarious "retranslation" from the French. 12 illustrations. 66pp. 5⅜ x 8½. 22686-7

BEST REMEMBERED POEMS, Martin Gardner (ed.). The 126 poems in this superb collection of 19th- and 20th-century British and American verse range from Shelley's "To a Skylark" to the impassioned "Renascence" of Edna St. Vincent Millay and to Edward Lear's whimsical "The Owl and the Pussycat." 224pp. 5⅜ x 8½. 27165-X

COMPLETE SONNETS, William Shakespeare. Over 150 exquisite poems deal with love, friendship, the tyranny of time, beauty's evanescence, death and other themes in language of remarkable power, precision and beauty. Glossary of archaic terms. 80pp. 5³⁄₁₆ x 8¼. 26686-9

THE BATTLES THAT CHANGED HISTORY, Fletcher Pratt. Eminent historian profiles 16 crucial conflicts, ancient to modern, that changed the course of civilization. 352pp. 5⅜ x 8½. 41129-X

THE WIT AND HUMOR OF OSCAR WILDE, Alvin Redman (ed.). More than 1,000 ripostes, paradoxes, wisecracks: Work is the curse of the drinking classes; I can resist everything except temptation; etc. 258pp. 5⅜ x 8½. 20602-5

SHAKESPEARE LEXICON AND QUOTATION DICTIONARY, Alexander Schmidt. Full definitions, locations, shades of meaning in every word in plays and poems. More than 50,000 exact quotations. 1,485pp. 6½ x 9¼. 2-vol. set.
Vol. 1: 22726-X
Vol. 2: 22727-8

SELECTED POEMS, Emily Dickinson. Over 100 best-known, best-loved poems by one of America's foremost poets, reprinted from authoritative early editions. No comparable edition at this price. Index of first lines. 64pp. 5³⁄₁₆ x 8¼. 26466-1

THE INSIDIOUS DR. FU-MANCHU, Sax Rohmer. The first of the popular mystery series introduces a pair of English detectives to their archnemesis, the diabolical Dr. Fu-Manchu. Flavorful atmosphere, fast-paced action, and colorful characters enliven this classic of the genre. 208pp. 5³⁄₁₆ x 8¼. 29898-1

THE MALLEUS MALEFICARUM OF KRAMER AND SPRENGER, translated by Montague Summers. Full text of most important witchhunter's "bible," used by both Catholics and Protestants. 278pp. 6⅝ x 10. 22802-9

SPANISH STORIES/CUENTOS ESPAÑOLES: A Dual-Language Book, Angel Flores (ed.). Unique format offers 13 great stories in Spanish by Cervantes, Borges, others. Faithful English translations on facing pages. 352pp. 5⅜ x 8½. 25399-6

GARDEN CITY, LONG ISLAND, IN EARLY PHOTOGRAPHS, 1869–1919, Mildred H. Smith. Handsome treasury of 118 vintage pictures, accompanied by carefully researched captions, document the Garden City Hotel fire (1899), the Vanderbilt Cup Race (1908), the first airmail flight departing from the Nassau Boulevard Aerodrome (1911), and much more. 96pp. 8⅞ x 11¾. 40669-5

OLD QUEENS, N.Y., IN EARLY PHOTOGRAPHS, Vincent F. Seyfried and William Asadorian. Over 160 rare photographs of Maspeth, Jamaica, Jackson Heights, and other areas. Vintage views of DeWitt Clinton mansion, 1939 World's Fair and more. Captions. 192pp. 8⅞ x 11. 26358-4

CAPTURED BY THE INDIANS: 15 Firsthand Accounts, 1750-1870, Frederick Drimmer. Astounding true historical accounts of grisly torture, bloody conflicts, relentless pursuits, miraculous escapes and more, by people who lived to tell the tale. 384pp. 5⅜ x 8½. 24901-8

THE WORLD'S GREAT SPEECHES (Fourth Enlarged Edition), Lewis Copeland, Lawrence W. Lamm, and Stephen J. McKenna. Nearly 300 speeches provide public speakers with a wealth of updated quotes and inspiration–from Pericles' funeral oration and William Jennings Bryan's "Cross of Gold Speech" to Malcolm X's powerful words on the Black Revolution and Earl of Spenser's tribute to his sister, Diana, Princess of Wales. 944pp. 5⅜ x 8⅜. 40903-1

THE BOOK OF THE SWORD, Sir Richard F. Burton. Great Victorian scholar/adventurer's eloquent, erudite history of the "queen of weapons"–from prehistory to early Roman Empire. Evolution and development of early swords, variations (sabre, broadsword, cutlass, scimitar, etc.), much more. 336pp. 6⅛ x 9¼.
25434-8